Laurence Sterne's
Sermons of Mr. Yorick

BY

LANSING VAN DER HEYDEN HAMMOND

ARCHON BOOKS
1970

[*Yale Studies in English, Vol. 108*]

SBN: 208 00922 1
Library of Congress Catalog Card Number: 72-91180
Printed in the United States of America

YALE STUDIES IN ENGLISH

Benjamin Christie Nangle · Editor

VOLUME 108

PUBLISHED ON
THE KINGSLEY TRUST ASSOCIATION
PUBLICATION FUND
ESTABLISHED BY
THE SCROLL AND KEY SOCIETY
OF YALE COLLEGE

To

CHAUNCEY BREWSTER TINKER

PREFACE

IN this study, for the first time, a list of sources has been compiled and a critical examination made of the corresponding passages in *The Sermons of Mr. Yorick* which betray indebtednesses to other writers. The results of an analysis of each sermon, to determine the amount of borrowed material contained and the differences observable in Sterne's use of such material, consistently point to two plausible hypotheses: first, that the sermons remaining in manuscript at the time of Sterne's death (subsequently published in Volumes v–vii) were written earlier than the others and that Volumes i–iv contain his later and most finished compositions for the pulpit; secondly, that all but one of the forty-five sermons had been committed to paper, at least in rudimentary form, prior to 1751.

As a consequence of these findings, several traditionally accepted opinions about Sterne must now be revised. First, since the most conspicuous instances of verbatim copying are strictly confined to the posthumously published discourses, whereas in the volumes Sterne himself prepared for the press the borrowings were transformed into something that was his own, the charges of plagiarism which have been brought against him, in the *Sermons,* lose much of their significance. Secondly, because many of the discourses written prior to 1751 distinctly foreshadow Yorick's later stylistic peculiarities, "Shandyism" is seen to be the result of a longer and slower development than has heretofore been realized. And finally, from the clearer understanding that emerges of when and how the sermons were probably composed, Sterne must now be accredited with a greater degree of sincerity and conscientiousness in the performance of his churchly duties than previously seemed possible.

Despite the fact that the whole story is not yet known, nor probably ever will be, and even though the available evidence cannot constitute positive proof, enough new material has been found, sufficiently persistent and pertinent in implication, to lend persuasive support to the hypotheses and conclusions here ventured. The belief that this may also be the reader's opinion is the reason for publishing the ensuing pages.

In its original form this study was presented as a dissertation for the degree of Doctor of Philosophy in Yale University. The subject was first suggested to me by Professor Chauncey Brewster Tinker, under whose direction it has been my privilege to work. It is difficult to acknowledge all the help I have received from him; I am, however, deeply grateful for his guidance and encouragement, and for permitting the dedication of these pages.

I wish also especially to thank Professors Wilbur L. Cross, Lewis P. Curtis, and Frederick A. Pottle for their many kindnesses and for the valuable suggestions they have made; and Professor Benjamin C. Nangle and Mrs. Frank McMullan for their assistance in preparing the final copy.

L. V. d. H. H.
New Haven, Connecticut,
  6 May 1947.

BIBLIOGRAPHICAL NOTE

THE text of Sterne's *Sermons of Mr. Yorick* used throughout this study is that of the first editions: Volumes I and II, London, 1760; Volumes III and IV, London, 1766; Volumes V, VI, and VII, London, 1769. The first two volumes contained fifteen sermons, numbered 1–15; Volumes III and IV, twelve sermons, numbered 1–12; and Volumes V, VI, and VII, eighteen sermons, numbered 1–18. To avoid confusion, hereafter, in referring to these sermons, Roman numerals will be used to indicate the volume; Arabic numerals, the number originally given to a sermon within that volume; and Arabic numerals within parentheses, the cumulative number of a sermon in the complete collection. Thus, the first sermon in Volume III will be designated "*Sermons*, III, 1 (16)." Since the first fifteen sermons, in Volumes I and II, also comprise the first fifteen in the complete collection, they will not be given the additional cumulative numbering.

LIST OF ABBREVIATIONS

Clarke, *Sermons*
   Clarke, Samuel. *Sermons*. Clarke, John, ed. London, 1730–31. 10 Vols.
D.N.B.
   Dictionary of National Biography.
Fitzgerald, *Life*
   Fitzgerald, Percy. *The Life of Laurence Sterne*. London, 1864. 2 vols.
Letters
   Curtis, Lewis Perry, ed. *Letters of Laurence Sterne*. Oxford, 1935.
Life
   Cross, Wilbur L. *The Life and Times of Laurence Sterne*. 3d ed. New Haven, 1929.
Sentimental Journey
   Sterne, Laurence. *A Sentimental Journey through France and Italy*. 1st ed. London, 1768. 2 vols.
Sermons
   The Sermons of Mr. Yorick. 1st ed. London, 1760–69. 7 vols.
Tillotson, *Works*
   Tillotson, John. *The Works of Dr. John Tillotson*. Birch, T., ed. London, 1820. 10 vols.
Todd and Sotheran, *Catalogue*
   Catalogue of a Curious and Valuable Collection of Books, among Which Are Included the Entire Library of the Late Reverend and Learned Laurence Sterne, A.M. York, 1768.
Tristram Shandy
   Sterne, Laurence. *The Life and Opinions of Tristram Shandy, Gentleman*. 1st ed. London, 1760–67. 9 vols.

CONTENTS

Preface   vii

Bibliographical Note   ix

I. The Problem   1

II. The Evidence   17
      Part I   17
      Part II   34
      Part III   50

III. Some Conjectures—Sterne in the Workshop   65

IV. In Extenuation   74

V. Yorick's Christianity   90

Appendix—Sources for *The Sermons of Mr. Yorick*   103

Index   193

Laurence Sterne's *Sermons of Mr. Yorick*

I

The Problem

WITH the exception of one specific gap, Laurence Sterne has fared well at the hands of modern scholarship. Unless new and hitherto unsuspected material comes to light, it is difficult to conceive of a more definitive and illuminating biographical study than Wilbur L. Cross's *Life;* or of a more authoritative edition of the *Letters* than the one edited by Lewis Perry Curtis.[1] *Tristram Shandy* and *A Sentimental Journey* have been reissued in many a modern edition[2] and subjected to psychoanalytical dissection.[3] Friedrich Behrmann has made a detailed study of the elements of Sterne's style[4] and Rudolf Maack's investigations have been of great service in establishing the relationship of Sterne's writings to eighteenth-century philosophies and schools of thought.[5] Even in the more popular field Sterne has had a full share of attention: two full-length biographies within the past five years[6] and at least two shorter studies since 1939 have done much toward keeping Yorick's memory fresh.[7]

The *Sermons*, however, have been curiously neglected, though for a few years after Sterne's death they shared some of the attention which literary detectives were paying to *Tristram Shandy*. The most important of these early investigations, and the one which had the greatest influence in inspiring like attempts, was Dr. John Ferriar's "Comments on Sterne," published in the *Manchester Philosophical and Literary Transactions for 1793* and reprinted the same year in Dodsley's *Annual Register*.[8] Here, for the first time, Sterne's indebt-

1. See the Bibliographical Note for the full titles of these works.
2. Particular attention is called to the edition of *Tristram Shandy* edited by James Aiken Work for the Odyssey Series (New York, 1940).
3. Arie de Froe, *Laurence Sterne and His Novels Studied in the Light of Modern Psychology* (Groningen, 1925).
4. Friedrich Behrmann, *Laurence Sterne und sein Einfluss auf die englische Prosa des achtzehnten Jahrunderts* (Zurich, 1936).
5. Rudolf Maack, *Laurence Sterne in Lichte seiner Zeit* (Hamburg, 1936).
6. Lodwick Hartley, *This Is Lorence* (Chapel Hill, 1943). Thomas Yoseloff, *A Fellow of Infinite Jest* (New York, 1945).
7. W. B. C. Watkins, *Perilous Balance* (Princeton, 1939). Peter Quennell, *The Profane Virtues* (New York, 1945).
8. *The Annual Register, or a View of the History, Politics, and Literature for the Year 1793*, xxxv, 379–98. Expanded, these "Comments" later were republished in book form.

edness in *Tristram Shandy* to Burton's *Anatomy of Melancholy* was definitely established; and, as a sort of parenthetical inclusion, convincing similarities between some of the *Sermons* and the *Contemplations* of Bishop Hall were pointed out.[9] But even earlier, anonymous correspondents to the leading periodicals had been commenting upon the same sort of thing, with varying degrees of conclusiveness. In the issue of the *European Magazine* for August, 1789, "O. P. Q." noted "interesting parallels" between Yorick's discourses and the sermons of the Dean of Salisbury and suggested a possible source in Swift for a passage in another discourse.[1] Three years later the *European Magazine* printed an article entitled "Various Supposed Plagiarisms of Sterne Detected and Pointed Out," which cited evidence to show that Sterne had helped himself to one of Richard Bentley's homilies before composing the famous "Abuses of Conscience Considered."[2] The opening paragraph of this article deserves quotation; it will be referred to again, in a later page of this study.

It is but little known or suspected, nor will it be readily believed, that the inimitable and never-to-be-excelled Author of *Tristram Shandy* made a very free use of those books which were "such reading as was never read," as accident threw into his way, or choice directed him to. The late Mr. Henderson, of Covent Garden Theatre, whose reading of Mr. Sterne's works will not be soon forgotten by those who had the pleasure of hearing him, perused with great attention, just before his death, a book formerly much celebrated, though now seldom looked into, entitled, "Burton's Anatomy of Melancholy," and from thence extracted various parallel passages, which Mr. Sterne had availed himself of in the course of his entertaining works. Some of these were so very striking, that I should have been much disposed to send them to the *European Magazine*, had I not been informed that a very learned Gentleman at Manchester had already been travelling over the same ground, and had communicated to the Society established there the result of his enquiries, which in due time will be given to the public in their Transactions. It is always pleasing to trace the origin and progress of the thoughts of eminent writers, and therefore I hope it will not be supposed, that I am possessed with the spirit of Lauder, if I point out a passage which Mr. Sterne appears to have read. I heartily wish to see any other writer employ his reading to as good purpose.

In the issue of the *Gentleman's Magazine* for May, 1794, it was suggested that Sterne had borrowed much from an English translation of the *Historia del famoso predicador fray Gerundio*, by José Francisco de Isla, but a careful examination of this work failed to

9. Joseph Hall, *Contemplations upon the Principal Passages of the Holy Story* (London, 1612–34).
1. *The European Magazine*, XVI, 118–19.   2. *Idem*, XXI, 167–9.

produce any convincing similarities.[3] Indebtednesses to John Norris[4] and again to Swift[5] were noted in subsequent issues of the same periodical.

These discoveries, in addition to the acknowledgments which Sterne himself had made in footnotes to his *Sermons* to Tillotson,[6] Wollaston,[7] and Steele,[8] and his reference to Samuel Clarke,[9] could have furnished anyone sufficiently interested with an abundance of clues for investigating the sources of *The Sermons of Mr. Yorick* and the use which had been made of borrowed material—certainly a fundamental aspect of the subject. Strange, is it not, that no one considered the task worthy the undertaking? The fact that two of Sterne's discourses had been printed more than a decade before the first installments of *Tristram Shandy*,[1] together with the improbability of Yorick's having had either much time or inclination for

3. *The Gentleman's Magazine*, Vol. LXIV, Pt. 1, 406–07. The writer of this article, signing himself "Eboracensis," after suggesting that Sterne had used parts of De Isla's book in *Tristram Shandy*, concluded his observations with the following comment: "Give me leave, Sir, to make another extract from the work itself, and which shews him [Sterne] to have had as little originality as a writer of sermons, as the preceding ones shew him to have had invention as a novelist.

'It was well known to be a favourite maxim with him,' says the author [of the *Historia*], speaking of the Predicadir [*sic*], 'to begin his sermon always with some jest . . . which at first sight, should seem blasphemy, impiety, or madness; and after having kept the audience for a while in expectation, he would finish the clause, or come out with an explanation which terminated in a miserable insipidity. Preaching one day on the mystery of the Trinity, he began with this period, "*I deny that there is in God, Unity of Essence, and Trinity of Persons;*" and there he stopped. The hearers began to look at one another as if scandalized . . . waiting for the issue of that blasphemous heresy; and, when our preacher thought that he had caught them, he proceeded with the poorness of adding: "Thus says the Arian, the Manichean, the Socinian; but I shall prove it against them by Scripture, by Councils, by Fathers." ' "

The resemblance "Eboracensis" had in mind was to the opening Yorick adopted for his discourse on "The House of Feasting" (*Sermons*, I, 2) where, after reading the text—"*It is better to go to the house of mourning, than to the house of feasting*"—he began with a startling "That I deny—" Though De Isla's *History of the Famous Preacher Friar Gerund de Campazas*, to give the work its translated title, was printed in Madrid in 1758, the earliest recorded English text is dated 1772. Percy Fitzgerald, it is true, in the 1896 edition of his *Life* (Appendix B, II, 214), asserted that there had been an earlier translation available to Sterne but no trace of such a publication has yet been found.

4. *The Gentleman's Magazine*, Vol. LXX, Pt. 2, 741.

5. *Idem*, Vol. LXXVI, Pt. 1, 407–08.

6. *Sermons*, II, 8, p. 35. See Bibliographical Note for an explanation of the method used in referring to these *Sermons*. See also *Sermons*, II, 11, p. 125.

7. *Idem*, II, 10, p. 102.   8. *Idem*, II, 12, p. 157.

9. *Idem*, VI, 8 (35), pp. 51–2.

1. "The Case of Elijah and the Widow of Zerephath, Considered" (York, 1747), *Sermons*, I, 5, and "The Abuses of Conscience" (York, 1750), *Sermons*, IV, 12 (27). As is well known, the latter sermon was also reprinted in *Tristram Shandy* (Bk. II, chap. XVII). It is worth noting that, with the exception of the stage directions added for Trim's benefit and the comments offered by Dr. Slop, Uncle Toby, and Walter Shandy, the basic text of the sermon underwent no significant changes between the time of its first printing, in 1750, and its last, in 1766.

sermon writing in the popularity which came to him after 1760, should further have suggested another possibility: that most of his homilies had been composed many years prior to their publication— possibly at the very beginning of his priesthood—and therefore offered a splendid opportunity for examining their unpredictable author, as it were, in the workshop, before his style had attained its full degree of subtle flexibility and economy, before his "strong imagination and sensible heart" had crystallized, or his humor ripened; in a word, while "Shandyism" was being evolved.

Percy Fitzgerald might have led the way, for in his two-volume *Life of Laurence Sterne* he listed the most comprehensive assemblage of sources for Yorick's sermons which has heretofore appeared in print. Noting the acknowledgments which Sterne himself had made,[2] he went on to add that

. . . while the originality of "Tristram Shandy" is in the main secure, I am afraid, in the case of the Sermons, he seems to have cast away all notions of literary morality. I find that the famous sermon on Conscience which was preached to the judges, and which Trim read aloud, is in manner, argument, order, and sometimes words, almost wholly from Swift's.[3] His depredations stretched in all directions. From Burnet's "Safe Way to Happiness" he took a passage in his twenty-eighth sermon, and from the same author's "Nature and Grace" he helped himself to a large passage in his thirty-first sermon.[4] From Norris he took many passages, as also from Bishop Hall; and in one of Bentley's sermons is to be found almost word for word the picture of the Inquisition.[5] The most daring, however, of all his plagiarisms, was that of some passages in his seventh posthumous sermon, which were literally transferred wholesale from Leighton's twelve sermons, the author of which was an obscure prebendary, not likely to attract notice.[6]

Fitzgerald, however, was not interested in pursuing the subject further, in verifying the accuracy of his statements, or in attempting to assess the quantity and importance of Sterne's borrowings. His concern with the sermons extended no further than to their Shandean

2. Fitzgerald, *Life*, I, 211.

3. This sentence was wisely omitted in the revised edition of the *Life* (London, 1896, 2 vols.), Appendix B, II, 214. Certainly the indebtedness to Swift was not nearly so great as Fitzgerald first implied.

4. The bibliography of Bishop Burnet's published writings, listed by T. E. S. Clarke and H. C. Foxcroft in their *Life of Gilbert Burnet* (Cambridge, 1907), Appendix II, contains nothing answering to Fitzgerald's description. Both sermons he mentions, however, are to be found in Dr. Edward Young's *Sermons on Several Occasions* (3d ed. London, 1720, 2 vols.).

5. Bentley's sermon was certainly known to Sterne, but Fitzgerald greatly overestimates the actual indebtedness.

6. The writer of this sermon was Walter Leightonhouse, an obscure prebendary of Lincoln Cathedral. Fitzgerald is confusing him with Robert Leighton, Archbishop of Glasgow, a theological writer to whom Sterne owed nothing.

elements, the arrangements for publication, and what various contemporaries, such as Gray, Lady Cowper, and Dr. Johnson had to say about them.[7] But he knew what he was writing about; it was at least obvious that he had read the sermons. So much cannot be said for many of Sterne's other critics. Sir Walter Scott, for example, contented himself with observing that Sterne's sermons "maintained the character of their author for wit, genius, and eccentricity"[8] and Thackeray, lecturing in 1851 on "The English Humourists of the Eighteenth Century," paused only long enough in his cursory flight to inform his listeners that "the whole polite world" of Sterne's day had subscribed for the sermons of that "delicious divine."[9]

Such brief and superficial generalities, wherein little information about the sermons themselves was given, became almost a standard form of commentary for the next half century. Paul Stapfer, with Fitzgerald avowedly in mind, commented in an abbreviated footnote on Sterne's obligations to some of his predecessors but then went on to indulge in rather vague speculations about the author's philosophy of modified optimism, his sincerity, and the unconventionality with which the texts were handled.[1] Walter Bagehot and Leslie Stephen were even less specific, confining their remarks to the expression of personal opinion, without illustration, about the morality preached by Sterne[2] or the "touches of Shandy style and efforts to escape from the dead level" in the printed discourses.[3] Henry D. Traill's perfunctory *Life* for the English Men of Letters series (1882), though devoting more pages to the subject, was equally unsatisfactory. Like Fitzgerald, Traill included a chapter on Sterne's plagiarisms, but he did little more than repeat what Dr. Ferriar had already written.[4] Completely ignoring the existence of the posthumously published sermons, Traill made only one reference to the first two volumes, describing their contents as being ". . . of the most commonplace character; platitudinous with the platitudes of a thousand pulpits,

---

7. Fitzgerald, *Life*, I, 200–10; II, 65–74.

8. Sir Walter Scott, "Biographical Memoirs of Eminent Novelists," *The Miscellaneous Prose Works* (Edinburgh, 1834, 30 vols.), III, 283.

9. William Makepeace Thackeray, *The English Humourists of the Eighteenth Century* (New York, 1853), p. 232.

1. Paul Stapfer, *Laurence Sterne, Étude biographique et littéraire* (Paris, 1870), p. 132, n.; p. 120; pp. 104–06; p. 107 ff. Fitzgerald's confusion of Leighton with Leightonhouse and of Bishop Burnet with Dr. Young is repeated.

2. Walter Bagehot, *Literary Studies* (London, 1879, 2 vols.), II, 110–11.

3. Leslie Stephen, *Hours in a Library* (London, 1892, 3 vols.), III, 157.

4. Henry D. Traill, *Sterne* (London, 1909), pp. 137–9: "Sterne's twelfth sermon, on the Forgiveness of Injuries, is merely a diluted commentary on the conclusion of Hall's 'Contemplation of Joseph'." Cf. J. Ferriar, *Illustrations of Sterne* (London, 1812, 2 vols.), I, 125–6: "Sterne's twelfth Sermon, on the Forgiveness of Injuries, is merely a dilated commentary on the beautiful conclusion of the *Contemplation* 'of Joseph'."

and insipid with the *crambe repetita* of a hundred thousand homiles."[5] He reserved his approval for the third and fourth volumes, feeling that because of their "daring quaintness of style and illustration" these discourses must be assigned to a later date of composition than those of the two earlier volumes.[6] George Saintsbury, on the other hand, in his edition of *The Letters, Sermons and Miscellaneous Writings of Laurence Sterne* (1894), considered the earliest volumes "the most carefully written things of his that we have in form," whereas the discourses which Traill commended suffer from the fact that Yorick was trying "experiments, to see how far Tristram in bands and gown could borrow the merits of Tristram in coat and *solitaire*."[7] As Mr. Cross observed, in noting these conflicting opinions, "Professor Saintsbury evidently read the first set, and Traill evidently read the second set.—That accounts for the charming disagreement."[8]

There is scarce need to give more than a passing glance to Walter Sichel's *Sterne, a Study* (London, 1910), whose appearance so soon after the first edition of Mr. Cross's *The Life and Times of Laurence Sterne* (1909) led many to wonder "where the second man got his materials on such short order";[9] or to Lewis Melville's *Life and Letters of Laurence Sterne* (London, 1911). Neither of these accounts contributed anything to a better understanding of Yorick's sermons. Melville did nothing more than quote without critical comment from a half dozen of the better-known discourses; Sichel only echoed, in modified form, what had been said by Fitzgerald, Bagehot, and Cross. Both repeated the inevitable references to the opinions of Gray, Lady Cowper, and Dr. Johnson and elaborated upon the arrangements for publication.

As might be supposed, the best discussion which has yet been published is to be found in Mr. Cross's *Life*. Though the acknowledgment of Sterne's indebtedness to Norris and Bentley, which Fitzgerald had given, is not included, Mr. Cross for the first time ventured an evaluation of the importance of the material borrowed from Tillotson, Young, Hall, Clarke, Wollaston, and Leightonhouse;[1] and this, with as sufficient a degree of completeness as could reasonably be demanded in a biographical study, before a systematic investigation had been made of these sources.

What has heretofore been written about *The Sermons of Mr.*

5. Traill, *op. cit.*, p. 56. Exception was made of the "Charity Sermon" (*Sermons*, I, 5), previously printed at York, 1747.

6. Traill, *op. cit.*, p. 97.

7. George Saintsbury, *Prefaces and Essays* (London, 1933), p. 191.

8. Wilbur L. Cross, *The Sermons of Mr. Yorick*, in *The Works of Laurence Sterne*, printed for the Members of the Jenson Club (New York, 1906, 12 vols.), I, xxxiv.

9. *Life*, p. x. 1. *Idem*, pp. 241–3. See also pp. 505–06.

Yorick emphasizes the need for and justifies the undertaking of such an investigation. It is, to be sure, always of interest to read what prominent critics have to say about a literary production. Unfortunately, in this case the comments have been largely restricted to the expression of purely personal opinion or to the repetition of what had already been said, without a previous determination of the degree of accuracy of these statements. It is obvious, for example, when Traill observes that Sterne's discourse on the "Forgiveness of Injuries" "is merely a diluted commentary on the conclusion of Hall's 'Contemplation of Joseph,' "[2] he is only echoing Dr. Ferriar; had he compared the sermon with the "Contemplation," he would surely have seen that such an appraisal overstated the degree of indebtedness. Equally fallacious is Fitzgerald's comment that "in one of Bentley's sermons is to be found almost word for word the picture of the Inquisition";[3] and in much the same vein Mr. Cross's assertion that "Our Conversation in Heaven" was "worked over from Tillotson" is misleading; Sterne unquestionably knew Tillotson's discourse, "Of the Happiness of a Heavenly Conversation," and was influenced by it; but there are more striking similarities in a sermon of Norris'.[4]

Or, to consider the problem from a slightly different angle, does it not seem rather futile to attempt discussing Sterne's ideas, as expressed in the *Sermons,* until one knows more precisely what was original and what was borrowed? Sichel quotes a paragraph from "The Rich Man and Lazarus" to show that Sterne "never dwelt on the goods of life as evils" and observes that "Here is the keynote of the *Sentimental Journey.*"[5] The passage he cites, however, was taken almost word for word from one of Clarke's discourses.[6] Similarly Traill, in dismissing the first two volumes of Mr. Yorick's *Sermons* as being "of the most commonplace character,"[7] quotes a single extract to illustrate the contention, from the discourse on "Evil-Speaking"; but the passage was largely derived from Tillotson.[8] Again, to support his belief that the third and fourth volumes were the best, Traill offers three quotations; one of these, however, from the conclusion to "The Prodigal Son," was a definite rephrasing of Locke.[9] Both Traill and Saintsbury might have been less positive in asserting the incontestable superiority of one group of Yorick's sermons over another, had they been aware of the fact that in the first four volumes Sterne had made use of the same sources, and with approximately the same

2. *Sermons,* II, 12.   3. See above, p. 4, n. 5, and below, p. 105.
4. *Sermons,* V, 2 (29). See *Life,* p. 95.
5. Walter Sichel, *Sterne, a Study* (London, 1910), p. 84, and *Sermons,* IV, 8 (23), pp. 51–2.
6. See below, p. 116.   7. Traill, *op. cit.,* p. 56.
8. *Sermons,* II, 11. For evidence that Sterne was acquainted with Tillotson's discourse, "Against Evil Speaking," see below, pp. 165–7.
9. *Sermons,* III, 5 (20). See below, pp. 140–1.

degree of indebtedness. It is true that the discourses contained in Volumes III and IV do have more Shandean touches than those of the two earlier volumes; but, in the light of new evidence about to be presented, it is difficult not to believe that practically all the forty-five extant sermons were written during the same general period, prior to 1760—possibly before 1750—though some may have been subjected to minor revision later.

It seemed logical that the first step in trying to evaluate Sterne's homiletic indebtedness should be a careful reading of the works of those predecessors from whom it was already known that he had borrowed; the list of names given by Fitzgerald should be fully investigated. For a point of departure there were Bentley, Butler, Clarke, Hall, Leightonhouse, De Isla, Locke, Norris, Steele, Swift, Tillotson, Wollaston, and Young—scholars, philosophers, theologians, essayists—a formidable array, including the names both of men familiar to Yorick's contemporaries, as well as their more obscure brethren, and extending back for more than a century. Obviously, Yorick had been browsing in variegated and unpredictable fields.

A careful examination of all the available writings of these predecessors revealed where Sterne found the inspiration for many ideas and paragraphs in his discourses and suggested the possibility, at least, that his borrowings had by no means been confined solely to them. Much had been found but there was every reason for believing that nearly as much yet remained undetected. The problem now was where to begin—how to select from the overwhelming wealth of material at hand. The Todd and Sotheran *Catalogue of a Curious and Valuable Collection of Books, among Which Are Included the Entire Library of the Late Reverend and Learned Laurence Sterne, A.M.* (York, 1768), with its twenty-five hundred entries, might afford interesting and valuable corroborative evidence; as a point of departure, however, its use was limited: it was, at once, too inclusive and not definite enough. Many of the listed items, on the one hand, such as "James's Theory and Practice of Gardening" or "Rauthmell's Roman Antiquities of Overborough" could not be regarded as likely sources for homiletic material; on the other hand, the catalogue contained many incompletely described volumes: "Sermons (18) by Bentley, Sharpe, Bishop of Worcester, &c. . . . ," "Sermons (23) by Patrick, Clagget, Lake, Lardner, Trimnel, Grove, &c. . . .";[1] and, following the last numbered item in the list, there was a note to the effect that "A large Collection of single Sermons" was available "at one Shilling per Dozen." Furthermore, no man's reading is ever restricted to those volumes which may happen to appear upon his

---

1. Todd and Sotheran, *Catalogue,* items 608 and 612; items 678 and 679. See, further, items 680–94 and 1102–11.

shelves; the names of Leightonhouse, Norris, and Rogers, three clergymen upon whom Sterne definitely levied toll, do not appear within the catalogue's pages.

Other approaches to the problem of selection fortunately suggested themselves; at least one clue demanded investigation. From various entries in the manuscript loan or issue book of the York Minster Library,[2] dating between 1741 and 1753, it is known that "L. Sterne" withdrew from the library and had in his possession certain volumes which might well have furnished him with illustrations and suggestions for his sermons. Not all the books thus charged against his name have been identified; for example, this entry for June 3, 1741: "2 vols. of tracts vs. Popery." Two other entries, however, appeared as likely sources: Bishop Simon Patrick's monumental *Commentaries* on the books of the Old Testament and William Burder's *Religious Ceremonies and Customs of the Several Nations of the Known World*, with numerous illustrations by Picart.[3] Although an examination of these two works, later, disclosed no evidence that Sterne had made use of them, they seemed rich in potentiality.

Another possible source might exist in the pages of some of those authors who had found their way into *Tristram Shandy*: Robert Burton and Sir Thomas Browne, Montaigne and Erasmus;[4] certainly, Yorick's passing reference to Daniel Waterland should be examined.[5]

Less specific but not to be ignored was the list of names suggested and commented upon by Dr. Johnson in answer to Boswell's query as to who were the best English sermon writers for style.

I took an opportunity today of mentioning several to him.—*"Atterbury?"* Johnson. "Yes, Sir, one of the best." Boswell. *"Tillotson?"* Johnson. "Why, not now. I should not advise a preacher at this day to imitate Tillotson's style. . . . *South* is one of the best, if you except his peculiarities. . . .

2. I am greatly indebted to Professor Lewis Perry Curtis of Yale University for first calling my attention to the existence of this document and for permitting me to make use of the transcript he had taken of it.

3. Sterne's withdrawal of this work was recorded in the York Minster Library's Loan Book as follows: "20 May 1753—3 vols. of Religious Ceremonies." Item 35 in the Todd and Sotheran *Catalogue* lists *Religious Ceremonies and Customs of all Nations*, 3 vols. *with fine Plates, by Picart*, &c. . . . 1731. Undoubtedly these were the volumes which attracted Yorick's attention. The edition used in preparation for this study was a later and enlarged one, published in London between 1731 and 1737: "Written Originally in French, and now published in English, with very considerable Amendments and Additions."

4. See the Introduction to Work's edition of *Tristram Shandy*, p. xxiii. See also Cross's chapter in *Life*, entitled "The Parson in His Library."

5. Cf. *Idem*, p. 242. In *Tristram Shandy*, Bk. vi, chap. xi, Sterne wrote that it was ever Yorick's custom, "on the first leaf of every sermon which he composed, to chronicle down the time, the place, and the occasion of its being preached: to this, he was ever wont to add some short comment or stricture upon the sermon itself, seldom, indeed, much to its credit:—For instance, *This sermon upon the jewish dispensation—I don't like it at all;—Though I own there is a world of* WATER-LANDISH *knowledge in it,—but 'tis all tritical, and most tritically put together."*

Seed has a very fine style; but he is not very theological.—*Jortin's* sermons are very elegant.—*Sherlock's* style too is very elegant, though he has not made it his principal study.—And you may add *Smallridge* [*sic*]. . . . I should recommend Dr. *Clarke's* sermons, were he orthodox. . . ." Boswell. "I like Ogden's *Sermons on Prayer* very much, both for neatness of style and subtilty of reasoning." Johnson. "I should like to read all that Ogden has written. . . . A Clergyman: (whose name I do not recollect.) "Were not Dodd's sermons addressed to the passions?" Johnson. "They were nothing, Sir, be they addressed to what they may."[6]

Sterne's indebtedness to Tillotson and Clarke had already been acknowledged; but might not Seed, just because Johnson found him "not very theological," and Dodd, whose sermons were "addressed to the passions," have been more appealing to Yorick? The reasons for Johnson's censure could well be the cause for Sterne's enjoyment and appreciation of these two clergymen.

Yorick's undeniable Latitudinarian tendencies also should be taken into account—tendencies underscored not only by what he himself had written but also by the fact that he had found so much that was congenial in Tillotson and Clarke, accepted leaders in this Low-Church movement. From the writings of these two clergymen, Sterne might easily have gone on to Stillingfleet, Chillingworth, Baxter, Whichcote, Hales, and Hoadly, men traditionally accepted as having shared, at least in part, in the propagation of Low-Church doctrines.

It is inconceivable that the Deist controversy could have been unknown to Sterne and that, at least in the early days of his priesthood, he had not read some of the tracts which that famous dispute called forth. Had he made free with Toland, Mudge, Shaftesbury, Bolingbroke? or had echoes from any of the defenders of Orthodox Christianity found their way into his sermons—had Nelson, Berkeley, Chandler, Sherlock, Atterbury, Cudworth, Smaldridge, or Blackall been laid under contribution? This was another possibility that required consideration.

Again. from the fact that Sterne is known to have consulted Bishop Patrick's *Commentaries* on the Old Testament. might he not also have looked into the biblical expositions of other well-known predecessors—Edward Wells, Henry Hammond, Dr. Jarmin, or Dr. Trapp? Several instances in *The Sermons of Mr. Yorick*, where difficult scriptural passages were expounded, would make this a not unlikely supposition; Yorick's speculations as to the probable meaning of "A voice was heard in Rama . . . Rachael weeping for her children" or upon our Saviour's statement, "I came not to send peace on earth, but a sword,"[7] suggest that his thoughts may not have been entirely original.

6. James Boswell, *Life of Johnson*, L. F. Powell, ed. (Oxford, 1934, 4 vols.), III, 247–8.
7. *Sermons*, II, 9, pp. 49–53; VII, 14 (41), pp. 41–4.

How early in his career had Sterne's acquaintance commenced with French writers, either in the original or in translation? Had Bishop Bossuet or La Bruyère or La Rochefoucauld been of any influence upon him? The sermons abound in generic character sketches and type portraits; had some of the "character" writers—John Earle, Joseph Hall, Sir Thomas Overbury, Theophrastus—supplied him with any details?

And finally, as the indebtednesses to Young and Leightonhouse would suggest, Sterne had also sampled the wares of obscure churchmen, whose names now are never included in the lists of their more famous contemporaries. From advertising sheets of "Books printed for" or "Books lately published by," so frequently to be found inserted at the end of eighteenth-century publications, or from bibliographies like John Veneer's "Books Made Use of, and Referred to in the Following Works"[8] one may quickly compile a register of minor clergymen about whom nothing is known today beyond the information contained in the title pages of their modest little volumes. To how many of these had Sterne also helped himself?

What began as an attempt to circumscribe the available material had, of necessity, expanded to nearly all-inclusive proportions. The only applicable restriction was to establish a definite time limit, at 1760—the year when the first two volumes of Mr. Yorick's *Sermons* were offered to the public; it is unlikely that Sterne would have availed himself of any theological writing which had not appeared in print before that time.

A word of comment and explanation is necessary at this point. Unusual difficulties beset anyone who is trying to determine whether or not a given sermon may have influenced or served as a model for another. In homiletic writing there are bound to be certain resemblances in the use of ideas; even an echoing of phraseology, not only between writer and writer but between the discourses of any one writer, cannot be avoided. After all, there are fixed limits to what can be said in the elucidation or expounding of a given scriptural text; too great a degree of originality is neither expected nor desirable. Well might Yorick, as had many another clergyman yielding to the temptation of going into print, warn "that the reader, upon old and beaten subjects, must not look for many new thoughts,—'tis well if he has new language."[9] The investigator of sources for Sterne's sermons must, therefore, be constantly upon his guard not to jump to hasty conclusions, however temptingly suspicious a similarity may appear.

8. John Veneer, *An Exposition on the Thirty-nine Articles of the Church of England* (London, 1725).
9. *Sermons*, Preface to Vol. i.

Two examples will serve both to illustrate these dangers and to provide the criterion by which sources have been judged in this study. In Bishop Patrick's *Commentary on Ecclesiastes* (chap. vii, pp. 2–3) there occurs this passage:

. . . it is our wisdom to think often of . . . and consequently, choose rather to converse with things that will make us serious, than with those which will make us merry: to go, for instance, into the company of those who are mourning for the dead, rather than of those who are feasting for joy. . . . for in the midst of those pleasures we are apt to be dissolute and forget ourselves: but that sad spectacle inclines us naturally to be considerate, and disposes our mind to humility, modesty, gentleness, sobriety, and charity . . . . Sadness, therefore, and sorrow, are much more profitable for us than mirth and jollity . . . because that grief which makes a man look sadly, whether it be for his own sins, or for other men's calamities, is apt to do his soul good: by giving him a right understanding of God, and of himself, and of all things else.

As has already been mentioned, there is evidence to show that Sterne knew the Bishop's *Commentary;* in the light of this circumstance, compare with the quotation from Patrick the following abridgment of "The House of Feasting and the House of Mourning Described."

Let us remember . . . that we have still set our faces towards Jerusalem —that we have a place of rest and happiness, towards which we hasten, and that the way to get there is not so much to please our hearts, as to improve them in virtue;—that mirth and feasting are usually no friends to atchievements of this kind—but that a season of affliction is in some sort a season of piety . . . that at certain times it is so necessary a man's mind should be turned towards itself, that rather than want occasions, he had better purchase them at the expence of his present happiness.—He had better, as the text expresses it, *go to the house of mourning,* where he will meet with something to subdue his passions, than to the house of feasting, where the joy and gaiety of the place is likely to excite them . . . .

This is the full force of the wise man's declaration.—But to do farther justice to his words . . . take a transient view of the two places here referred to . . . . Give me leave therefore, I beseech you, to recall both of them for a moment, to your imaginations, that from thence I may appeal to your hearts . . . .

Imagine then, such a house of feasting . . . . When the gay and smiling aspect of things has begun to leave the passages to a man's heart . . . thoughtlessly unguarded— . . . when music likewise has lent her aid . . . the voice of singing women with the sound of the viol and the lute have broke in upon his soul . . . that moment let us dissect and look into his heart—see how vain! how weak! how empty a thing it is! . . .

Thus much for the house of feasting . . . . Let us turn aside, from this gay scene; and suffer me to take you with me for a moment to one much fitter for your meditation. Let us go into the house of mourning . . . where perhaps, the aged parents sit broken hearted . . . . A transient scene of distress, such as is here sketch'd, how soon does it furnish materials to set the mind at work? how necessarily does it engage it to the consideration of the miseries and misfortunes . . . to which the life of man is subject. . . . take notice, to what a serious and devout frame of mind every man is reduced . . . . see, the light and easy heart . . . how pensive it is now, how soft, how susceptible, how full of religious impressions . . . .

. . . upon this single evidence [we rest our cause] and appeal to the most sensual, whether Solomon has not made a just determination here, in favour of the house of mourning?—not for its own sake, but as it is fruitful in virtue, and becomes the occasion of so much good.[1]

It does not require a great stretch of the imagination to conceive of Yorick's having found the germinal idea for his sermon in the *Commentary*. This particular passage from Bishop Patrick, however, has not been included in the list of sources printed in the Appendix, not only because there were no verbal similarities but also because nothing else in the Bishop's published writings comes under the slightest suspicion of having influenced any of Sterne's other discourses. If prototype there was for "The House of Feasting," it is more likely to be found in Bishop Hall's "Mourner in Sion"—a probability which is heightened by the existence of evidence showing that Sterne had helped himself to other portions of Hall's writing.

Even when one or more paragraphs have been found, containing ideas and expressions sufficiently similar to Yorick's to justify the belief that here was a definite source, it is not always easy to determine the full extent of the confiscations. How much Sterne borrowed from John Rogers' "Twelfth Sermon" is a case in point. There can be no doubt that sentences from the opening and concluding paragraphs of this discourse were incorporated into the sermon on "Humility";[2] further indebtednesses, however, may admit of dispute. In Rogers' homily, Sterne read this observation:

. . . it is from Christ we must learn Humility.

But especially are we to learn it from him, because he not only prescrib'd this Virtue, but was himself meek and lowly, the great Pattern and Example of it. . . . Humility is a Virtue which shines with a peculiar Eminence in his Example, and is exhibited to us in every part of his Life and Character. . . . the blessed Jesus came not in a Character to share the Pleasures or Glories of Life with us, to be a Prince or a Ruler on Earth: No, the Meanness of his Birth, the Toils and Indigence of his Life, and the Shame and Ignominy of his Death, are all convincing Arguments that his Kingdom was not of this World. . . . he voluntarily . . . took upon him the Form of a Servant, and, as the Prophet had foretold in that mournful Description of him, he had no Form nor Comliness, nor any Beauty, that

---

1. *Idem*, I, 2, pp. 27-45.
2. John Rogers, *Twelve Sermons, Preached upon Several Occasions* (London, 1730). See below, pp. 145-6.

we should desire him. . . . [He] submitted to a Condition, below even the common Provisions of Life: *Foxes had Holes, and the Birds of the Air Nests, but the Son of God had not where to lay his Head. . . . He came not,* as he says, *to be minister'd unto, but to minister, and to give his Life a Ransom for many.* He gave his Life, and with amazing Resignation humbled himself to the Death of the Cross, the Death of a Slave and a Malefactor.

In his discourse on "Humility" Yorick commented:

. . . every believer must receive some tincture of the character [of Humility] . . . from the example of so great, and yet so humble a Master, whose whole course of life was a particular lecture to this one virtue; and in every instance of it shewed, that he came not to share the pride and glories of life . . . but . . . appearing himself rather as a servant than a master,————coming, as he continually declared, not to be ministred unto, but to minister; and as the Prophet had foretold in that mournful description of him,————to have no form, or comeliness, nor any beauty that they should desire him. The voluntary meanness of his birth,————the poverty of his life,————the low offices in which it was engaged . . . the inconveniences which attended the execution of it, in having no where to lay his head,————all spoke the same language . . . the tender and pathetick proof he gave of the same disposition at the conclusion and great catastrophe of his suffering,—when a life full of so many instances of humility was crowned with the most endearing one of *humbling himself even to the death of the cross;*————the death of a slave,————a malefactor———— drag'd to *Calvary* without opposition,————insulted without complaint.————[3]

Most of the verbal similarities in the two paragraphs originate from a common source in the Bible; in what remains there is little of that word-for-word sort of transcription that makes obligation indisputable. The resemblances in the selection of details, however, and the persistency with which comments from Rogers are echoed in Sterne's phraseology, when combined with the knowledge that Sterne had already made use of other portions of this same sermon, justify the conclusion that there was a further instance of indebtedness in the paragraph under consideration. For similar reasons, two or three additional extracts from Rogers have been reprinted with the other parallel passages in the Appendix.

Exception to these standards of judgment has been made by the inclusion of quotations from three of James Foster's and one of Thomas Wise's sermons as among those writings from which Yorick plagiarized. Although none of the selections from Foster betray more definite indications of having influenced Sterne than the passage just quoted from Rogers, and are therefore without the benefit of

3. *Idem,* pp. 339–43, and *Sermons,* IV, 10 (25), pp. 120–2. See also Matthew 20.28; Isaiah 66.2–3; Matthew 8.20; and Philippians 2.8.

that firm anchorage which a more verbatim repetition affords, the similarities in thought and the echoes of phraseology are too numerous and too suggestive to be explained away on the grounds of sheer coincidence.[4]

Since a systematic examination of all the available writings of those authors to whom Sterne himself acknowledged indebtedness and whom earlier commentators had discovered to have been of influence produced such interesting and proportionately satisfactory results, it seemed highly probable that a continued investigation, along the lines just suggested, would be almost equally rewarding. Such, unfortunately, was not the case. Despite the existence of what promised to be a wealth of clues and possibilities, a careful reading of more than six thousand new sermons and of well over one hundred thousand pages of additional miscellaneous theological, philosophi-

4. It is tempting to identify La Rochefoucauld as the anonymous satirical writer quoted by Sterne (*Sermons,* IV, 9 [24], p. 83) as having said, "That all mankind at the bottom were proud alike;—that one man differed from another, not so much in the different portions which he possessed of it, as in the different art and address by which he excells in the management and disguise of it to the world . . . ." Cf. La Rochefoucauld, *Maximes* (London, 1902), p. 14: "L'orgueil est égal dans tous les hommes, et il n'y a de différence qu'aux moyens et à la manière de le mettre à jour." Again, from an allusion to "the great Addison" in that section of *Tristram Shandy* where the merits of various travel writers are discussed (Bk. VII, chap. IV), there is reason for assuming that Sterne knew the *Remarks on Several Parts of Italy* (London, 1705); it is equally tempting, therefore, to believe that a passage from this book may have been in the back of Sterne's mind while he was composing his discourse on "Penances."

ADDISON

"From Rome to Naples," pp. 179–83

In my way from *Rome* to *Naples* I found nothing so remarkable as the Beauty of the Country, and the extreme Poverty of its Inhabitants . . . . One can scarce imagine how so plentiful a Soil should become so miserably unpeopled, in Comparison of what it once was. . . . This desolation appears no where greater than in the Pope's Territories . . . [where] there is not a more miserable People . . . . These ill Effects may arise, in a great measure, out of the Arbitrariness of the Government, but I think they are chiefly to be ascrib'd to the very Genius of the *Roman* Catholick Religion, which here shows it self in its Perfection.

STERNE

Sermons, VI, 10 (37), pp. 100–01

. . . in many countries where popery reigns,—but especially in that part of Italy where she has raised her throne,— though, by the happiness of its soil and climate, it is capable of producing as great variety and abundance as any country upon earth;—yet so successful have its spiritual directors been in the management and retail of these blessings, that they have found means to allay, if not entirely to defeat, them all, by one pretence or other.—Some bitterness is officiously squeezed into every man's cup for his soul's health, till, at length, the whole intention of nature and providence is destroyed.

Since there are no further indications that Sterne might have been indebted either to La Rochefoucauld or Addison, and in the absence of more definite verbal similarities, the selections here quoted have not been included with the other source-material passages in the Appendix. There is no more reason for believing that Yorick appropriated these observations directly from the works in which they originally appeared than that he came upon them already embodied in some intermediary sermon, so far undetected.

cal, and general literature disclosed only five hitherto unsuspected sources, of which Yorick had made comparatively limited use: Rogers' "Twelfth Sermon," another sermon by Stillingfleet, two more by James Blair, three by James Foster, and probably one by Thomas Wise. In so far as the shedding of new light upon either Sterne's sources or practices was concerned, the law of diminishing returns definitely had become operative. Without doubt, continued research would ultimately uncover more sources and reveal the identities of those "witty divines" whom Yorick quoted as having said that enthusiasts "were much fitter to *make* a pulpit, than get into one" and "That covetousness is the shirt of the soul,—the last vice it parts with."[5] Admittedly, the available evidence today is still incomplete. But it is not likely that a full count will ever be reckoned: from what is known of Sterne's reading habits, it would probably be necessary, before completeness were achieved, to read nearly every book printed in English prior to 1760; and the list might have to be extended to include all French, Latin, and Greek publications as well. It is partially because of the obvious impossibility of such an undertaking but more largely because of a conviction that enough new material has already been assembled to warrant publication that the investigation of sources has been pursued no further. From the not inconsiderable amount of evidence, assembled here for the first time, a much clearer picture emerges of how Yorick went about the task of sermon writing and of the books he used in the process; of the varying degrees to which he was influenced by the materials appropriated and what bearing this has upon his originality as a writer. As a result of this clearer picture, we are now in a better position to determine when most of the discourses were probably written, to see how they differed from those of Sterne's predecessors and contemporaries, to estimate the sincerity with which Sterne undertook his priestly duties, and to appraise with more understanding and sympathy the Christianity he preached.

In other words—though the complete story is not yet known, and probably never will be—it will nevertheless still be possible to show that much of the vilification which has been heaped upon Sterne the Churchman is without justification; and in other instances, where complete exoneration is more difficult, to point to extenuating considerations. That at least some of the unfortunate misconceptions which have stood between Yorick and his twentieth-century reader may now be dispelled is the justification for the ensuing chapters.

5. *Sermons*, IV, 10 (25), p. 128, and III, 4 (19), p. 115. Cf. Owen Feltham, "Of Fame," *Resolves or, Excogitations. A Second Century* (London, 1628), p. 43: "Desire of *Glory,* is the last *garment,* that, even *wise men,* lay aside."

II

The Evidence

IT has long been recognized that in the character of Parson Yorick, which emerges from the pages of *Tristram Shandy,* Sterne was drawing a portrait of himself as Vicar of Sutton.[1] Not that one is to accept every detail in a strictly autobiographical sense; allowance must be made, always, for the novelist's inclination to exaggeration and whimsicality. But in the two instances where Yorick's methods of composing sermons are commented upon, there is every likelihood that Sterne was depicting his own practices with an unusual degree of fidelity. One of these pictures discloses the Parson in his study, writing "on the first leaf of every sermon which he composed" such a comment as

—N.B. . . . —For this sermon I shall be hanged,——for I have stolen the greatest part of it. Doctor Paidagunes *found me out. . . . Set a thief to catch a thief.——*[2]

The other picture shows us Yorick astride his "meek-spirited jade of a broken-winded horse," from which point of vantage

. . . he could spend his time, as he rode slowly along,——to as much account as in his study;—that he could draw up an argument in his sermon, —or a hole in his breeches, as steadily on the one as in the other; . . . upon his steed—he could unite and reconcile every thing,—he could compose his sermon,—he could compose his cough,——and, in case nature gave a call that way, he could likewise compose himself to sleep.——[3]

Despite the seeming contradiction, there is really no inconsistency in the two accounts, for they are representative of two entirely different periods in the preacher's career. The first picture characterizes Yorick's earliest manner of sermon writing when, "be hanged" or not, he had only his rural congregation to consider; there was no need to do more for them than piece together a series of paragraphs from the discourses of others; untroubled by thoughts of possible publication, why encumber his remarks with painstaking acknowledgments of sources? The second picture, of Yorick upon horseback meditating

---

1. *Life,* p. 61. See also *Sentimental Journey,* II, 70–2, where Sterne explains to the Count de B*** that he is Yorick but not "the king of Denmark's jester."
2. *Tristram Shandy,* Bk. VI, chap. xi. 3. *Idem,* Bk. I, chap. x.

various matters, reveals the Parson several years later, after his conception of sermon writing had undergone a change. In response to a growing consciousness of his own literary abilities, he was no longer content to copy what had been written by others; he now preferred to see for himself what could be done with a text. Though still susceptible to suggestion, his liberated imagination was carrying him far beyond the walls of his study and the beaten paths of his predecessors, constantly suggesting how a borrowed phrase or idea could be transformed into something more striking, more truly his own. The pleasure of seeing his discourses in print had become a definite possibility.

Such contrasting aims would naturally lead to strikingly different results, which in turn should make it possible to separate Sterne's sermons into two easily distinguishable groups: in the one, those parish homilies which contained a large amount of borrowed material and were generally perfunctory in character; in the other, those discourses showing a greater flexibility and originality and stamped with a clearer reflection of the writer's personality. That all the sermons are not of equal merit is no new discovery; but what has not heretofore been considered is the possibility that this definite inequality, separating the sermons into two distinct groups, could be accounted for principally by the preacher's changed attitude toward his task. In other words, instead of taking it for granted that good and poor discourses were alternately produced from year to year, might it not be possible that the poorer discourses were the first to have been written and consistently antedate the others? That there are plausible grounds for making such a distinction—more specifically, that practically all of Yorick's earliest sermons are to be found in the three posthumously published volumes,[4] while the discourses written later were the ones selected for inclusion in the first four volumes which Sterne himself supervised through the press[5]—is one of the major premises to be advanced in this study.

The evidence which will be used to support this supposition results from two different bases of comparison. First, if it can be shown that the sermons remaining in manuscript at the time of Sterne's death (included later in Volumes v–vii) are consistently less creative and distinctive in character and invariably betray more striking instances of verbatim copying from older writers than those which the preacher selected for printing (contained in Volumes i–iv); and, secondly, if there exists a convincingly large number of passages appearing once in the posthumously published homilies and again, reworked and improved, in those of earlier issue, then it would seem reasonable to conclude that Volumes I–IV, though first to be printed, were of later composition than the last three volumes.

In attempting to substantiate the first part of this premise—that those discourses which Sterne did not select for publication comprise his earliest attempts at sermon writing—a certain amount of repetition is unavoidable. The parallel passages listed in the Appendix, though revealing the nature and extent of Yorick's plagiarisms in general, do not indicate how much appropriated material any one discourse contained; more important, they fail to indicate in which volumes the borrowings were most pronounced. To exemplify these points and, in so doing, to stress the very real differences separating the posthumous from the earlier-printed discourses, let us examine in detail one representative from each group. Consider first the "Temporal Advantages of Religion," a sermon altogether mechanical and platitudinous in character and justifiably left unpublished by Sterne at the time of his death.[6] It is reprinted in its entirety because, as the following pages will show, Yorick contributed little that was his own; four fifths of this homily consist of literal transcripts, selected from the writings of five different clergymen.

YOUNG

"The Safe Way to Happiness," Sermon 11, P. 1, pp. 366–8 [7]

There are Two Opinions which the Devil has been always busy to propagate in the World, as the Two main Pillars of his Kingdom: The First is, That a Sinful Life is a State of true Liberty, and sincere Pleasures, and happy Advantages; The Second is (on the contrary) That a Religious Life is a Servile and Uncomfortable State.

He made the first Breach upon humane Innocence by the former of these Suggestions; when he told *Eve*, That by Eating of the Tree of Knowledge *she should be as God*, that is, she should reap some high and strange felicity from doing that which was forbidden her to do. But we know the Success: *Eve* learnt the difference between *Good* and *Evil* by her Transgression, which she knew not before; but she learnt the Difference to be this, That Good is that that gives the Mind pleasure

STERNE

"Temporal Advantages of Religion," *Sermons*, v, 1 (28), pp. 3–6

There are two opinions which the inconsiderate are apt to take upon trust.— The first is—a vicious life, is a life of liberty, pleasure, and happy advantages.— The second is—and which is the converse of the first—that a religious life is a servile and most uncomfortable state.

The first breach which the devil made upon human innocence, was by the help of the first of these suggestions, when he told Eve, that by eating of the tree of knowledge, she should be as God, that is, she should reap some high and strange felicity from doing what was forbidden her.—But I need not repeat the success— Eve learnt, the difference between good and evil by her transgression, which she knew not before—but then she fatally learnt at the same time, that the difference was only this—that good is that which can only give the mind pleasure and comfort

6. *Sermons*, v, 1 (28). Cf. *Life*, pp. 621–2: "A perfunctory sermon . . . clearly belonging to the Sutton period. . . ." Sterne was officially in residence at Sutton from 1738 to 1760.

7. Page references are to the *Sermons on Several Occasions*, I.

and assurance; and Evil is that that must necessarily be attended, sooner or later, with shame and sorrow.

As he thus began his Kingdom, so he has carried it on ever since by the same Imposture; that is, by possessing men's minds with vast Expectations of the present Incomes of Sin; and making them dream of golden Mountains, mighty gratifications and advantages they shall meet with in following their Appetites the forbidden way. Whereas on the contrary, there are Seasons wherein all Sinners are ready to confess, that their Counsellor has been a Deceiver, that their Foolish Hearts have been darkened, that their Hopes have been Vain, their Gains no Profit, and all their Enjoyments leading to Bitterness. So little trust is to be given to all the promising Overtures of sin.

—and that evil is that, which must necessarily be attended sooner or later with shame and sorrow.

As the deceiver of mankind thus began his triumph over our race—so has he carried it on ever since by the very same argument of delusion.—That is, by possessing men's minds early with great expectations of the present incomes of sin,—making them dream of wondrous gratifications they are to feel in following their appetites in a forbidden way—making them fancy, that their own grapes yield not so delicious a taste as their neighbours, and that they shall quench their thirst with more pleasure at his fountain, than at their own. This is the opinion which at first too generally prevails—till experience and proper seasons of reflections make us all at one time or other confess—that our counsellor has been (as from the beginning) an imposture—and that instead of fulfilling these hopes of gain and sweetness in what is forbidden—that on the contrary, every unlawful enjoyment leads only to bitterness and loss.

pp. 368–9

To promote the second Opinion, That a Religious Life is a Servile and Uncomfortable State, the Devil suggests to our Thoughts, That true Freedom is to follow our own Humour; That to deny our Appetites is to be Miserable? That not to prosecute our Passions is to be Cowards . . . . That to live by moderate and prescribed Rules is to have no Joy; and therefore that when the Religious Man looks for Joy, he can only see it at the tedious distance of a Future Life: Which were it true, our Nature that is so importunately goaded on with the desire of present Happiness, could not but languish under the discouragement of so Remote an Expectation. But in the mean time the Holy Scriptures give us a quite different prospect of this matter: there we are told, that the *service of* God is true *Liberty;* that the *Yoak of Christ is easy,* in comparison of that which any other Form of Living will bring upon us; that *Religion has Pleasantness in its ways,* as well as Glory in its End; that it will bring us in *Peace and Joy, such as the World cannot give;* and therefore that the Religious Man's Joy does not stand at so tedious a distance, but is so present and at hand that it may be felt and tasted every moment.

pp. 6–9

The second opinion, or, That a religious life is a servile and uncomfortable state, has proved a no less fatal and capital false principle in the conduct of unexperience through life—the foundation of which mistake arising chiefly from this previous wrong judgment—that true happiness and freedom lies in a man's always following his own humour—that to live by moderate and prescrib'd rules, is to live without joy—that not to prosecute our passions is to be cowards—and to forego every thing for the tedious distance of a future life.

Was it true that a virtuous man could have no pleasure but what should arise from that remote prospect—I own we are by nature so goaded on by the desire of present happiness, that was that the case, thousands wou'd faint under the discouragement of so remote an expectation.— But in the mean time the Scriptures give us a very different prospect of this matter. —There we are told that the service of God is true liberty;—that the yoke of Christianity is easy in comparison of that yoke which must be brought upon us by any other system of living,—and the text tells of wisdom—by which he means Religion, that it has pleasantness in its way,

pp. 381-2

Moral Delight is that which springs from the Conscience of *Well doing:* And though this be a Pleasure that properly belongs to the Good; yet even the Vicious can hardly be insensible of it; because it may be felt to spring from any Single or Casual Act of *Virtue*. As for Example: Let a Man but refresh the Bowels of the needy, or comfort the afflicted, or check an Appetite, or overcome a Temptation, or forgive an Injury, or receive an Affront with Temper and Meekness, and he shall immediately find the tacit Praise of what he has done, darting through his Mind, accompanied with a sincere Delectation. And thus Conscience plays the *Monitor* ev'n to the Loose and Unregenerate in their most Casual Acts of *Well-doing;* and *is like a voice whispering behind them, and saying, This is the way, walk in it.*

Cf. P. 2, pp. 423-4

. . . *God* has provided . . . indulgently for those that love him: *Godliness has the Promise of this Life, as well as of that which is to come:* and this in the Text has peculiar Respect to *this Life;* and therefore I shall only treat of it here in reference to its Accomplishment *here;* and shew how, and in what manner the *Goodness of God* will infallibly make it good to every one that *delights in Him.*

TILLOTSON

"The Advantages of Religion to Particular Persons," Sermon 4, p. 441[8]

God has not been so hard a master to us that we have reason . . . to complain of

as well as glory in its end—that it will bring us peace and joy such as the world cannot give.—So that upon examining the truth of this assertion, we shall be set right in this error, by seeing that a religious man's happiness does not stand at so tedious a distance—but is so present and indeed so inseparable from him, as to be felt and tasted every hour—and of this even the vicious can hardly be insensible, from what he may perceive to spring up in his mind, from any casual act of virtue. And tho' it is a pleasure that properly belongs to the good—yet let any one try the experiment, and he will see what is meant by that moral delight, arising from the conscience of well-doing.—Let him but refresh the bowels of the needy—let him comfort the broken-hearted—or check an appetite, or overcome a temptation—or receive an affront with temper and meekness—and he shall find the tacit praise of what he has done, darting thro' his mind, accompanied with a sincere pleasure—conscience playing the monitor even to the loose and most inconsiderate, in their most casual acts of well-doing, and is, like a voice whispering behind and saying—this is the way of pleasantness—this is the path of peace—walk in it.—

pp. 10-13

But to do further justice to the text, we must look beyond this inward recompence which is always inseparable from virtue—and take a view of the outward advantages, which are as inseparable from it, and which the Apostle particularly refers to, when 'tis said, Godliness has the promise of this life, as well as that which is to come—and in this argument it is, that religion appears in all its glory and strength—unanswerable in all its obligations—that besides the principal work which it does for us in securing our future well-being in the other world, it is likewise the most effectual means to promote our present—and that not only *morally,* upon account of that reward which virtuous actions do entitle a man unto from a just and wise providence,—but by a natural tendency in themselves, which the duties of religion have *to procure* us riches, health, reputation, credit, and all those things, wherein our temporal happiness is

8. Page references are to T. Birch's edition of Tillotson, *Works* (London, 1820, 10 vols.), 1. Cf. Norris, "A Discourse Concerning Doing God's Will on Earth," from *Prac-*

him. He hath given us no laws but what are for our good; nay, so gracious hath he been to us as to link together our duty and our interest, and to make those very things the instances of our obedience, which are the natural means and causes of our happiness.

Sermon 6, pp. 469–70

. . . there is nothing in all those laws but what is most reasonable and fit to be done by us, nothing but what if we were to consult our own interest and happiness, and did rightly understand ourselves, we would chose for ourselves . . . . Some virtues plainly tend to the preservation of our health, others to the improvement and security of our estates, all to the peace and quiet of our minds; and . . . to the advancement of our esteem and reputation . . . .

BLAIR

Sermon 8, p. 157 [9]

. . . *Justice* and *Honesty* in our Dealings is the surest way to guard against Want . . . . For the better imprinting of which Truth in your Minds and Memories, there are these few things I would briefly offer to your Consideration.

1. The *First* is, That *Justice* and *Honesty* contribute very much towards the Improvement of all the Faculties of the Soul; I mean, that it clears up the Understanding from that Mist, which crooked

thought to consist,—and this not only in promoting the well-being of particular persons, but of public communities and of mankind in general,—agreeable to what the wise man has left us on record, that righteousness exalteth a nation:—insomuch,—that could we, in considering this argument, suppose ourselves to be in a capacity of expostulating with God, concerning the terms upon which we would submit to his government,—and to chuse the laws ourselves which we would be bound to observe, it would be impossible for the wit of man to frame any other proposals, which upon all accounts would be more advantageous to our own interests than those very conditions to which we are obliged by the rules of religion and virtue. —And in this does the reasonableness of christianity, and the beauty and wisdom of providence appear most eminently towards mankind, in governing us by such laws, as do most apparently tend to make us happy,—and in a word, in making that (in his mercy) to be our duty, which in his wisdom he knows to be our interest,— that is to say, what is most conducive to the ease and comfort of our mind,—the health and strength of our body,—the honour and prosperity of our state and condition,—the friendship and good will of our fellow creatures;—to the attainment of all which, no more effectual means can possibly be made use of, than that plain direction,—to lead an uncorrupted life, and to do the thing which is right, to use no deceit in our tongue, nor do evil to our neighbour.

For the better imprinting of which truth in your memories, give me leave to offer a few things to your consideration.

The first is,—that justice and honesty contribute very much towards all the faculties of the mind: I mean, that it clears up the understanding from that mist, which dark and crooked designs are apt

tical *Discourses upon Several Divine Subjects* (5th ed. London, 1707, 3 vols.), II, 272: ". . . God is so good and kind as to enjoyn nothing but what is pursuant of the End for which he Created us; that is, our Happiness and perfection: so kind as to link our Duty and Interest together, and to make those very things the Instances of our Obedience, which are the natural Means and necessary Causes of our Happiness: So that were we to contrive a way to make our Condition Happy, we could pitch upon no better than what he has already prescribed to us in the Laws which he has given us. So highly consonant and *agreeable* are they to the frame of our Natures, and so absolutely *necessary* are they both to the order of this present World, and to the Happiness of the next."

9. Page references are to *Our Saviour's Divine Sermon on the Mount* (London, 1722, 5 vols.), I.

dark Designs are apt to raise in it: That it preserves the Rectitude of the Will . . . and that it keeps up a regularity in the Affections, by suffering no sinister Design of Lusts or By-ends to disorder them. It likewise preserves the Conscience from all Damps of Grief and Melancholy, which are the Natural and Infallible Consequences of Unjust Designs and Actions. And by this Improvement of the Faculties, **it makes a Man so much the Abler to discern,** and so much the more Chearful, Active, and Diligent to Mind his Business. *Light is sown for the Righteous,* says the Psalmist, and *Gladness for the upright in Heart* . . . .

to raise in it,—and that it keeps up a regularity in the affections, by suffering no lusts or *by-ends* to disorder them.—That it likewise preserves the mind from all damps of grief and melancholy, which are the sure consequences of unjust actions; and that by such an improvement of the faculties, it makes a man so much the abler to discern, and so much the more chearful, active and diligent to mind his business.—Light is sown for the righteous, says the prophet, and gladness for the upright in heart.—

CLARKE

"Uprightness a Man's Greatest Security," Sermon 13, p. 281 [1]

. . . In the *continuance* and whole course of his affairs, he has the greatest probability not to fall into any considerable disappointment or calamity. . . . 1*st,* Because the way of Uprightness is in itself freest from danger . . . . 2*dly,* Because it is moreover guarded and protected, by the peculiar favour and providence of God.

pp. 15–17

Secondly, let it be observed,—that in the continuance and course of a virtuous man's affairs, there is little probability of his falling into considerable disappointments or calamities;—not only because guarded by the providence of God, but that honesty is in its own nature the freest from danger.

p. 280

The upright man lays no projects which it is the interest of his neighbour to hinder from succeeding; and therefore he needs no indirect methods, no fraudulent and deceitful practices, to secure his own Interest by undermining his neighbour's . . . .

First, because such a one lays no projects, which it is the interest of another to blast, and therefore needs no indirect methods or deceitful practices to secure his interest by undermining others.—

pp. 279–80

The paths of Virtue and Righteousness are plain and streight; so that the Blind, *i.e.* persons of the meanest capacity . . . shall not err therein. The ways of iniquity and injustice, of fraud and deceit, are infinitely various and uncertain . . . . It requires great skill and industry to find out such methods of overreaching our neighbours, as will have any probability of success . . . and it cannot but cause much solicitude of mind, to be always in fear of being disappointed by a discovery. How many do we meet with in the world who (out of a greedy desire of a little

The paths of virtue are plain and strait, so that the blind, persons of the meanest capacity, shall not err.—

Dishonesty requires great skill to conduct it, and as great art to conceal—what 'tis every one's interest to detect. And I think I need not remind you how oft it happens in attempts of this kind—where worldly men, in haste to be rich, have overrun the only means to it,—and for want of laying their contrivances with proper cunning, or

1. Page references are to Clarke, *Sermons,* VIII.

greater gain) endeavouring to over-reach and deceive their neighbours, have for want of laying their contrivances cunningly enough . . . fallen short of that gain which they might without farther trouble have gotten in the plain way of Honesty and Uprightness? . . .

managing them with proper secrecy and advantage, have lost for ever, what they might have certainly secured by honesty and plain-dealing.—

p. 282

. . . the general causes of mens misfortunes and disappointments, lie manifestly in their own Irregularities and Disorders; and the ruine of most men be evidently owing, to their own deceitful and indirect practices . . . .

pp. 282-3

Then is Uprightness undeniably the securest and least dangerous course.

p. 284

. . . as uprightness is *in itself* the safest and least dangerous course; so is it moreover guarded by the peculiar favour and providence of God.

The general causes of the disappointments in their business, or of unhappiness in their lives, lying but too manifestly in their own disorderly passions, which by attempting to carry them a shorter way to riches and honour, disappoint them of both for ever, and make plain their ruin is from themselves, and that they eat the fruits, which their own hands have watered and ripened.

Consider, in the third place, that as the religious and moral man (one of which he cannot be without the other) not only takes the surest course for success in his affairs, but is disposed to procure a help, which never enters into the thoughts of a wicked one:

BLAIR

Sermon 8, p. 158

. . . being conscious to himself of his sincere upright Intentions, he [the honest man] can with good Assurance recommend his Affairs to Gods Blessing and Direction; whereas the Dishonest Fraudulent Man dares not call for Gods Blessing upon his Wicked Designs, or if he does, he knows it is in vain to expect it. Now a Man who believes that he has God on his side, acts with another sort of Life and Chearfulness, and with another Vigour and Resolution, than he who knows he is alone in what he does . . . . *The Eyes of the Lord, says the Psalmist, are upon the Righteous, and his Ears are open unto their Cry. The Face of the Lord is against them that do Evil . . . .*

pp. 17-21

for being conscious of upright intentions, he can look towards heaven, and with some assurance recommend his affairs to God's blessing and direction:—whereas the fraudulent and dishonest Man, dares not call for God's blessing upon his designs,—or if he does, he knows it is in vain to expect it.—Now a man who believes that he has God on his side, acts with another sort of life and courage, than he who knows he stands alone;—like Esau, with his hand against every man, and every man's hand against his.

The eyes of the Lord are upon the righteous, and his ears are open to their cry,—but the face of the Lord is against them that do evil.

p. 159

. . . In all good Governments, such as understand their own Interest, the Upright Honest Man stands much fairer for Preferment than the Knave , ...

Consider, in the fourth place, that in all good governments who understand

p. 158

. . . The Honest Man is most likely to be kept in Business and Employ; For all Men, whatever they may be themselves, love to find Honesty in those they deal with; and hate to be tricked and cheated. This is so true an observation, that the greatest Knaves and Cheats have no other way to get into Business, but by Counterfeiting Honesty, and pretending to be what they are not. And if they happen to be discovered, as it is a thousand to one but that they will, they are presently blown upon, and discountenanced; and every one is cautious of having any further Dealings with such a Person.

The Honest Man has this great advantage, that the more and the longer he is known, so much the better is he Liked, and Trusted; so that his Reputation and his Wealth have a gradual Increase, as he comes to be better acquainted with Mankind, and they with him . . . .

Cf. p. 160

. . . all Men are apt to pity an Honest Man, if he falls into Troubles thro' Misfortune . . . .

NORRIS

"The Importance of a Religious Life, Considered," pp. 110–11 [2]

Indeed a bad Conscience is a Companion troublesom enough even in the midst of the most high-set Enjoyments; 'tis then

2. Norris, *op. cit.*, II.

their own interest, the upright and honest man stands much fairer for preferment, and much more likely to be employed in all things when fidelity is wanted:—for all men, however the case stands with themselves, they love at least to find honesty in those they trust; nor is there any usage we more hardly digest, than that of being outwitted and deceived.—This is so true an observation, that the greatest knaves have no other way to get into business, but by counterfeiting honesty, and pretending to be what they are not; and when the imposture is discovered, as it is a thousand to one but it will, I have just said, what must be the certain consequence:—for when such a one falls,—he has none to help him, —so he seldom rises again.—

This brings us to a fifth particular in vindication of the text,—That a virtuous man has this strong advantage on his side (the reverse of the last) that the more and the longer he is known, so much the better is he loved,—so much the more trusted;—so that his reputation and his fortune have a gradual increase:—and if calamities or cross accidents should bear him down,—(as no one stands out of their reach in this world)—if he should fall, who would not pity his distress,—who would not stretch forth his hand to raise him from the ground—wherever there was virtue, he might expect to meet a friend and brother.—And this is not merely speculation, but fact, confirmed by numberless examples in life, of men falling into misfortunes, whose character and tried probity have raised them helps, and bore them up, when every other help has forsook them.

pp. 21–3

Lastly, to sum up the account of the temporal advantages which probity has on its side,—let us not forget that greatest of all happiness, which the text refers to,— in the expression of all its paths being peace,—peace and content of mind, arising from the consciousness of virtue, which is the true and only foundation of all earthly satisfaction; and where that is wanting, whatever other enjoyments you bestow upon a wicked man, they will as soon add a cubit to his stature as to his happiness.—In the midst of the highest

like the *Hand writing* upon the Wall, enough to spoil and disrelish the *Feast;* but much more when the tumult and hurry of Delight is over, when all is still and silent, when the Sinner has nothing to do, but attend to its lashes and remorses. And this in spite of all the common Arts of Diversion, will be very often the case of every wicked Man; for we cannot live always upon the *Stretch;* our Faculties will not bear constant Pleasure any more than constant Pain; there will be some *Vacancies,* and when there are, they will be sure to be filled up with uncomfortable Thoughts and black Reflections . . . . So that setting aside the great *After-reckoning,* its Pleasures are over-bought even in this World . . . .

entertainments,—this, like the hand-writing upon the wall, will be enough to spoil and disrelish the feast;—but much more so, when the tumult and hurry of delight is over,—when all is still and silent,—when the sinner has nothing to do but attend its lashes and remorses;—and this, in spite of all the common arts of diversion, will be often the case of every wicked man;—for we cannot live always upon the stretch;—our faculties will not bear constant pleasure any more than constant pain;—there will be some vacancies; and when there are, they will be sure to be filled with uncomfortable thoughts and black reflections.—So that, setting aside the great after-reckoning, the pleasures of the wicked are over-bought, even in this world.—

pp. 23–6

I conclude with one observation upon the whole of this argument, which is this—

Notwithstanding the great force with which it has been often urged by good writers,—there are many cases which it may not reach,—wherein vicious men may seem to enjoy their portion of this life,—and live as happy, and fall into as few troubles as other men:—and, therefore, it is prudent not to lay more stress upon this argument than it will bear:—but always remember to call into our aid, that great and more unanswerable argument, which will answer the most doubtful cases which can be stated,—and that is, certainty of a future life, which christianity has brought to light.—However men may differ in their opinions of the usefulness of virtue for our present purposes,—no one was ever so absurd, as to deny it served our best and our last interest,—when the little interests of this life were at an end:—upon which consideration we should always lay the great weight which it is fittest to bear, as the strongest appeal, and most unchangeable motive that can govern our actions at all times.—However, as every good argument on the side of religion should in proper times be made use of,—it is fit sometimes to examine this,—by proving virtue is not even destitute of a present reward,—but carries in her hand a sufficient recompence for all the self-denials she may occasion:—she is pleasant in the way,—as well as in the end;—her ways being ways of pleasantness, and all her paths peace.—But it is her greatest

p. 111

. . . the practice of . . . Virtue . . . is not destitute even of a *Present* Reward, but carries in hand a sufficient Recompense for all the trouble she occasions. She is pleasant in the *Way* as well as in the *End,* for even her very Ways are Ways of Pleasantness, and all her Paths are Peace. But 'tis her greatest and most distinguishing Glory and Commendation, that she befriends us *Hereafter,* and brings us Peace at the last. And this is a Portion she can never be dis-inherited of, however the Malice of Men or an ill Combination of Accidents may defraud her of the Other.

and most distinguished glory,—that she befriends us hereafter, and brings us peace at the last;—and this is a portion she can never be disinherited of,—which may God of his mercy grant us all, for the sake of Jesus Christ.

An analysis of the "Temporal Advantages of Religion" shows quite clearly why Sterne had not selected this discourse for printing! Not only is it commonplace and dull but the extent of the borrowings left little room for the preacher to express either his own ideas or sentiments.

In contrast to such a mosaic of extended quotations, it is revealing to examine the earlier-printed "Parable of the Rich Man and Lazarus Considered."[3] Though this sermon betrays greater obligations to older writers than any of the discourses which Sterne himself prepared for publication, it will not be necessary here to reproduce it in its entirety, with accompanying columns of parallel source passages; less than a quarter of the whole stands in need of such comparison. Of even greater significance is the fact that, for the most part, the specific passages which Sterne appropriated from others have, to some degree, been reworked and stamped with a new imprint.

The text was one frequently preached upon by clergymen in the seventeenth and eighteenth centuries: "If they hear not Moses and the prophets, neither will they be persuaded, tho' one should rise from the dead."[4] What could such a messenger say, Yorick asks, as others had queried before him, "which had not been proposed and urged already?" He could

. . . prove it by a thousand arguments, that to be temperate and chaste, and just and peaceable, and charitable and kind to one another,—was only doing that for Christ's sake, which was most for our own; and that were we in a c[ap]acity of capitulating with God upon what terms we would submit to his government,—he would convince us, 'twould be impossible for the wit of man, to frame any proposals more for our present interests, than *to lead an uncorrupted life—to do the thing which is lawful and right,* and lay such restraints upon our appetites as are for the honour of human nature, and the refinement of human happiness.[5]

This paragraph is the first of nine instances in the "Lazarus" sermon where Yorick utilized another's writings; possibly Norris, but more probably Tillotson, suggested the basic thought. It is still more likely, however, that instead of copying directly from either primary source Sterne was improving upon a section he had included in one of the posthumously published discourses; the same thought had been

3. *Sermons,* IV, 8 (23).   4. Cf. Luke 16.31.
5. *Sermons,* IV, 8 (23), pp. 39–40.

voiced in the "Temporal Advantages of Religion,"[6] though neither
so concisely nor so pointedly as here. The presumably earlier-written
passage read:

. . . agreeable to what the wise man hath left us on record, [it is notable]
that righteousness exalteth a nation:—insomuch,—that could we, in considering this argument, suppose ourselves to be in a capacity of expostulating with God, concerning the terms upon which we would submit to his
government,—and to chuse the laws ourselves which we would be bound
to observe, it would be impossible for the wit of man to frame any other
proposals, which upon all accounts would be more advantageous to our
own interests than those very conditions to which we are obliged by the
rules of religion and virtue.—And in this does the reasonableness of christianity, and the beauty and wisdom of providence appear most eminently
towards mankind, in governing us by such laws, as do most apparently tend
to make us happy,—and in a word, in making that (in his mercy) to be our
duty, which in his wisdom he knows to be our interest,—that is to say,
what is most conducive to the ease and comfort of our mind,—the health
and strength of our body,—the honour and prosperity of our state and
condition,—the friendship and good will of our fellow creatures;—to the
attainment of all which, no more effectual means can possibly be made use
of, than that plain direction,—to lead an uncorrupted life, and to do the
thing which is right, to use no deceit in our tongue, nor do evil to our
neighbor.[7]

Not only does the paragraph just quoted betray more evidence of
indebtedness to Tillotson but it is more rambling in structure and
less forceful in expression than the corresponding passage from the
"Lazarus" sermon. Can there be any doubt as to which of the two
paragraphs was the first to have been written?

A still more interesting and impressive example of this reworking
of borrowed material, probably through the medium of an earlier-
written discourse, is to be found in the closing pages of "The Rich
Man and Lazarus." Yorick had been asked to preach on behalf of the
Foundling Hospital, in Holborn,[8] and in order to intensify his plea
for generous contributions he envisaged for his auditors a series of
afflicting scenes, such as might be expected to stir their hearts and
loosen their pocketbooks. The sequence of pictures, unmistakably,
was based on passages from the posthumously published "Trust in
God"[9] which, in turn, had been transcribed from Leightonhouse's
"Twelfth Sermon,"[1] with scarcely a change of word. The contrast
between these two discourses in the use of borrowed material is indeed striking. When compiling "Trust in God," Yorick had been
content to purloin entire paragraphs from Leightonhouse, without

6. See above, p. 22.
7. *Sermons*, v, 1 (28), pp. 11–13.
8. *Idem*, iv, 8 (23), p. 63, n.
9. *Idem*, vi, 7 (34), pp. 25–7.
1. See below, p. 137.

bothering substantially to alter or add to what he took; in the "Lazarus" sermon, on the other hand, what was borrowed served but as a theme, around which original variations were woven; the material was expanded, dramatized, and the pathos of the scenes heightened. In the following passages Yorick's changed attitude toward the use of appropriated material is seen clearly reflected in his increasing independence and originality. Words printed in small capital letters indicate where Leightonhouse's phraseology has been retained, unchanged.

"Trust in God," *Sermons*, VI, 7 (34), pp. 25-8

HAST THOU EVER LAID UPON THE BED OF LANGUISHING, OR LABOURED UNDER A GRIEVOUS DISTEMPER which threatened thy life? CALL TO MIND THY SORROWFUL and PENSIVE SPIRIT AT THAT TIME; AND ADD TO IT, WHO IT WAS THAT HAD MERCY ON THEE, THAT BROUGHT THEE OUT OF DARKNESS, AND THE SHADOW OF DEATH, AND MADE ALL THY BED IN THY SICKNESS.—

HATH THE SCANTINESS OF THY CONDITION HURRIED THEE INTO GREAT STRAITS and difficulties, AND BROUGHT THEE ALMOST TO distraction?—CONSIDER WHO IT WAS THAT SPREAD THY TABLE IN THAT WILDERNESS OF THOUGHT,—who was it MADE THY CUP TO OVERFLOW,—WHO ADDED A FRIEND OF CONSOLATION TO THEE, AND THEREBY SPAKE PEACE TO THY TROUBLED MIND.—HAST THOU EVER SUSTAINED ANY CONSIDERABLE DAMAGE IN THY STOCK OR TRADE?—BETHINK THYSELF WHO IT WAS THAT GAVE thee A SERENE AND CONTENTED MIND UNDER THOSE LOSSES.—If thou hast recovered,—consider WHO IT WAS THAT REPAIRED THOSE BREACHES,—when thy own skill and endeavours failed:—call to mind whose providence has blessed them since,—whose hand it was that has set a hedge about thee, and made all that thou hast done to prosper.—HAST THOU EVER BEEN WOUNDED IN THY MORE TENDER PARTS, THROUGH THE LOSS OF AN OBLIGING HUSBAND?—or hast thou been torn away from the embraces of a dear and PROMISING CHILD, by its unexpected death?—

O CONSIDER, WHETHER THE GOD OF TRUTH DID NOT APPROVE HIMSELF A FATHER TO THEE, WHEN FATHERLESS,—OR A HUSBAND to thee, WHEN A WIDOW,—AND HAS EITHER GIVEN THEE A NAME BETTER THAN OF SONS AND DAUGHTERS, OR

"The Rich Man and Lazarus," *Sermons*, IV, 8 (23), pp. 65-8

HAST THOU EVER LAID UPON THE BED OF LANGUISHING, OR LABOURED UNDER A DISTEMPER which threatened thy life? CALL TO MIND THY SORROWFUL AND PENSIVE SPIRIT AT THAT TIME, and say, What it was that made the thoughts of death so bitter:—if thou had'st children,———I affirm it, the bitterness of death lay there; ———if unbrought up, and unprovided for, What will become of them? Where will they find a friend when I am gone, who will stand up for them and plead their cause against the wicked?

———Blessed God! to thee, who art a father to the fatherless, and a husband to the widow,—I entrust them.

HAST THOU EVER SUSTAINED ANY CONSIDERABLE shock IN THY fortune? or, HAS THE SCANTINESS OF THY CONDITION HURRIED THEE INTO GREAT STRAITS, AND BROUGHT THEE ALMOST TO distraction? CONSIDER what WAS IT THAT SPREAD A TABLE IN THAT WILDERNESS OF THOUGHT, ———who MADE THY CUP TO OVERFLOW? Was it not a FRIEND OF CONSOLATION who stepped in,———saw thee embarrassed with tender pledges of thy love, and the partner of thy cares,———took them under his protection?———Heaven! thou will reward him for it!———and freed thee from all the terrifying apprehensions of a parent's love.

Hast thou———

———But how shall I ask a question which must bring tears into so many eyes? HAST THOU EVER BEEN WOUNDED in a more affecting manner still, BY THE LOSS OF A most OBLIGING FRIEND,—or been torn away from the embraces of a dear and PROMISING CHILD by the stroke of death? ———bitter remembrance! nature droops at it—but nature is the same in all conditions and lots of life.———A child thrust

EVEN BEYOND THY HOPE, MADE THY RE-
MAINING TENDER BRANCHES TO GROW UP
TALL AND beautiful, LIKE THE CEDARS OF
LIBANUS.—

Strengthened by these CONSIDERATIONS, suggesting the same or LIKE PAST DELIV-ERANCES, OR ACQUAINTANCE,—thou wilt learn this great lesson in the text, in all thy exigencies and difficulties,—to TRUST GOD . . . .

forth in an evil hour, without food, without raiment, bereft of instruction, and the means of its salvation, is a subject of more tender heart-aches, and will awaken every power of nature:———as we have felt for ourselves,———let us feel for Christ's sake———let us feel for theirs: and may the God of all comfort bless you. Amen.

Though the obligation to Leightonhouse, in the "Lazarus" sermon, is still present, the actual indebtedness is far less pronounced than it had been in "Trust in God." As a result, whereas "Trust in God" contains little to distinguish it from the run of the mill homily, there is much in "The Rich Man of Lazarus" to remind us of the mature Sterne; the concluding paragraphs might easily have been extracts from either *Tristram Shandy* or *A Sentimental Journey*. It requires too wide a flight of the imagination to believe the order of composition was reversed; that, after experiencing the freedom of imaginative writing, Sterne would have been content to revert to a source and copy more closely than he had done before.

Three additional paragraphs in the "Lazarus" sermon may be accounted for by a similar explanation; that is, they can best be described as resulting from this increasingly dramatic and sentimental approach to and handling of material which Yorick had earlier been content to appropriate with very few changes. From an extended paragraph in his discourse on "God's Forbearance Abused," lifted quite literally from Stillingfleet's "Danger and Deceitfulness of Sin,"[2] Sterne extracted a few lines which, in contracted form, reveal further indications of the artist, rather than the transcriber, at work.[3] In like manner, a passage taken from Young, in the posthumously published

2. See below, p. 148.

3. *Sermons*, v, 6 (33), "God's Forbearance abused," pp. 151–2. ". . . whoever considers the state and condition of human nature, and upon this view, how much stronger the natural motives are to virtue than to vice, would expect to find the world much better than it is, or ever has been.—For who would suppose the generality of mankind to betray so much folly, as to act against the common interest of their own kind, as every man does who yields to the temptation of what is wrong.—But on the other side, —if men first look into the practice of the world, and there observe the strange prevalency of vice, and how willing men are to defend as well as commit it,—one would think they believed that all discourses of virtue and honesty were mere matter of speculation for men to entertain some idle hours with;—and say truly, that men seemed universally to be agreed in nothing but in speaking well and doing ill.—" Compare with this the following passage from "The Rich Man and Lazarus" (*Sermons*, IV, 8 [23], p. 43: ". . . indeed, were we only to look into the world, and observe how inclinable men are to defend evil, as well as to commit it,—one would think, at first sight, they believed, that all discourses of religion and virtue were mere matters of speculation, for men to entertain some idle hours with; and conclude very naturally, that we seemed to be agreed in no one thing, but speaking well—and acting ill."

"Temporal Advantages of Religion,"[4] and another from Norris, in "Our Conversation in Heaven,"[5] reappear in "The Rich Man and Lazarus," combined and refashioned.[6]

Comparable to the way in which borrowed material had been filtered through the posthumously published discourses, and then given more original treatment, was Yorick's procedure when making direct use of the writings of other clergymen. Three of the four remaining instances of indebtedness, in "The Rich Man and Lazarus," illustrate the same intention to improve upon what was being appropriated.[7] In one of John Norris' sermons, Sterne had come upon the following observation.

4. See below, p. 186.
6. "Temporal Advantages of Religion," *Sermons*, v, 1 (28), pp. 8–9

5. See below, p. 142.
"The Rich Man and Lazarus," *Sermons*, IV, 8 (23), pp. 59–61

. . . and of this even the vicious can hardly be insensible, from what he may perceive to spring up in his mind, from any casual act of virtue. And tho' it is a pleasure that properly belongs to the good —yet let any one try the experiment, and he will see what is meant by that moral delight, arising from the conscience of well-doing.—Let him but refresh the bowels of the needy—let him comfort the broken-hearted—or check an appetite, or overcome a temptation—or receive an affront with temper and meekness—and he shall find the tacit praise of what he has done, darting thro' his mind, accompanied with a sincere pleasure . . . .

Let us then for a moment, my dear auditors! . . . consider the traces which even the most insensible man may have proof of, from what he may perceive springing up within him from some casual act of generosity; and tho' this is a pleasure which properly belongs to the good, yet let him try the experiment;—let him comfort the captive, or cover the naked with a garment, and he will feel what is meant by that moral delight arising in the mind from the conscience of a humane action.

"Our Conversation in Heaven," *Sermons*, v, 2 (29), pp. 38–9

And here, not to feign a long hypothesis, as some have done, of a sinner's being admitted into heaven, with a particular description of his condition and behaviour there,—we need only consider, that the supreme good, like any other good, is of a relative nature, and consequently the enjoyment of it must require some qualification in the faculty, as well as the enjoyment of any other good does;—there must be something antecedent in the disposition and temper, which will render that good a good to that individual,—otherwise though (it is true) it may be possessed,—yet it never can be enjoyed.—

But to know it right, we must call upon the compassionate;———Cruelty gives evidence unwillingly, and feels the pleasure but imperfectly; for this, like all other pleasures, is of a relative nature, and consequently the enjoyment of it, requires some qualification in the faculty, as much as the enjoyment of any other good does: —there must be something antecedent in the disposition and temper which will render that good,———a good to that individual; otherwise, tho' 'tis true it may be possessed,———yet it never can be enjoyed.

7. The fourth and last instance was a short comment of Tillotson's to the effect that "there is not a greater paradox in the world, than that so good a religion [as the Christian] should be no better recommended by its professors." This comment was appropriated, without change, on p. 42 of the "Lazarus" sermon.

. . . generally are Men most Covetous . . . when they have most Wealth
. . . [and are] the more *Empty* for being *Full.* . . . Strange, that Men
should *contract* their *Spirits* upon the *inlargement* of their *Fortunes!* Many
indeed are the Temptations and Snares of Wealth; but of all Vices one
would think it should not dispose Men to Covetousness, but rather be an
Antidote against it . . . .[8]

In utilizing this observation, though retaining Norris' very words,
Sterne has reworked the passage into something more pointed and
polished than it was when he first saw it.

. . . nay, what is strange, do they [riches] not often tempt men even to
covetousness; and tho' amidst all the ill offices which riches do us, one
would last suspect this vice, but rather think the one a cure for the other;
yet so it is, that many a man contracts his spirits upon the enlargement of
his fortune, and is the more empty for being full.[9]

Similarly, two extracts from Clarke underwent the same reshaping
process before reappearing in the sermon under consideration.[1]

If the indications of conscious artistry and a more original treatment of borrowed material are not so apparent in the passages appropriated from Clarke as in those taken from Leightonhouse, the

---

8. John Norris, *op. cit.*, II, 209–10.   9. *Sermons,* IV, 8 (23), p. 57.
1. In the two following quotations, small capital letters have again been used to indicate where Sterne retained the phraseology of his source.
"In this state he [Lazarus] is described as desiring to be fed with the crumbs which
fell from the rich man's table; AND THO' THE CASE IS NOT EXPRESSLY PUT, THAT HE WAS
REFUSED, YET AS THE CONTRARY IS NOT AFFIRMED IN THE HISTORICAL PART OF THE
PARABLE,————OR PLEADED AFTER BY THE OTHER, THAT HE SHEWED MERCY TO THE
MISERABLE, WE MAY CONCLUDE HIS REQUEST WAS UNSUCCESSFUL,————like too many
others in the world, either so high lifted up in it, that they cannot look down distinctly
enough upon the sufferings of their fellow creatures,————or by long surfeiting in a
continual course of banqueting and good cheer, they forget there is such a distemper as
hunger, in the catalogue of human infirmities" (*Idem,* IV, 8 [23], pp. 47–8).
"————That he had received his good things,—'twas from heaven,————and could be
no reproach: with what severity soever the scripture speaks against riches, IT DOES NOT
APPEAR, THAT THE LIVING OR FARING SUMPTUOUSLY EVERY DAY, WAS THE CRIME OB-
JECTED TO THE RICH MAN; or that it is a real part of a vicious character: the case might
be then, as now: HIS QUALITY AND STATION IN THE WORLD MIGHT BE SUPPOSED TO BE
SUCH, as not only to have justified his doing this, but, in general, to have required it
WITHOUT ANY IMPUTATION OF DOING WRONG; FOR DIFFERENCES OF STATIONS THERE
MUST BE IN THE WORLD, WHICH MUST BE SUPPORTED BY SUCH MARKS OF DISTINCTION AS
CUSTOM IMPOSES. The exceeding great plenty and magnificence, in which Solomon is
described to have lived, who had ten fat oxen, and twenty oxen out of the pastures,
and a hundred sheep, besides harts, and roebucks, and fallow deer, and fatted fowl,
with thirty measures of fine flower [*sic*], and three score measures of meal, for the daily
provision of his table;*————all this is not laid to him as a sin, but rather remarked as
an instance of God's blessing to him;————and whenever these things are otherwise,
'tis from a WASTFUL and dishonest PERVERSION OF THEM to pernicious ends,————and
oft times, to the very opposite ones for which they were granted,————to glad the
heart, to open it, and render it more kind.————" (*Idem,* IV, 8 [23], pp. 51–3.)

*Cf. I Kings 4.22–3. It was quite in character that Yorick should have chosen to ex-
pand the passage by the inclusion of such a biblical quotation.

explanation may well be that the "Lazarus" sermon must be considered as having been composed during a transitional period in the writer's development. "The Rich Man and Lazarus" is neither so commonplace and imitative, on the one hand, as the "Temporal Advantages of Religion"; nor yet is it uniformly so distinctive and typically Shandean as some of the other discourses which came from Yorick's pen. It is worth noting that this sermon was not included among those first selected for publication in 1760. Quite possibly Yorick recognized its uneven character and, for that reason, did not make use of it until 1766, when Volumes III and IV were being prepared for the press and he found himself hard put to it to assemble a sufficient number of acceptable discourses. As it was, these last two volumes to appear during Sterne's lifetime contained only twelve instead of the sixteen sermons that had been planned for the previous summer.[2]

Despite such reservations, however, there is in the "Lazarus" sermon sufficient evidence to justify assigning it to a later period of composition than the "Temporal Advantages of Religion." If it can be shown, further, that the differences distinguishing these two sermons are, in general, characteristic and representative as a whole of the two groups in which they are found—those discourses which Sterne himself selected for inclusion in Volumes I–IV, on the one hand, and those of posthumous publication, on the other—then a basis will have been established for determining a rough chronology of the sermons which, in turn, will make it possible to advance additional and still more discriminating conjectures.

2. Cf. *Life,* p. 372.

PART II

Sterne's change in attitude toward the use of borrowed material which now, for the first time, can be shown clearly reflected in many of the sermons, together with the degree of imagination used in his handling of biblical texts, provides the most reliable and satisfactory criterion that has yet been found for gauging his emergence as an original and creative writer. Unfortunately, the full extent of Yorick's plagiarisms is not yet known; nor is it likely that it ever will be. But an examination of those discourses where appropriations have been discovered leads consistently and convincingly to but one conclusion: the differences which made it possible to assume a later period of composition for "The Rich Man and Lazarus" than for the "Temporal Advantages of Religion" are quite representative, in general, of the differences separating the two groups of printed sermons from which each was taken. The average posthumously published discourse displays little originality or distinction; and, though the "Temporal Advantages of Religion" will probably always remain the most striking example of how profoundly Sterne could obligate himself, several of the other sermons from this group betray nearly as great a degree of uninspired borrowing. Everything of importance in "The Sin of Murder" was either copied directly from or else suggested by Samuel Clarke's discussion, "Of the Heinousness of the Sin of Wilful Murder";[1] "Trust in God" could much more appropriately have been entitled, "Leightonhouse's Twelfth Sermon."[2] Tillotson and Stillingfleet, together, contributed the substance for "God's Forbearance Abused";[3] Tillotson, Young, and Locke, for the discourse on "Enthusiasm."[4] From Wollaston, Leightonhouse, Clarke, and Locke was taken more than half of "The Ways of Providence Justified to Man."[5] "The Ingratitude of Israel," "Description of the World," and "Thirtieth of January"[6] bear unmistakable traces of being variations upon some common source, which so far has eluded detection; they share long paragraphs in common, with only slight verbal alterations to distinguish them from one another.[7]

Six additional discourses in this posthumously published group are

1. *Sermons,* VI, 8 (35). See below, pp. 119–22.
2. *Sermons,* VI, 7 (34). See below, pp. 133–7.
3. *Sermons,* V, 6 (33). See below, pp. 148–50 and 170.
4. *Sermons,* VI, 11 (38). See below, pp. 139–40, 169–70, and 189–91.
5. *Sermons,* VII, 17 (44). See below, pp. 113, 134–5, 138, and 178–80.
6. *Sermons,* VII, 18 (45); V, 3 (30); and V, 5 (32). See also *Life,* p. 505. Some of these repetitions were noted by a correspondent to *The Gentleman's Magazine,* LXXVI, Pt. 1, 409.
7. Cf. *Sermons,* V, 3 (30), p. 68; V, 5 (32), p. 134; and VII, 18 (45), p. 152. Also, V, 3 (30), pp. 56–7; and V, 5 (32), pp. 131–3. And V, 5 (32), pp. 122–6 and 131–6 with VII, 18 (45), pp. 141 ff. and 152–5.

to be differentiated from those already mentioned, chiefly by the lesser amount of borrowed material which they contain;[8] in other respects they are quite mechanical and commonplace, almost completely without the stamp of individuality. For the three remaining sermons left among "the sweepings of the Author's study" at the time of his death—"The Eternal Advantages of Religion," "Asa: A Thanksgiving Sermon," and "Search the Scriptures"[9]—there is no applicable evidence to show whether or not they were also influenced by older writers. Two or three paragraphs in the last of these, a discourse which won approving words from Cardinal Newman,[1] might have been modeled after Jeremiah Seed's "The Intrinsic Excellency of the Scriptures" or one of Archbishop Secker's sermons;[2] but the similarities are neither sufficiently extended nor close enough to warrant their inclusion here as probable sources.

It should not be assumed, however, from the observations which have just been made, that none of the sermons remaining in manuscript at the time of Sterne's death betrays any evidences of originality or that every time Yorick helped himself to something he had seen in print he was content to incorporate what he found into the posthumously published discourses, without change. Mr. Cross mentions several instances where he feels that Yorick is "visible . . . at his very best"[3] and cites with good reason the opening remark in the sermon on "Evil" where the preacher, having read two texts, began his discourse by saying: "Take either as you like it, you will get nothing by the bargain."[4] Further, a careful examination of the parallel passages contained in the Appendix will disclose repeated (if not always striking) attempts on Yorick's part to increase the effectiveness of the material he was transcribing. Note, for example, the use made of this passage from Wollaston's *Religion of Nature*.

It rarely happens, that we are competent judges of the *good* or *bad fortune* of other people. That, which is disagreeable to one, is many times agreeable to another, or disagreeable in a less degree. The misery accruing from any inflection or bad circumstance of life is to be computed . . . according to the resistance and capacity of bearing it, which it meets with. If one man can carry a weight of four or five hundred pounds as well as another can

8. *Idem*, v, 2 (29); v, 4 (31); vi, 9 (36); vi, 10 (37); vii, 14 (41); and vii, 16 (43).
9. *Idem*, vi, 12 (39); vii, 13 (40); and vii, 15 (42).   1. *Life*, p. 508 and note.
2. *Discourses on Several Important Subjects* (4th ed. London, 1751, 2 vols.), ii, 174. *The Works of Thomas Secker* (new ed. London, 1825, 6 vols.), iii, 245–6.
3. *Life*, pp. 506–08. Of the four sermons specifically mentioned, two (*Sermons*, v, 3 [30], and vii, 15 [42]) contain no clues which might indicate when they were written; the third (*idem*, vii, 13 [40]), giving a portrait "of the young George the Third under the guise of Asa," obviously postdates 1760; from the fourth (*idem*, vii, 15 [42]), only the opening sentence is quoted; but this might well have been a later addition to a discourse otherwise quite commonplace in character.
4. *Sermons*, v, 6 (33), p. 147.

carry the weight of one hundred, by these *different* weights they will be *equally* loaded. And so the same poverty or disgrace, the same wounds, &c. do not give the *same pain* to all men. The apprehension of but a *vein* to be opened is worse to some, than the *apparatus* to an execution is to others: and a *word* may be more terrible and sensible to tender natures, than a *sword* is to the senseless, or intrepid breed. The same may be said with respect to the injoyments: men have different tastes, and the use of the same thing does not beget *equal pleasure* in all.[5]

The reader will have no difficulty in deciding where the suggestion came from for the following paragraph in "The Ways of Providence Justified to Man":

Besides this, a man's unhappiness is not to be ascertained so much from what is known to have befallen him,—as from his particular turn and cast of mind, and capacity of bearing it.—Poverty, exile, loss of fame or friends, the death of children, the dearest of all pledges of a man's happiness, make not equal impressions upon every temper.—You will see one man undergo, with scarce the expence of a sigh,—what another, in the bitterness of his soul, would go mourning for all his life long:—nay, a hasty word, or an unkind look, to a soft and tender nature, will strike deeper than a sword to the hardened and senseless.—If these reflections hold true with regard to misfortunes,—they are the same with regard to enjoyments:—we are formed differently,—have different tastes and preceptions of things;—by the force of habit, education, or a particular cast of mind,—it happens that neither the use or possession of the same enjoyments and advantages, produce the same happiness and contentment . . . .[6]

Certainly Yorick had revised the material before including it in his discourse: several of Wollaston's illustrations were omitted and the sentimental appeal has been substantially heightened. If a comparison of these two passages does not add much to Sterne's reputation as an original thinker, at least it shows the selective processes of a maturing artist at work.

What appears in the posthumously printed discourses as somewhat of an exception becomes the usual practice in those sermons included in the four volumes which Sterne himself saw through the press. Though it is still possible to find sentences and even short paragraphs appropriated from others with very little change, most of the indebtednesses are suggestive or stimulative in character and noticeably less literal or repetitious; the borrowings betray less of their source and reveal more of Yorick's personality, often making it impossible to be sure which one of several writers he has drawn upon.[7]

5. Wollaston, *The Religion of Nature, Delineated* (6th ed. London, 1738), Sec. 5, Pt. xviii.

6. *Sermons*, VII, 17 (44), pp. 124–6.

7. For example, an idea often voiced by Yorick was the inseparability of religion and virtue, if a man was to be consistently humane and upright in his actions. A typical

An analysis of the contents of the first four volumes of *The Sermons of Mr. Yorick* shows Tillotson's influence to have been predominant, affecting eighteen of the twenty-seven discourses. What Sterne appropriated from the Archbishop, however, rarely amounted to more than suggestions for developing a text[8]—short, generalized statements, such as the comment that Seneca, "at the same time he was writing against riches . . . was enjoying a great estate, and using every means to make that estate still greater,"[9] or pertinent illustrations which could be varied, as fancy and a growing sense of the dramatic might direct. The discourse on "Evil-Speaking," it is true, contains little which Tillotson's "Against Evil Speaking" could not have supplied; but whereas in the posthumously published "Sin of Murder" more than half of the sermon was made up of close verbal repetitions from the sole source—Clarke's homily, "Of the Heinousness of the Sin of Wilful Murder"—in this discourse only three out of twenty-six pages echo Tillotson with sufficient literalness to make possible direct comparisons.

Again, it is likely that a half dozen or so of the biblical stories which Sterne found recounted in Bishop Hall's *Contemplations* suggested to him the more expanded framework which a sermon requires; but in the resulting discourses[1] direct indebtednesses to the Bishop seldom exceed an appropriation of more than three or four short sentences. In that homily which followed Hall most closely—"The

expression of this idea occurs in the "Advantages of Christianity to the World" (*idem,* IV, 11 [26], p. 159): ". . . I firmly deny, that . . . religion and morality are independent of each other: they appear so far from it, that I cannot conceive how the one, in the true and meritorious sense of the duty, can act without the influence of the other . . . ."

The suggestion for this could have come from Stillingfleet (*The Works of That Eminent and Most Learned Prelate, Dr. Edw. Stillingfleet* [London, 1709–10, 6 vols.], I, 218): "When once the people had swallowed that pernicious principle, that Morality was no part of Religion, they had no great regard to the good or evil of their actions . . . ." Sterne might have had Swift in mind (*Three Sermons* [London, 1744], pp. 27–9): ". . . there is no solid, firm Foundation for Virtue, but on a Conscience which is guided by Reason. . . . It is found by Experience, that those Men who set up for Morality without regard to Religion, are generally but virtuous in part. . . ." Or, the idea might have come from Locke (*The Reasonableness of Christianity* [London, 1836], sec. 170): ". . . it is too hard a task for unassisted reason, to establish morality in all of its parts, upon its true foundations, with a clear and convincing light. . . . human reason, unassisted, failed men in its great and proper business or morality." There is definite proof that Sterne read all three of the writings in which these ideas were voiced; one of the three undoubtedly suggested the idea to him. The chances are, had the passage in question appeared in one of the posthumously published discourses, the particular source would have been copied with such closeness that no uncertainty could have remained.

8. Tillotson probably suggested to Sterne the general plan for *Sermons,* I, 1; II, 8; II, 15; and V, 2 (29).

9. *Sermons,* III, 4 (19), p. 114.

1. The following sermons of Sterne probably owe their outlines to Hall's *Contemplations: Sermons,* I, 5; II, 12 and 13; III, 1 (16), 2 (17), and 3 (18).

Case of Hezekiah and the Messengers"—less than ten per cent of Yorick's sermon imitates its source with recognizable approximation.[2]

In like manner, "Self Knowledge" contains a sufficient number of ideas shared in common with discourses by Swift and Butler to justify a belief that Sterne knew and made use of both these writers; verbal similarities, however, rarely exceed a slight echoing of occasional phrases.[3]

Locke's *Thoughts Concerning Education* undoubtedly prompted the idea for that most unusual and unexpected conclusion to Yorick's sermon on "The Prodigal Son,"[4] in which the advantages and disadvantages of making the "Grand Tour" are weighed in the balance; but once more the actual indebtedness extends no further than to a general agreement with Locke about the dangers and ill consequences usually attending such peregrinations. There is no real appropriation of Locke's phraseology.

Bentley appears to have exercised a more pronounced influence upon "The Vindication of Human Nature," particularly in that section where Sterne is discussing and illustrating the underlying assumption that "No man liveth to himself."[5] But instead of copying the example contained in the source—"even monarchs and princes of the world, with their chief ministers under them," cannot be self-sufficient unto themselves—Sterne made the major portion of the discourse his own by a more pertinent and applicable substitution: "To illustrate this, let us take a short survey of the life of any one

---

2. *Sermons*, iii, 2 (17). See below, pp. 128–30.

3. Note, for example, Sterne's use of the following paragraph from Swift's sermon on "The Difficulty of Knowing One's-Self," *The Works of Jonathon Swift, D.D.*, Walter Scott, ed. (Edinburgh, 1814), iii, Sermon No. 1:

SWIFT	STERNE
"The Difficulty of Knowing One's-Self," pp. 10–11	"Self Knowledge," *Sermons*, i, 4, p. 93
. . . however it cometh to pass, they [men] are wonderfully unacquainted with their own temper and disposition, and know very little of what passeth within them: for, of so many proud, ambitious, revengeful, envying, and ill-natured persons that are in the world, where is there one of them, who, although he hath all the symptoms of the vice appearing upon every occasion, can look with such an impartial eye upon himself, as to believe that the imputation thrown upon him is not altogether groundless and unfair?	Of the many revengeful, covetous, false and ill-natured persons which we complain of in the world, though we all join in the cry against them, what man amongst us singles out himself as a criminal, or ever once takes it into his head that he adds to the number?—or where is there a man so bad, who would not think it the hardest and most unfair imputation to have any of those particular vices laid to his charge? If he has the symptoms never so strong upon him, which he would pronounce infallible in another, they are indications of no such malady in himself.

4. *Sermons*, iii, 5 (20), pp. 155–60. See below, 140–1.

5. *Sermons*, ii, 7, p. 10. See also Richard Bentley, *Works* (London, 1838), iii, 269.

man, (not liable to great exceptions, but such a life as is common to most) let us examine it merely to this point, and try how far it will answer such a representation."[6] The ensuing six pages appear to be entirely original.

In addition to "The Parable of the Rich Man and Lazarus," which has already been analyzed, the ten discourses just enumerated contain the most striking, as well as the most extensive, indications of obligation to the writings of others which are to be met with in the first four volumes of Mr. Yorick's *Sermons*. There is scarcely need, therefore, to continue such résumés of minor indebtednesses for the remaining discourses of this group: to point out, for instance, that in another of Bentley's sermons Sterne probably found the suggestion for his more famous and essentially original description of the Inquisition in "The Abuses of Conscience Considered" but that, as the picture stands, it is almost completely the product of Yorick's imagination;[7] or that the concluding paragraph of "The Pharisee and Publican in the Temple" is reminiscent of a longer passage in Clarke's discourse "Of the Spirituality of God," although otherwise Sterne's homily appears to be of his own making.[8] Enough, surely, has been said to reveal how slight, how relatively unimportant, is the amount of borrowed material contained in these earlier-printed sermons, especially when they are compared with those of posthumous publication.

Yorick's self-emancipation from a more-or-less slavish dependence upon others, as exemplified by the decreased proportion of indebtednesses contained in the discourses of the first four volumes, is further emphasized by the changed attitude toward his work which his treatment of specific appropriations betrays. Though indications of this change have already been cited and illustrated by various quotations from the "Lazarus" sermon, it will not be amiss at this point to examine in some detail the handling of biblical texts. Even more clearly than by his use of older sermon writers, Sterne's manipulation of scripture material provides a means for measuring the artistic and intellectual differences which so clearly separate the earlier from the posthumously printed group.

Throughout the last three volumes, where there is no evidence to show that the passages may have been copied from some intermediary writer rather than directly from the Bible, Sterne did little

6. Bentley, it is true, had suggested a somewhat similar illustration (*idem*, p. 272): ". . . let such a one consider, that even in the most private life there are various relations and duties arising: as a husband, as a father, a master, a neighbor, a member of the community . . . ." But the idea was left undeveloped, preference being given to the illustration mentioned above.

7. *Sermons*, IV, 12 (27), pp. 201–03. See below, p. 105.

8. *Sermons*, I, 6, pp. 175–6.

more than transcribe brief phrases into his text or string together series of quotations to emphasize an idea; it was the same procedure he had followed when borrowing from nonscriptural writings. The two following examples may be taken as representative. In the post-humously published discourse, "Follow Peace," Yorick commented:

Look into private life,—BEHOLD HOW GOOD AND PLEASANT A THING IT IS TO LIVE TOGETHER IN UNITY;—IT IS LIKE THE PRECIOUS OINTMENT POURED UPON THE HEAD OF AARON, THAT RUN DOWN TO HIS SKIRTS;—[9] importing, that this balm of life is felt and enjoyed, not only by governors of kingdoms, but is derived down to the lowest rank of life, and tasted in the most private recesses;—all, from the king to the peasant, are refreshed with its blessings . . . . It is this blessing gives every one to SIT QUIETLY UNDER HIS VINE,[1] and reap the fruits of his labor and industry . . . .

How inconsistent the whole body of sin is, with the glories of the celestial body that shall be revealed hereafter,—and that in proportion as we fix the representation of these glories upon our minds, and in the more numerous particulars we do it,—the stronger the necessity as well as persuasion to DENY OURSELVES ALL UNGODLINESS AND WORLDLY LUSTS, TO LIVE SOBERLY, RIGHTEOUSLY AND GODLY IN THIS PRESENT WORLD,[2] as the only way to entitle us to that blessedness spoken of in the Revelations—of those who do his commandments, and have a RIGHT TO THE TREE OF LIFE, AND SHALL ENTER INTO THE GATES OF THE CITY[3] of the living God, the heavenly Jerusalem, and to an innumerable company of angels;—TO THE GENERAL ASSEMBLY AND CHURCH OF THE FIRST-BORN, THAT ARE WRITTEN IN HEAVEN, AND TO GOD THE JUDGE OF ALL, AND TO THE SPIRITS OF JUST MEN MADE PERFECT,[4]—who have WASHED THEIR ROBES, AND MADE THEM WHITE IN THE BLOOD OF THE LAMB.—[5]

In contrast to this obvious and conventional use of the Scriptures, witness what was done with a text, in the earlier-published discourses, once Yorick's fancy was awakened. Recounting the story of the Good Samaritan, each biblical verse was lingered over, expanded, and amplified; from every suggestion was wrung the uttermost in drama and sentiment.

AND BY CHANCE THERE CAME DOWN A CERTAIN PRIEST!—merciful God! that a teacher of thy religion should ever want humanity — or that a man whose head might be thought full of the one, should have a heart void of the other! —This however was the case before us— . . .[6]

But it is painful to dwell long upon this disagreeable part of the story; I

9. Cf. Psalms 133.1–2. Small capital letters are used to indicate where biblical phrase-ology has been retained.
1. Cf. I Kings 4.25. See also *Sermons*, VII, 14 (41), pp. 40–1.
2. Cf. Titus 2.12.   3. Cf. Revelation 22.14.   4. Cf. Hebrews 12.23.
5. Cf. Revelation 7.14. The second quotation is taken from *Sermons*, V, 2 (29), pp. 47–9.
6. *Idem*, I, 3, pp. 57–69. Cf. Luke 10.30–6. Small capital letters again have been used to indicate where Sterne was quoting directly from the Bible.

therefore hasten to the concluding incident of it, which is so amiable that one cannot easily be too copious in reflections upon it.—AND BEHOLD, says our Saviour, A CERTAIN SAMARITAN AS HE JOURNEYED CAME WHERE HE WAS; AND WHEN HE SAW HIM HE HAD COMPASSION ON HIM—AND WENT TO HIM— BOUND UP HIS WOUNDS, POURING IN OIL AND WINE—SET HIM UPON HIS OWN BEAST, BROUGHT HIM TO AN INN AND TOOK CARE OF HIM. . . .

. . . because it is a pleasure to look into a good mind, and trace out as far as one is able what passes within it on such occasions, I shall beg leave for a moment, to state an account of what was likely to pass in his, and in what manner so distressful a case would necessarily work upon such a disposition.

As he approached the place where the unfortunate man lay, the instant he beheld him, no doubt some such train of reflections as this would rise in his mind. "Good God! what a spectacle of misery do I behold—a man stripped of his raiment—wounded—lying languishing before me upon the ground just ready to expire,—without the comfort of a friend to support him in his last agonies . . . . But perhaps my concern should lessen when I reflect on the relations in which we stand to each other—that he is a Jew and I a Samaritan.—But are we not still both men?—partakers of the same nature—and subject to the same evils?—let me change conditions with him for a moment and consider, had his lot befallen me as I journeyed in the way, what measure I should have expected at his hands.—Should I wish when he beheld me wounded and half-dead, that he should shut up his bowels of compassion from me, and double the weight of my miseries by passing by and leaving them unpitied?—But I am a stranger to the man —be it so,—but I am no stranger to his condition—misfortunes are of no particular tribe or nation, but belong to us all, and have a general claim upon us, without distinction of climate, country or religion. Besides, though I am a stranger—'tis no fault of his that I do not know him, and therefore unequitable he should suffer by it:—Had I known him, possibly I should have had cause to love and pity him the more—for aught I know, he is some one of uncommon merit, whose life is rendered still more precious, as the lives and happiness of others may be involved in it: perhaps at this instant that he lies here forsaken, in all this misery, a whole virtuous family is joyfully looking for his return, and affectionately counting the hours of his delay. Oh! did they know what evil hath befallen him—how would they fly to succour him.—Let me then hasten to supply those tender offices of binding up his wounds, and carrying him to a place of safety—or if that assistance comes too late, I shall comfort him at least in his last hour—and, if I can do nothing else,—I shall soften his misfortunes by dropping a tear of pity over them."

'Tis almost necessary to imagine the good Samaritan was influenced by some such thoughts as these, from the uncommon generosity of his behaviour . . . .

Similarly, the thoughts of the Pharisee were dissected, as he looked down upon the Publican in the Temple; or the Levite's mental agonies were analyzed, while he reflected upon the wrongs done him by his concubine.[7] Again, it was the departure of the Prodigal Son that stimulated Sterne's imagination.

He gathers all together————

————I see the picture of his departure:—the camels and asses loaden with his substance, detached on one side of the piece, and already on their way:————the prodigal son standing on the fore ground, with a forced sedateness, struggling against the fluttering movement of joy, upon his deliverance from restraint:————the elder brother holding his hand, as if unwilling to let it go:————the father,————sad moment! with a firm look, covering a prophetic sentiment, "that all would not go well with his child," —approaching to embrace him, and bid him adieu.————Poor inconsiderate youth! From whose arms art thou flying? . . .[8]

The prodigal's return was still more fancifully described: "Alas! How shall he tell his story?" But Yorick, with or without biblical suggestion, was equally at no loss for words in which to enumerate "the sad *Items* of his extravagance and folly."

———— The feasts and banquets which he gave to whole cities in the east, —the costs of Asiatick rarities,—and of Asiatick cooks to dress them———— the expences of singing men and singing women,————the flute, the harp, the sackbut, and of all kinds of musick—the dress of the Persian courts, how magnificent! their slaves how numerous!————their chariots, their horses, their palaces, their furniture, what immense sums they had devoured! ————what expectations from strangers of condition! what exactions!
How shall the youth make his father comprehend, that he was cheated at Damascus by one of the best men in the world;—that he had lent a part of his substance to a friend at Nineveh, who had fled off with it to the Ganges;—that a whore of Babylon had swallowed his best pearl, and anointed the whole city with his balm of Gilead;— . . . that all had gone wrong since the day he forsook his father's house.[9]

There was no possibility of predicting what might be done with a text in these earlier-published discourses. Since the "uses" of the parable of the Prodigal Son, Yorick observed, "have been so ably set forth, in so many good sermons, . . . I shall turn aside from them at present, and content myself with some reflections upon that fatal passion which led him,—and so many thousands after the example, *to gather all he had together, and take his journey into a far country.*"[1] In treating of "The History of Jacob," "the second great occurrence in the patriarch's life.—The imposition of a wife upon him which he

7. *Sermons,* I, 6, p. 162, and III, 3 (18), pp. 77–80.
8. *Idem,* III, 5 (20), pp. 135–6.
9. *Idem,* pp. 142–4. Traill comments (*Sterne,* in English Men of Letters Series [New York, 1900], p. 100): "All this, it must be admitted, is pretty lively for a sermon."
1. *Sermons,* III, 5 (20), p. 151.

neither bargain'd for or loved" suggested a digressive plea to all who were contemplating matrimony: "Be open————be honest: give yourself for what you are; conceal nothing————varnish nothing, ————and if these fair weapons will not do,————better not conquer at all, than conquer for a day:————when the night is passed, 'twill ever be the same story,————*And it came to pass, behold it was Leah!*"[2] And then there was the occasion when Yorick came to preach on the subject of "The Levite and His Concubine."

————A CONCUBINE!—but the text accounts for it, *for in those days there was no king in Israel,* and the Levite, you will say, like every other man in it, did what was right in his own eyes,————and so, you may add, did his concubine too—*for she played the whore against him, and went away.*————[3]

————Then shame and grief go with her, and whereever she seeks a shelter, may the hand of justice shut the door against her.————

Not so . . . .

. . . let us stop a moment, and give the story . . . a second hearing: like all others much of it depends upon the telling; and as the Scripture has left us no kind of comment upon it, 'tis a story on which the heart cannot be at a loss for what to say, or the imagination for what to suppose—the danger is, humanity may say too much.

And it came to pass in those days when there was no king in Israel, that a certain Levite sojourning on the side of mount Ephraim, took unto himself a Concubine.————

O Abraham, thou father of the faithful! if this was wrong,————Why didst thou set so ensnaring an example before the eyes of thy descendants? and, Why did the God of Abraham, the God of Isaac and Jacob, bless so often the seed of such intercourses, and promise to multiply and make princes come out of them?

God can dispense with his own laws; and accordingly we find the holiest of the patriarchs, and others in Scripture whose hearts cleaved most unto God, accommodating themselves as well as they could to the dispensation: that Abraham had Hagar;—that Jacob, besides his two wives, Rachael and Leah, took also unto him Zilpah and Bilhah, from whom many of the tribes descended:—that David had seven wives and ten concubines;———— Rehoboam, sixty,—and that, in whatever cases it became reproachable, it seemed not so much the thing itself, as the abuse of it, which made it so; this was remarkable in that of Solomon, whose excesses became an insult upon the privileges of mankind; for by the same plan of luxury, which made it necessary to have forty thousand stalls of horses,—he had unfortunately miscalculated his other wants, and so had seven hundred wives, and three hundred concubines.————

2. *Idem,* IV, 7 (22), pp. 20–1.
3. *Idem,* III, 3 (18), pp. 63–4. Cf. Judges 19.1, 2. Though this and three other small selections were borrowed from Hall (see below, p. 126), there was nothing in the Bishop's *Contemplation* to suggest the treatment which Yorick gave to the story.

Wise———deluded man! was it not that thou madest some amends for thy bad practice, by thy good preaching, what had become of thee!——— three hundred———but let us turn aside, I beseech you, from so sad a stumbling block.[4]

Finally, in much the same vein as the discourse about "The Levite and His Concubine," there is the misquoted reference at the beginning of "Philanthropy Recommended." "What is written in the law, how readest thou?" replied Christ, to the lawyer who tempted him: "—upon which the enquirer reciting the general heads of our duty to God and Man as delivered in the 18th of Leviticus and the 6th of Deuteronomy,—namely—*That we should worship the Lord our God with all our hearts, and love our neighbor as ourselves;* our blessed Saviour tells him, he had answered right . . . ."[5] If the reader turns to "the 18th [chapter] of Leviticus," however, he will find not the verse which the lawyer correctly quoted from the nineteenth chapter but a series of pronouncements upon quite a different topic. The "error" was not rectified in any of the later editions which appeared during Yorick's lifetime; its presence is probably best explained by considering it just another manifestation of the preacher's curious sense of humor.[6] No such use had been made of the Scriptures in any of the posthumously published discourses.

Thus, a comparison of the two different groups of sermons, on a basis of the proportion and use made of material borrowed either from other clergymen or from the Bible, consistently demonstrates

---

4. *Sermons,* III, 3 (18), pp. 63–71. In the presence of such a passage, it is revealing to read a letter written by Yorick in 1765, shortly before the publication of those volumes of sermons in which "The Levite" appeared: ". . . have you seen my 7 & 8 graceless Children [Vols. VII and VIII of *Tristram Shandy,* published in 1765]—but I am doing penance for them, in begetting a couple of more ecclesiastick ones—which are to stand penance [again] in their turns—in Sheets ab^t the middle of Sept^r—they will appear in the Shape of the 3^d and 4 Vol^s of Yorick. These you must know are to keep up a kind of balance, in my shandaic character, & are push'd into the world for that reason by my friends . . . ." (*Letters,* p. 252.) A curious way of doing penance! With this letter, however, should be taken the comments made by two of Yorick's contemporaries. In 1765 Mrs. Montagu, writing to her sister, characterized Sterne as beng "harmless as a child, but often a naughty boy, and a little apt to dirty his *frock.*" (*Idem,* p. 238.) The second comment appeared in a communication to *The Morning Chronicle and London Advertiser* (Friday, September 3, 1773). At the close of a letter written in praise of Samuel Foote's *Piety in Pattens,* the correspondent remarked: "I have . . . followed Sterne's method; I have talked incoherently in this essay, but I hope not altogether without reason. Some men are enticed to read lucubrations, which are introduced with an air of levity and inattention. Yorick's sermons owe their success to such a mode of conveyance."

5. *Sermons,* I, 3, pp. 50–1.

6. Cf. John Seward, *The Spirit of Anecdote and Wit* (London, 1823), IV, 239–40. An anecdote is here related about "the whimsical and immortal author of Tristram Shandy" which, if true, would strengthen the probability that the misquoted reference to "the 18th of Leviticus" was not accidental. On the first Sunday following his marriage, Sterne is reported to have mounted the pulpit in Sutton Church and, when "every eye

the more imitative, perfunctory, and commonplace character of the discourses remaining in manuscript at the time of Sterne's death. The reader will discover in them little to arrest his attention—little that was not to be found in the hundreds of other collections of sermons which the eighteenth-century presses were constantly turning out; almost nothing which might foreshadow *Tristram Shandy*. In the four earlier-published volumes, on the other hand, the majority of discourses could have been composed by no one but Yorick. Here one constantly encounters most of those features which made *Tristram Shandy* and *A Sentimental Journey* so distinctive: the same ability to conceive dialogue, create characters, and furnish a scene with sharply etched backgrounds; the digressions and the eccentricities of punctuation; the obvious delight in alternately shocking and then moving people to tears by deft portrayals of the soft and delicate states of emotion; and the whole, clothed in a style as subtle and flexible in texture and showing as great an economy of means as any that English prose had yet known. Surely, there can be no reason for doubting that these sermons which Sterne himself edited were written after those which his wife and daughter assembled for publication.

A final and equally convincing criterion, which lends added support to the hypothesis that practically all the posthumously published sermons must have been written prior to those included in his first four volumes, may be obtained by examining a small but revealing collection of repetitious passages, shared in common by both groups. In discussing Sterne's use of borrowed material in "The Rich Man and Lazarus," attention was called to his freer, more imaginative handling of certain appropriations from Leightonhouse, which he had been content to transcribe, quite slavishly, in "Trust in God"; and reasons were advanced, at that time, for believing that Sterne, in writing the "Lazarus" sermon, had probably drawn directly upon "Trust in God" rather than revert to the primary source in Leightonhouse.[7] In like manner it seems almost certain that the discourse on "Penances" was later made use of for material in the more original and characteristically Shandean "The House of Feasting and the House of Mourning Described." In the following set of passages, the presumably earlier-written exposition has been contracted and reappears much more strikingly in its revised form.

---

was directed to him, and every ear ready to catch the words of the text," he commenced his discourse by reading the fifth verse from the fifth chapter of St. Luke: "We have toiled all the night and have taken nothing." The sermon, however, Mr. Seward assures us, "turned out, as usual, very instructive; and all went home highly delighted with the text, except poor Mrs. Sterne, who blushed down to her finger ends every step of the way to her house." This anecdote is also referred to in *Letters*, p. 15, n. 1.

7. See above, pp. 28–30.

"Penances," *Sermons*, VI, 10 (38), pp. 85-7

I John v. 3. *And his commandments are not grievous.*

NO,—they are not grievous, my dear auditors.—Amongst the many prejudices which at one time or other have been conceived against our holy religion, there is scarce any one which has done more dishonour to christianity, or which has been more opposite to the spirit of the gospel, than this, in express contradiction to the words of the text, "That the commandments of God *are* grievous."—That the way which leads to life is not only strait, for that our Saviour tells us, and that with much tribulation we shall seek it;—but that christians are bound to make the worst of it, and tread it barefoot upon thorns and briers,—if ever they expect to arrive happily at their journey's end.— And in course,—during this disastrous pilgrimage, it is our duty so to renounce the world, and abstract ourselves from it, as neither to interfere with its interests, or taste any of the pleasures, or any of the enjoyments of this life.—

Nor has this been confined merely to speculation, but has frequently been extended to practice, as is plain, not only from the lives of many legendary saints and hermits,—whose chief commendation seems to have been "That they fled unnaturally from all commerce with their fellow creatures, and then mortified, and piously —half starved themselves to death;"— but likewise from the many austere and fantastic orders which we see in the Romish church, which have all owed their origin and establishment to the same idle and extravagant opinion.

pp. 89-91

If this, or some such account, was not to be admitted, how is it possible to be conceived that christianity, which breathed out nothing but peace and comfort to mankind, which professedly took off the severities of the Jewish law, and was given us in the spirit of meekness, to ease our shoulders of a burthen which was too heavy for us;—that this religion, so kindly calculated for the ease and tranquility of man, and enjoins nothing but what is suitable to his nature, should be so misunderstood;—or that it should ever be supposed,—that he who is infinitely

"The House of Feasting and the House of Mourning Described," *Sermons*, I, 2, pp. 24-5

Ecclesiastes vii. 2, 3. *It is better to go to the house of mourning, than to the house of feasting.*—

THAT I deny—but let us hear the wise man's reasoning upon it—*for that is the end of all men, and the living* will *lay it to* his *heart: sorrow is better than laughter*— for a crack'd-brain'd order of Carthusian monks, I grant, but not for men of the world: For what purpose do you imagine, has God made us? for the social sweets of the well watered vallies where he has planted us, or for the dry and dismal deserts of a *Sierra Morena?* are the sad accidents of life, and the uncheery hours which perpetually overtake us, are they not enough, but we must sally forth in quest of them—belie our own hearts, and say, as your text would have us, that they are better than those of joy?

pp. 25-6

did the Best of Beings send us into the world for this end—to go weeping through it,—to vex and shorten a life short and vexatious enough already? do you think my good preacher, that he who is infinitely happy, can envy us our en-

happy, could envy us our enjoyments;—or that a Being infinitely kind, would grudge a mournful passenger a little rest and refreshment, to support his spirits through a weary pilgrimage;—or that he should call him to an account hereafter, because, in his way, he had hastily snatched at some fugacious and innocent pleasures, till he was suffered to take up his final repose.—

pp. 91–5

. . . The apostle tells us in the text,—That God's commandments are not grievous. . . . That he has proposed peace and plenty, joy and victory, as the encouragement and portion of his servants; thereby instructing us,—that our virtue is not necessarily endangered by the fruition of outward things . . . .

If this was not so, why, you'll say, does God seem to have made such provision for our happiness?—Why has he given us so many powers and faculties for enjoyment, and adapted so many objects to gratify and entertain them?—Some of which he has created so fair,—with such wonderful beauty, and has formed them so exquisitely for this end,—that they have power, for a time, to charm away the sense of pain,—to chear up the dejected heart under poverty and sickness, and make it go and remember its miseries no more.—Can all this, you'll say, be reconciled to God's wisdom, which does nothing in vain;—or can it be accounted for on any other supposition, but that the author of our Being, who has given us all things richly to enjoy, wills us a comfortable existence ever *here,* and seems moreover so evidently to have ordered things with a view to this, that the ways which lead to our future happiness, when rightly understood, he has made to be ways of pleasantness and all her paths peace.

From this representation of things we are led to this demonstrative truth, then, that God never intended to debar man of pleasure, under certain limitations.

Travellers on a business of the last and most important concern, may be allowed to please their eyes with the natural and artificial beauties of the country they are passing through, without reproach of forgetting the main errand they were sent upon;—and if they are not led out of their road by variety of prospects, edifices and ruins, would it not be a senseless piece of

joyments? or that a being so infinitely kind would grudge a mournful traveller, the short rest and refreshments necessary to support his spirits through the stages of a weary pilgrimage? or that he would call him to a severe reckoning, because in his way he had hastily snatch'd at some little fugacious pleasures, merely to sweeten this uneasy journey of life, and reconcile him to the ruggedness of the road, and the many hard justlings he is sure to meet with?

p. 26

Consider, I beseech you, what provision and accomodation, the Author of our being has prepared for us, that we might not go on our way sorrowing—how many caravansera's of rest—what powers and faculties he has given us for taking it—what apt objects he has placed in our way to entertain us;—some of which he has made so fair, so exquisitely for this end, that they have power over us for a time to charm away the sense of pain, to cheer up the dejected heart under poverty and sickness, and make it go and remember its miseries no more.

pp. 26–7

I will not contend at present against this rhetorick; I would choose rather for a moment to go on with the allegory, and say we are travellers, and, in the most affecting sense of that idea, that like travellers, though upon business of the last and nearest concern to us, may surely be allowed to amuse ourselves with the natural or artificial beauties of the country we are passing through, without reproach of forgetting the main errand we are sent upon; and if we can so order it, as not to be led out of the way, by the variety of

severity to shut their eyes against such gratifications? *For who has required such service at their hands?*

prospects, edifices, and ruins which solicit us, it would be a nonsensical piece of saint errantry to shut our eyes.

That "The House of Feasting" was written after "Penances" must be apparent to the critical reader. Not only has Yorick fitted neatly into the first three and a half pages of the earlier-published sermon everything of importance to the subject, which had occupied twice as many pages in "Penances," but the very omissions are significant. The preacher's growing tolerance is reflected in the suppression of irrelevant digressions on Methodists and the "Strange force of enthusiasm"; a paragraph devoted to the "fantastic orders" of the Roman Church reappears condensed into a single phrase; and the allegory, used in "Penances" as a loose, connecting thread for stringing together a series of divergent thoughts, is unified and kept intact, thus giving it the emphasis it deserves. It is inconceivable that from a sermon usually regarded as one of Yorick's most brilliant studies, and which the writer himself referred to as "one of the best,"[8] passages should have been extracted and deliberately made less effective so that they could be fitted into a discourse of inferior quality.

There are eleven additional instances of this reworking of older material and putting it to new uses;[9] and in every case the sequence of antecedency is the same: the version showing the greater degree of originality, polish, and effectiveness is invariably to be found in a discourse from one of the first four volumes.[1] Though the presence of such revisions provides a definite means for judging which of two

8. Cf. *Life*, p. 244, and *Letters*, p. 301.

9. *Sermons.* Compare:

II, 11, pp. 130–1, with v, 3 (30), pp. 64–6.
II, 13, pp. 186–8, with vII, 17 (44), pp. 128–30.
III, 1 (16), pp. 21–3, with vI, 9 (36), pp. 62–8.
III, 4 (19), p. 127, with vI, 10 (37), p. 111.
III, 4 (19), p. 123, with vI, 10 (37), pp. 98–9.
III, 6 (21), pp. 191–2, with v, 5 (32), pp. 142–3.
IV, 7 (22), p. 25, with vI, 10 (37), p. 109.
IV, 7 (22), pp. 26–7, with vI, 10 (37), pp. 110–11.
IV, 10 (25), pp. 120–2, with v, 4 (31), pp. 88–91.
IV, 11 (26), p. 162, with v, 6 (33), p. 172.
IV, 11 (26), pp. 163–4, with v, 6 (33), pp. 153–4.

This list does not include those instances already mentioned, from the "Lazarus" sermon or from "The House of Feasting."

1. As a final illustration, compare these two "definitions" of Popery. The first occurs in "Penances" (*Sermons*, vI, 10 [37], pp. 98–9): ". . . when you examine it [the Romish Religion] minutely, [it] is little else than a mere pecuniary contrivance.—And the truest definition you can give of popery—is,—that it is a system put together and contrived to operate upon men's weaknesses and passions,—and thereby to pick their pockets,—and leave them in a fit condition for its arbitrary designs." The second "definition" is given in "Felix's Behaviour towards Paul, Examined" (III, 4 [19], p. 123): "Consider popery well; you will be convinced, that the truest definition which can be given of it, is,—That it is a pecuniary system, well contrived to operate upon men's passions and weakness, whilst their pockets are o'picking . . . ."

given sermons antedates the other, such a measure can, unfortunately, be applied to only ten of the twenty-seven discourses which Sterne prepared for publication and is not sufficient, by itself, to constitute positive proof. This test does, however, contribute convincing substantiating testimony in support of one of the major premises of this study.

PART III

The varying degrees of indebtedness and independence which have been found consistently to differentiate the contents of the last three from the first four volumes of Yorick's sermons and the ease with which it is possible to classify most of these discourses as belonging either to the imitative and platitudinous group or to the original and Shandean group should leave little doubt as to which were written first. If this be granted—and the reader is once again reminded that all available evidence consistently supports such a conclusion—then a second and more discriminating hypothesis may now be ventured; namely, that most of the sermons from both groups were probably composed many years before their respective dates of publication, very likely as early as 1751. This conjecture is not wholly speculative.

Four of Sterne's discourses are known to have been written before 1751: the "Charity Sermon," printed at York in 1747;[1] the "Abuses of Conscience," also printed at York, in 1750;[2] the discourse on "Penances," inscribed by Sterne on the original manuscript, "preached April 8th, 1750";[3] and "Our Conversation in Heaven," likewise inscribed by the author, "Made for All Saints and preach'd on that Day 1750."[4] An examination of the borrowings in the first betrays indebtednesses to Clarke, Hall, Tillotson, and Wollaston; in the second, to Bentley, Butler, Swift, and Tillotson; in the third, to Locke, Tillotson, and Wollaston; and, in the fourth, to Clarke, Norris, and Tillotson. From these two sets of facts, therefore, it can be established that Sterne was indebted to certain predecessors in four of his sermons written prior to 1750; and this certitude, in turn, suggests a means for determining what additional sermons may also have been in existence before this date. If it can be shown for any given discourse, first, that use was made of one or more of the writers just enumerated; secondly, that the borrowed material was woven into its basic framework and was not likely, therefore, to have been added later; and, thirdly, that

1. *Sermons*, I, 5. See *Life*, pp. 597–8.   2. *Sermons*, IV, 12 (27). See *Life*, p. 598.
3. *Sermons*, VI, 10 (37). See *Life*, p. 619. It is much to be regretted that so little is known about the present location of Sterne's *Sermon* manuscripts. To the definite information supplied by Mr. Cross, that the "Penances" manuscript is now in the Pierpont Morgan Library, New York City, I have only been able to add that the undated manuscript for the "Temporal Advantages of Religion" may be found in the Henry E. Huntington Library, Pasadena, California. The rest seem entirely to have disappeared. Advertisements inserted in British and American publications and innumerable letters of inquiry addressed to private libraries and public institutions, both in this country and abroad, have failed to elicit any further information.
4. *Sermons*, V, 2 (29). See *Life*, p. 620. The present location of this manuscript is not known.

the discourse contains nothing to invalidate such a conclusion, then there is good reason for believing that such a discourse was probably composed during the same general period as those four definitely dated sermons. The presence of a stray quotation from Clarke or Hall or Tillotson, to be sure, is not significant; short paragraphs or illustrative anecdotes might well have been later additions;[5] but, when a borrowed passage occupies a fundamental structural position in the main argument, the probability is that the borrowing was made while the sermon was in the original process of being formulated. This type of indebtedness constitutes evidence of a highly relevant character.

To illustrate: an analysis of the "Charity Sermon" indicates that the first part was inspired by one of Bishop Hall's *Contemplations:* three direct quotations are woven into Yorick's retelling of the story of Elijah and the widow of Zarephath, and in such a manner as to make it unlikely that they were inserted after the account was first written. It is probable, therefore, that Sterne made use of Bishop Hall in the original draft of the "Charity Sermon," which, in turn, implies that his acquaintance with the Bishop's work antedates 1747. Since materials from the *Contemplations* were also utilized in six additional discourses,[6] as they had been in Sterne's version of the story of Elijah, it may be assumed that all seven sermons, showing this comparable use of material from Hall, belong to the same approximate period of composition. Again, in the latter portion of the "Charity Sermon," Sterne drew upon Wollaston's *Religion of Nature* to illustrate one of his principal contentions—that Nature has "sown the seeds of compassion in every man's breast."[7] Without the appropriation, the argument loses much of its force; it is inconceivable that the exposition was not inspired by Wollaston's illustration and that both were not simultaneously included in the discourse at the time when it was first being written. Five additional sermons betray

5. Cf. *Life*, pp. 244–5. Mr. Cross believes that the sermons in the first two volumes were probably "published practically as they had been written at sundry times for his cathedral congregation and afterwards repeated at Sutton and Stillington. This is not to say that he did not make many minor changes in them as they were going through the press. . . . Such was his method, as we may see by comparing the three printed versions we have of the sermon on conscience. 'That I deny' [*Sermons*, I, 2], it may be, was an afterthought in place of a more general repudiation of Solomon. But that Sterne's revision of his sermons for Dodsley went beyond details is really impossible. Had he wished it, there was no time for rewriting them during the months he was in London marching from one great house to another."

Most of the discourses in Volumes III–IV, Mr. Cross observes elsewhere (*Life*, p. 372), "were doubtless old sermons, recast or stretched out for the closet"; exception was made, however, of "two or three, like 'The Prodigal Son,' [which] may have been prepared solely for the press." The nonexistence of manuscripts for any sermon in the first four volumes makes it impossible to do much more than speculate upon this aspect of the problem.

6. *Sermons*, II, 12; II, 13; III, 1 (16); III, 2 (17); III, 3 (18); and IV, 7 (22).

7. *Idem*, I, 5, pp. 138–9.

equally basic and significant indebtednesses to Wollaston;[8] hence there is good reason for believing that these six were also written at about the same time that Yorick was preparing his Elijah discourse (*circa* 1747).

In like manner, from the fact that two of the four definitely dated discourses are under fundamental structural obligation to both Clarke and Tillotson, it is probable that the ten additional sermons in which the joint influence of these two clergymen is similarly manifest[9] were also in existence before mid-century. And when this test, or measure, has been extended to include all those sermons of Yorick's whose structures contain material borrowed from one or more of the writers known to have influenced him during the seventeen-forties,[1] the results—even in the light of incomplete evidence—would indicate that only fourteen of the forty-five are lacking in sufficiently significant indebtednesses to make it possible to assign them to the early period here suggested.[2]

A critical appraisal of other features exhibited by the fourteen discourses temporarily excluded from this conjectural, early-written group, moreover, discloses additional means for further reducing the number of those which would otherwise have to be considered as written later than 1750. For example: "Trust in God" and "On Enthusiasm"[3] were appropriated from Leightonhouse and Young, respectively, and with such literalness that there can be little objection to classifying them with the earliest of Yorick's parish homilies; their lack of originality and the absence of any Shandean touches certainly imply their having been compiled before the "Charity Sermon" or the "Abuses of Conscience."

Then, if use is made of inferences such as those suggested by Mr. Cross, good reasons can be advanced for assigning eight of the remaining twelve sermons to this same early period of composition. In discussing the contents of the posthumously published volumes, Mr. Cross observed: ". . . other sermons like 'Penances' and 'On Enthusiasm,' whether original or not in their phrasing, merely reflect the violent hatred against the Church of Rome prevalent in '45, a phase of passion through which Sterne had long since passed."[4] Three of the

---

8. *Idem*, I, 1; I, 2; II, 10; VI, 10 (37); and VII, 17 (44).

9. *Idem*, I, 1; I, 3; I, 5; I, 8; II, 15; IV, 8 (23); IV, 9 (24); V, 2 (29); VII, 14 (41); and VII, 16 (43).

1. Passages from Norris are to be found in basic sections of *Sermons*, V, 1 (28), and VI, 9 (36); from Locke and Tillotson, jointly, in *idem*, II, 14, and IV, 11 (26); from Swift and Butler in *idem*, I, 4; from Swift and Tillotson in *idem*, II, 11; from Tillotson, alone, in *idem*, V, 4 (31), and V, 6 (33); from Bentley in *idem*, I, 7.

2. *Idem*, I, 6; II, 9; III, 4 (19); III, 5 (20); III, 6 (21); IV, 10 (25); V, 3 (30); V, 5 (32); VI, 7 (34); VI, 11 (38); VI, 12 (39); VII, 13 (40); VII, 15 (42); and VII, 18 (45).

3. *Idem*, VI, 7 (34), and VI, 11 (38).   4. *Life*, pp. 506, 88.

four discourses known to have been written prior to 1750 betray evidences of this "violent hatred," either in open denunciations of or slurring references to Roman Catholicism;[5] so also do six others of the twelve now under consideration.[6] The virulency with which Popery is attacked and ridiculed suggests that Sterne was voicing his own aroused sentiments at a time of general excitement rather than recollecting at a later period what his feelings had been several years before. Again, Mr. Cross points out that Sterne regarded "The long wars of his time, the high tax rate in consequence of them, and the pestilence that swept over the cattle after the insurrection of 1745, leaving 'no herd in the stalls,' . . . as the last judgment of the Almighty upon a people who had forgotten the ways of righteousness, and were listening to the seductions of Jesuit missionaries."[7] Certainly the two posthumously printed discourses which concern themselves with the state of affairs outlined by Mr. Cross—"Thirtieth of January" and "The Ingratitude of Israel"[8]—must have been written at a time when the sharpness of these public calamities was still vivid in the minds of Yorick's parishioners, so that the preacher would have to do no more in his plea for a reformation of manners than merely to make mention of what so obviously should be interpreted as marks of the Almighty's displeasure.

The presence of an additional comment in the latter of these two discourses might suggest that the time of composition could be yet more definitely determined. "You have just felt two dreadful shocks in your metropolis of a most terrifying nature," Yorick reminded his listeners;[9] the reference, clearly, was to the earthquakes of March 8, 1749/50, which so startled Londoners and called forth so many similar warnings from contemporary clergymen. On the authority of Archbishop Secker, such tremors were unusual in England; it was "fifty-seven years ago, when the last earthquake before these was felt here. . . ."[1] But the relevancy of Sterne's comment, as a means for establishing precisely when the sermon, as a whole, may have been written, is somewhat impaired when the passage is examined in relation to its setting. Both "The Ingratitude of Israel" and "Thirtieth of January" share a large number of identical paragraphs, probably derived from some common source not yet identified; and, as the fol-

5. *Sermons*, I, 5, p. 144; IV, 12 (27), pp. 183–5, 119–204; VI, 10 (37), pp. 96–100, 100–03.
6. *Idem*, I, 6, p. 175; II, 9, pp. 50–1; III, 4 (19), pp. 123–4; III, 5 (20), p. 188; III, 6 (21), pp. 183, 188; VII, 15 (42), pp. 75–8.
7. *Life*, p. 87.   8. *Sermons*, V, 5 (32), p. 136; and VII, 18 (45), pp. 152–3.
9. *Idem*, VII, 18 (45), p. 153.
1. Thomas Secker, Archbishop of Canterbury, in a sermon "Preached in the Parish-Church of St. James, Westminster, March 11, 1749/50, on occasion of the earthquake, March 8." *The Works of Thomas Secker*, V, 158.

lowing comparisons will suggest, it is likely that the allusion to earth-quakes was a later insertion into the framework of a discourse which had already been in existence for several years.

"Thirtieth of January," *Sermons*, v, 5 (32), pp. 134-5

But this licentiousness, he [a stranger visiting England] would say, may be chiefly owing to a long course of pros-perity, which is apt to corrupt mens minds.—God has since tried you with af-flictions;—you have been visited with a long and expensive war:—God has sent, moreover, a pestilence amongst your cat-tle, which has cut off the stock from the fold,—and left no herd in the stalls.—Surely he'll say,—two such terrible scourges must have awakened the con-sciences of the most unthinking part of you, and forced the inhabitants of your land—from such admonitions,—though they failed with the Jews, to have learnt righteousness for themselves.—

"The Ingratitude of Israel," *Sermons*, vii, 18 (45), pp. 152-3

But this licentiousness, he'll say, may be chiefly owing to a long course of pros-perity, which is apt to corrupt mens minds.—God has since tried you with af-flictions;—you have had lately a bloody and expensive war;—God has sent, more-over, a pestilence amongst your cattle, which has cut off the stock from the fold, and left no herd in the stalls;—besides,—you have just felt two dreadful shocks in your metropolis of a most terrifying na-ture;—which, if God's providence had not checked and restrained within some bounds, might have overthrown your cap-ital, and your kingdom with it.

Surely, he'll say,—all these warnings must have awakened the consciences of the most unthinking part of you, and forced the inhabitants of your land, from such admonitions, to have learned right-eousness.—

Were the manuscript for "The Ingratitude of Israel" available, it would probably be seen that the earthquake reference was a later (and timely) addition; both this discourse and its variant, "Thirtieth of January," abound in colorless platitudes and are otherwise lacking in individuality; they must be considered as belonging to the earliest period of Yorick's homiletic compositions.

An interesting piece of documentary evidence, discovered by Canon S. L. Ollard, provides the ground for assigning one of the four remaining discourses to the same early years of Sterne's priest-hood. In going through the diocesan records which form part of the manuscript library of the Archbishop of York, at Bishopsthorpe, Canon Ollard came upon a collection of answers to a questionnaire which had been sent out by Archbishop Herring of York to the clergy of his diocese, in advance of his primary visitation in May, 1743; and among these answers was the reply which Sterne, as Vicar of Sutton-in-the-Forest, had submitted.[2] The Archbishop requested specific information on twelve different points; one in particular concerns us here. Question vii read, in part: "Do you know of any who come to Church in your Parish who are not Baptized?" Sterne answered: "No. Except one Quaker-Woman whom I have prevaild with to

2. S. L. Ollard and P. C. Walker, eds., *Archbishop Herring's Visitation Returns, 1743*, in The Yorkshire Archaeological Society's Record Series, iii, 92-3.

come to Church, but have not yet been able to gain her Consent to be Baptised." The Vicar's admitted concern for the spiritual welfare of this "Quaker-Woman" and his efforts to bring her into the fold make it probable that the one sermon of his in which there is a direct reference to the mistaken tenets of those "harmless quiet people"[3] was written at a time when he was taking so personal an interest in the subject.

Three of the forty-five *Sermons of Mr. Yorick* remain to be accounted for. For two of these no positive internal evidence has yet been discovered which might be of use in determining when they were composed;[4] since they are nothing more than routine homilies, however, dull and unenlivened, there is no reason why they should not be considered as belonging to the early Sutton period, the uninspired products of the village parson's labors. Only one of Sterne's extant discourses—"Asa: A Thanksgiving Sermon"[5]—could not have been written as early as 1751; under the guise of Asa, Yorick drew "a portrait of the young George the Third . . . the peaceful king"; very probably this eulogy was specially prepared for the king's coronation on September 22, 1761.[6]

Admittedly, the reasons which have been advanced to substantiate the theory that all but one of Sterne's sermons were probably written before 1750 do not constitute proof; they are, however, sufficiently numerous and consistent to lend strong plausibility to such a supposition. And there are further considerations to strengthen this belief. The picture of Sterne as Vicar of Sutton in 1743, which Canon Ollard's discovery has given us, shows that at this time, however unclerically he may have behaved later, Yorick was performing his duties as parish priest with more than average conscientiousness. In an article appearing in the London *Times Literary Supplement* for March 18, 1926, Canon Ollard analyzed Sterne's report of his activities, comparing it with the hundreds of other replies which Archbishop Herring's questionnaire had evoked. The results are quite different from what one who knows Yorick only as the literary and drawing-room figure of later years might have expected. Here are some of Sterne's answers.

I do reside Personally upon my Cure, and in my Parsonage-House.
I have no Curate.
public Service is duely perform'd twice every Lord's Day.
I Catechise every Sunday in my Church during Lent, But explain our Religion to the Children and Servants of my Parishioners in my own House every Sunday Night during Lent, from Six o'clock till nine. I mention the Length of Time as my Reason for not doing it in Church.

3. *Sermons*, IV, 10 (25), p. 129.   4. *Idem*, V, 3 (30), and VI, 12 (39).
5. *Idem*, VII, 13 (40).   6. *Life*, p. 506. See also *Letters*, pp. 145–6, n. 6.

The Sacrament is administered five Times every Year in my Church. There are about 250 Communicants above one Half of wch. communicated last Easter.

As Mr. Cross rightly comments, "Over against gossip about Sterne should always be set the portrait of a faithful parish priest, solicitous for the spiritual welfare of the souls committed to his care . . . ."[7]

Consider, for a moment, the implications of this portrait in the bearing they have upon those four sermons of Yorick's which are known to have been written during the fourth decade of the century. The two discourses which had appeared in print before 1751 were both distinctive and characteristic of his mature writing; and the fact that the "Abuses of Conscience," ten years later, could be fitted without change into the second volume of *Tristram Shandy*—and not suffer by comparison when so inserted—certainly indicates that at least by mid-century Sterne had already attained considerable literary skill. Would he have been satisfied to produce sermons of a markedly inferior order—would he have been willing slavishly to imitate and copy from others after he had experienced the pleasures of original and creative writing? More specifically: if he was able before 1747 to write such a discourse as the "Charity Sermon," is it likely that thereafter he could have turned out anything so flat and uninspired, so filled with repetitions, as the discourses on "Penances" or "Our Conversation in Heaven"? What, then, more reasonable to suppose than that all the distinctly inferior, more platitudinous sermons preceded by several years those which are more characteristically Shandean; further, that the period when Yorick was conscientiously performing his other parish duties was also the period when most of his discourses were written? In other words, are there not plausible grounds for believing that most of the poorer sermons antedate 1747; most of the better ones, 1750?

There is another bit of corroborative evidence, not without its relevancy in this connection. With the single exception of Swift's *Sermons*, apparently first published in 1744,[8] Sterne made no use in his own discourses of any writing which had not already appeared in print before 1733. The significance of this circumstance lies not so much in its indication of what Yorick may have done as in what he did not do. Just because a book was available to him before a certain date is no guarantee that he might not have read it many years later. What is of significance is that he appears to have appropriated noth-

7. *Life*, p. 68.
8. 1744 is the earliest-listed appearance in print for any of Swift's sermons. Cf. the bibliographies compiled by W. Spencer Jackson (*The Prose Works of Jonathan Swift*, Scott, ed. [London, 1908], Vol. XII) and Herman Teerink (*A Bibliography of the Writings in Prose and Verse of Jonathan Swift* [The Hague, 1937]).

ing from the innumerable volumes of discourses and general theological and philosophical writings of later issue. For example: in making use of material from James Foster's *Sermons,* Sterne borrowed
only from the first of the four volumes, which was published in 1732;
he took nothing whatsoever from any of the three later ones, appearing between 1735 and 1744.

Against the objection that he would have preferred not to plagiarize from up-to-the-minute, contemporary publications, there is the
fact, as will be shown later,[9] that two of the three predecessors to
whom he was most indebted—John Tillotson and Samuel Clarke—
were clergymen whose works were constantly being read and discussed by Sterne's generation. Fear of detection, then, could not have
acted as too strong a deterrent. The inferences seem rather to point
to the conclusion which is being advanced in this chapter; and upon
two counts: first, that as Yorick's originality developed and he felt
his own literary powers stirring within him he would be increasingly
dissatisfied with borrowing from anyone; and, secondly, that as his
interests expanded and he began to venture upon new undertakings
there would naturally be less and less time for consulting the pages
of older writers. The period concurrent with his first admittance to
the priesthood would be the normal time for his most serious and sustained attention to his churchly duties; he would then have felt the
greatest need for reading and for compiling sermons. It must have
been during the years between 1737 and 1745 that practically all his
discourses, at least in rudimentary form, were set down on paper.

There remain to be considered several possible objections to so
sweeping and arbitrary a generalization as the one just proposed. Mr.
Cross, for example, conjectures that of the discourses making up the
contents of the third and fourth volumes, "two or three, like 'The
Prodigal Son,' may have been prepared solely for the press."[1] Were
this supposition correct, then "The Prodigal Son" would have to be
assigned to a period of composition between the publication of Volumes I–II (1760) and III–IV (1766). Yorick's imaginative handling of
his text, in the particular discourse mentioned by Mr. Cross, and the
whimsicality which characterizes his treatment of the prodigal's adventures are not inconsistent with such a suggestion. On the other
hand, the concluding pages of this sermon are based largely upon
Locke's *Thoughts Concerning Education* and the influence of Locke
is apparent in the structure of a discourse which Sterne himself had
dated 1750; though Yorick's indebtedness to the philosopher is discernible throughout all of his later writing, the extent and nature of
the borrowings in "The Prodigal Son" suggest Sterne's earlier rather
than his later practice.

9. See below, pp. 78–81.   1. *Life,* p. 372.

Reasons for believing that any other discourse in the third and fourth volumes "may have been prepared solely for the press" are still less convincing. Though "The Levite and His Concubine" might appear to be another exception, the basic indebtednesses to Hall and Tillotson, closely paralleling Sterne's use of these same predecessors in the "Charity Sermon," would argue against such a supposition. In the absence of manuscript evidence, of course, it is impossible to prove that these particular sermons may not have been subjected to later revision; but, even if such were the case, it is my conviction that such revisions were not extensive and were superimposed upon the framework of homilies, basically at least a decade older.

A second objection which might be raised against the theory that all but one of Mr. Yorick's sermons had been written before 1751, and most of them probably several years before then, is the information possessed as to when certain of these discourses were preached. "The Parable of the Rich Man and Lazarus," for example, was delivered on May 3, 1761, at St. Andrew's, Holborn;[2] "National Mercies Considered," "On the Inauguration of His Present Majesty," September 22, 1761;[3] "The Case of Hezekiah and the Messengers," "before his Excellency the Earl of Hertford. At Paris, 1763";[4] and Mr. Curtis believes that "The Character of Herod," "Preached on Innocent's Day," is the discourse referred to in a letter of Sterne's, dated "December, 1758."[5] All these dates are fully ten years later than the ones which have been suggested in this chapter as the probable times of composition. But it does not necessarily follow, because a sermon was preached on a certain day, that it had only just been written, and for that particular occasion. An examination of the internal evidence provided by the four discourses in question, on the contrary, tends to confirm a belief that they had been composed many years earlier and that, at most, they could have been subjected to no more than minor revision. In "Hezekiah and the Messengers," the sermon preached at Paris in 1763, there are extended and verbatim transcripts from Hall, Tillotson, and Young. Is it not more likely that when Lord Hertford's messenger came to Yorick "On a Saturday afternoon . . . with a request that he preach, on the next morning, in the chapel at the new embassy in place of Dr. James Traill,"[6] Sterne's recourse was to draw upon a previously written discourse rather than compose a new one upon such short order? From what is known of Yorick's health and habits at this time, it is difficult to picture his having packed volumes of Hall, Tillotson, and Young in his valise when he left for the Continent, so that he could make desired transcripts from these predeces-

2. Sermons, IV, 8 (23), p. 63. See also Life, pp. 272–4, and Letters, pp. 134–5.
3. Sermons, III, 6 (21), p. 161. See also Life, pp. 276–7.
4. Sermons, III, 2 (17), p. 27. See also Life, pp. 345–8, and Letters, pp. 218–20.
5. Sermons, II, 9 (45). See Letters, p. 65, n. 2.   6. Life, p. 347.

sors in case he were asked to conduct a service; or, even granting the existence of a "commonplace book"[7]—which would have permitted his leaving these volumes at home—to believe he had either the strength or the inclination to prepare a brand-new homily when an older one was available. Further, the conventional use made of the Bible in the "Hezekiah" sermon, as well as the tone and general structure of the discourse as a whole, invites comparison with "The Case of Elijah and the Widow of Zerephath"; for all its brilliance of characterization and occasional flashes of scintillating whimsicality, there is nothing in the discourse preached before Lord Hertford which cannot be matched in the latter, justly described by Mr. Cross as revealing Sterne "already a master of his art."[8]

No sources have as yet been discovered which might serve to indicate when "The Character of Herod" was written, save one minor illustration derived from Wollaston.[9] But, inasmuch as most of the factual details around which the sermon is woven were admittedly based upon Josephus,[1] it is probable that some convenient "intermediary" saved Yorick the trouble of perusing the pages of the Jewish historian for himself; an examination of *The Antiquities* failed to bring forth any indication that Sterne had gone directly to the original for the material he used. The unimaginative treatment given to the factual parts of this sermon, the unusually extended and probably appropriated commentary upon the text, with its echoing of what "the Jewish interpreters say upon this," the dragged-in aspersion of "Romish dreamers" and their "doctrine of intercessions,"[2] as well as the generally serious tone which characterizes the homily as a whole, combine to imply that this sermon was written by Sterne, the young priest, rather than Yorick, the famous jester.

In like manner, although "The Parable of the Rich Man and Lazarus Considered" was inscribed as having been preached in May, 1761, it is difficult not to believe, in the light of what has already been shown regarding the amount and use made of borrowed material, that this sermon, also, must have been written during the seventeen-forties—at a time contemporaneous with or even earlier than "Elijah and the Widow of Zerephath" or "The Abuses of Conscience." With his head full of new ideas for succeeding volumes of *Tristram Shandy* and his days and nights taken up with engrossing social engagements, there would have been little time or inclination for sermon writing; so that when he agreed to preach on behalf of the St. Andrew's Foundling Hospital, in May, 1761, our parson in all probability did little more than rummage through his papers and pull out a discourse sufficient for the occasion, which would require only minor revision. The

7. See below, pp. 67–8.   8. *Life*, p. 90.   9. *Sermons*, II, 9, p. 70.
1. *Idem*, II, 9, pp. 62, 64, and 67.   2. *Idem*, II, 9, pp. 50–1.

temptation to repeat such a procedure would have reoccurred in the fall of the same year, when it became necessary to deliver an address "On the Inauguration of His Present Majesty." Certainly, "National Mercies Considered" is a thoroughly colorless, unimaginative piece of writing; the appropriations from Tillotson, as well as the somewhat forced allusion to "the arts of Jesuitry," are more characteristic of the earlier than of the later Sterne.[3]

A final objection which might seem to threaten the validity of the assumption that all but one of the *Sermons of Mr. Yorick* were existent before 1751 arises from the presence of a small but provocative number of similarities, shared in common by the discourses and Sterne's other writings. Two passages in the fourth book of *Tristram Shandy*, for example, would seem to be improved versions of material which later appeared in the posthumously published "Trust in God" and which, in turn, had been taken out of Leightonhouse's "Twelfth Sermon."

"Trust in God," *Sermons*, vi, 7 (34), pp. 3–4

Tristram Shandy, Bk. iv, chap. vii

Whoever seriously reflects upon the state and condition of man, and looks upon that dark side of it, which represents his life as open to so many causes of trouble;—when he sees, how often he eats the bread of affliction, and that he is born to it as naturally as the sparks fly upwards;—. . . when one sits down and looks upon this gloomy side of things, with all the sorrowful changes and chances which surround us,—at first sight, —would not one wonder,—how the spirit of a man could bear the infirmities of his nature, and what it is that supports him, as it does, under the many evil accidents which he meets with in his passage through the valley of tears?—Without some certain aid within us to bear us up, —so tender a frame as ours, would be but ill-fitted to encounter what generally befals it in this rugged journey . . . .

When I reflect, brother *Toby*, upon Man; and take a view of that dark side of him which represents his life as open to so many causes of trouble—when I consider, brother *Toby*, how oft we eat the bread of affliction, and that we are born to it, as to the portion of our inheritance—. . . when one runs over the catalogue of all the cross-reckonings and sorrowful *items* with which the heart of man is overcharged, 'tis wonderful by what hidden resources the mind is enabled to stand it out, and bear itself up, as it does against the impositions laid upon our nature.—

pp. 5–6

Bk. iv, chap. viii

This expectation,—though in fact it no way alters the nature of the cross accidents to which we lay open, or does at all pervert the course of them,—yet imposes upon the sense of them, and like a secret spring in a well-contrived machine, though it cannot prevent, at least it counterbalances the pressure . . . .

—Figuratively speaking, dear *Toby* . . . said my father . . . the spring I am speaking of, is that great and elastic power within us of counterbalancing evil, which like a secret spring in a well-ordered machine, though it can't prevent the shock—at least it imposes upon our sense of it.

3. *Idem*, iii, 6 (21), pp. 168, 188.

Compare, also, this passage from the posthumously published discourse on "The Ways of Providence Justified to Man," with a final comment in *Tristram Shandy*.

Sermons, VII, 17 (44), p. 134	Tristram Shandy, Bk. IV, chap. xvii
—Nay, have not the most obvious things that come in our way dark sides, which the quickest sight cannot penetrate into; and do not the clearest and most exalted understandings find themselves puzzled, and at a loss, in every particle of matter?	—But mark, madam, we live amongst riddles and mysteries—the most obvious things, which come in our way, have dark sides, which the quickest sight cannot penetrate into; and even the clearest and most exalted understandings amongst us find ourselves puzzled and at a loss in almost every cranny of nature's works . . . .

Reflections of the *Sermons* in *A Sentimental Journey* are neither so literal nor so extensive as these examples from *Tristram Shandy;* they consist entirely of similarities in thought and are limited exclusively to discourses appearing in the third and fourth volumes, published two years earlier. In "The Levite and His Concubine," for example, Sterne had exclaimed:

. . . notwithstanding all we meet with in books, in many of which, no doubt, there are a good many handsome things said upon the sweets of retirement, &c. . . . . Yet still, *"it is not good for man to be alone:"* nor can all which the coldhearted pedant stuns our ears with upon the subject, ever give one answer of satisfaction to the mind; in the midst of the loudest vauntings of philosophy, Nature will have her yearnings for society and friendship;—a good heart wants some object to be kind to—and the best parts of our blood, and the purest of our spirits suffer most under the destitution.

Let the torpid Monk seek heaven comfortless and alone—God speed him! For my own part, I fear, I should never so find the way: let me be wise and religious—but let me be MAN: wherever thy Providence places me, or whatever be the road I take to get to thee—give me some companion in my journey, be it only to remark to, How our shadows lengthen as the sun goes down;—to whom I may say, How fresh is the face of nature! How sweet the flowers of the field! How delicious are these fruits![4]

These sentiments find echoes in two different places in *A Sentimental Journey.*

—Surely—surely man! it is not good for thee to sit alone—thou wast made for social intercourse and gentle greetings, and this improvement of our natures from it, I appeal to, as my evidence.

If nature has so wove her web of kindness, that some threads of love and desire are entangled with the piece—must the whole web be rent in drawing them out?—Whip me such stoics, great governor of nature! said I to myself—Wherever thy providence shall place me for the trials of my virtue

4. *Idem,* III, 3 (18), pp. 72–4.

—whatever is my danger—whatever is my situation—let me feel the movements which rise out of it, and which belong to me as a man—and if I govern them as a good one, I will trust the issues to thy justice, for thou hast made us, and not we ourselves.[5]

The bearing which such similarities have upon the problem of dating the sermons may best be illustrated by comparing a section from the discourse on "God's Forbearance Abused" with a letter to Dr. Topham, inscribed by Sterne, "January 20, 1759." In both, use was made of an observation and a supporting quotation, which had come from Tillotson.[6] In the discourse Yorick wrote:

. . . as the merciful man does good to his own soul, so he that is cruel troubleth his own flesh.—

In all which cases there is a punishment . . . which a man's own mind takes upon itself, from the remorse of doing what is wrong.—*Prima est haec ultio . . . .*[7]

and in the letter:

. . . As for the many coarse and unchristian Insinuations scatter'd throughout your *Reply,* . . . Believe me, Dr *Topham,* they hurt yourself more than the Person they are aimed at; and when the *first Transport* of Rage is a little over, they will grieve you too.——*prima est haec Ultio.*[8]

In the presence of these likenesses, it might seem reasonable to assume that both the letter and the discourse had been composed at approximately the same time, shortly after the borrowing was made from Tillotson and while the passage in question was still fresh in the preacher's mind; in other words, a previously undated sermon might now be assigned, tentatively, to the year in which the letter was written—1759. Similarly, one might assume that "Trust in God" and "The Ways of Providence Justified to Man" had been compiled while Yorick was busying himself with the fourth volume of *Tristram Shandy* (1760–61); or that the discourses containing ideas in common with *A Sentimental Journey* (1768) also shared this later period of composition.

More likely explanations, however, may be found for these occasional and not too important similarities. The only ones that are close enough to warrant serious attention are those existing between the posthumously published discourses and Book iv of *Tristram Shandy;* and here the time element is of significance: the first two

---

5. *A Sentimental Journey,* I, 172, and II, 100–01. Compare also the following passages from the *Sermons,* respectively, with paragraphs in *A Sentimental Journey:*

III, 5 (20), pp. 147–8, with II, pp. 191–2.

III, 5 (20), pp. 152–4, with II, p. 66.

III, 12 (27), pp. 201–03, with II, pp. 30–2.

6. See below, p. 174–5.   7. *Sermons,* v, 6 (33), p. 164.   8. *Letters,* p. 72.

volumes of sermons did not appear in print until the end of May, 1760; by the first week in August of the same year—Sterne tells us— he had completed the writing of Book III of *Tristram* and may already have begun work on Book IV.[9] Undoubtedly, before deciding which of the discourses should go to make up the contents of the first two volumes, Yorick must have taken into consideration all the manuscripts available at the moment; it would only be natural that he should still have had in mind certain ideas and illustrations from the rejected sermons a few months later, when continuing with the adventures of Uncle Toby and Walter Shandy. The likenesses shared in common by other of the *Sermons* and *A Sentimental Journey,* or the *Letters,* as has already been shown, are too vague and coincidental to bear much weight as evidence one way or the other; they could easily be accounted for by Locke's theory of the association of ideas. Such an interpretation was, in fact, offered by an anonymous correspondent to the *Gentleman's Magazine* in 1806 as an explanation for the more provocative and less defensible series of repetitious passages to be found in the *Sermons* themselves. The comment is worth considering.

. . . in those extracts, where the phraseology is almost literally the same, it is not, I presume, to be inferred that Sterne copied from a former Sermon what he afterwards wrote in a latter; perhaps he might not at the time have even recollected the passage. The coincidence may be rather attributed to a previous impression, which, being excited by the same ideas occurring to the mind of the writer, though at a later period, and on a different occasion, insensibly led him to cloath them in the same dress.[1]

No cogent objection, thus, stands in the way of accepting the conclusions toward which all the newly assembled evidence points. Admittedly, this evidence is incomplete and, as such, cannot constitute proof; but it does lend convincing support to the suppositions that practically all *The Sermons of Mr. Yorick* had been written before 1751 and that those of posthumous publication preceded the ones which Sterne himself prepared for the press. On the basis of these distinctions, a better opportunity is now provided for observing the development of Sterne's literary artistry. In the earliest of the discourses, as has been shown, Yorick's practice was to copy, often slavishly, from the pages of others; apparently he was content if the resulting compilations were but long enough. From the fact that he did not select any of these for publication, it may be assumed that he recognized his first efforts for what they were—transcriptions to be delivered orally, not literary productions for the closet. Then, in response to a growing consciousness of latent powers within him, Sterne

9. *Idem,* p. 111, n. 8, and p. 120.
1. *The Gentleman's Magazine,* Vol. LXXVI, Pt. 1, 409.

began experimenting: phrases were refashioned and given greater effectiveness; new ways were found for heightening the dramatic or emotional possibilities of a scene; character sketches became more sharply etched. Most important of all, Yorick's individuality was permitted free play in determining how a text should be interpreted and developed. That this changed conception of sermon writing must have taken place earlier than has commonly been supposed is apparent from the artistry displayed in the "Charity Sermon" and the ease whereby "The Abuses of Conscience" was later inserted into the second book of *Tristram Shandy*. In these two discourses are to be found, clearly revealed, many of the peculiarities in thought and expression which one usually associates exclusively with the preacher's later novels; and "Shandyism" thus is seen to be not a drastic and sudden stylistic change which came into being simultaneously with Sterne's conception of "the HOMUNCULUS" but the result of a steady development which had clearly manifested itself at least a decade before the opening chapters of *Tristram Shandy* were set down on paper.

III

Some Conjectures—
Sterne in the Workshop

T HE existence of phrases and ideas shared in common by
Tristram Shandy, A Sentimental Journey, the *Letters,* and
the *Sermons* and the manner in which diverse borrowed materials were sometimes worked into a discourse raise interesting conjectures as to how Yorick went about the business of sermon writing,
the methods he adopted for taking notes on or recording references
to whatever may have attracted him in his reading, and the sort of
book he felt would be most useful to him. Speculations such as these
are always hazardous; frequently they can be misleading; and here,
once more, the dearth of sermon manuscripts is a serious obstacle.
Yet, in spite of these difficulties and dangers, an examination of the
evidence in hand does suggest several things sufficiently plausible
and illuminating to justify their inclusion in this study. The curiosity
which naturally attaches itself to the formative years of an artist, the
all but impenetrable mystery surrounding the creative process are
considerations of such interest in themselves that any attempt to
throw new light upon them, however slight, is in need of no apology.

As an approach to some of these matters, there are, first of all, the
implications suggested by Sterne's ability harmoniously to weave together verbatim transcripts from five different sources in that homily
of his which has already been discussed as a typical representative
of the last three posthumously published volumes, the "Temporal
Advantages of Religion." The first seven of the twenty-four pages
which this sermon occupies in the first edition are made up solidly
of transcripts from Young; the eighth page and part of the ninth
would seem to be original. An extract from Young fills the tenth; Blair
occupies the last paragraph of the eleventh and all of the twelfth; and
Clarke takes up where Blair stops, filling the thirteenth, fourteenth,
and half of the fifteenth. Then Blair reappears and continues without
break into the eighteenth page. Most of the eighteenth and nineteenth are Yorick's; but Norris supplies the paragraphs for most of
the twentieth and twenty-first; Tillotson probably suggested what
appears on the twenty-second and twenty-third; and Norris provides
the conclusion. From Blair had been taken the first, third, fourth, and
fifth "considerations," in "vindication of the text"; Clarke supplied

the second; Norris provided a summary of the account, in addition
to the conclusion; Young the introduction, and Tillotson an illustrative warning. And yet these various fragments were joined together
so skillfully that, when combined, they read as though one man had
written them all, and at one time—truly an amazing performance.[1]
An examination of the manuscript reveals corrections of only a trifling
nature: slight verbal changes, three or four short deletions, and one
addition;[2] on the verso of the last page a further borrowing was made
from the same discourse of Norris that Yorick had already used, to
double the length of the third paragraph from the end. In so far as it
is possible to judge from the handwriting and the ink used, the
changes were probably made at the same time the sermon was first
compiled; at latest, very soon thereafter.

How had Sterne been able to assemble such a mosaic? Were there
in front of him, as he wrote, the five volumes containing those homilies which he had found so useful? The Todd and Sotheran catalogue
lists many different editions of both Tillotson and Clarke, single editions of Young and Blair, but does not include Norris. Even assuming that these volumes were readily available at the moment of composition, by what association of ideas would Yorick have been likely
to recollect that from discourses with such dissimilar titles as Blair's
"A Competency Promised to the Just," Young's "Safe Way to Happiness, Present as Well as Future," Clarke's "Uprightness a Man's Greatest Security," Tillotson's "Advantages of Religion to Particular Persons," and Norris' "Importance of a Religious Life Considered"
materials could be extracted, harmoniously pieced together, and
used to develop and illustrate the particular topic he wished to dis-
cuss? Were there no additional examples of this joiner's skill in the
Sermons of Mr. Yorick, exception might be made of the "Temporal
Advantages of Religion"; but, though this discourse remains unique,
even in the list of Sterne's achievements, many other instances can
be cited where extracts from different sources have been combined
and put to new uses. Tillotson and Steele are thus united in "Joseph's
History Considered."

TILLOTSON   STERNE

Vol. vii, Sermon 147, pp. 67–8   *Sermons,* ii, 12, pp. 155–7

And we continually stand in need of   Without derogating from the merit of
mercy both from God and man. We are   his [Joseph's] forbearance, he might be
liable one to another; and in the change supposed to have cast an eye upon the
of human affairs, we may be all subject to change and uncertainty of human affairs
one another by turns, and stand in need   which he had seen himself, and which

1. This was also Sir Walter Scott's opinion. See the edition of his *Miscellaneous Prose
Works* (Edinburgh, 1834, 30 vols.), iii, 293.
2. For two examples of the deletions, see below, pp. 185 and 186.

of one another's pity and compassion . . . . To restrain the cruelties, and check the insolences of man, God has so ordered, in his providence, that very often, in this world, men's cruelties "return upon their own heads, and their violent dealings upon their own pates."

STEELE

Christian Hero, chap. iv, p. 70

. . . to forgive is the most arduous Pitch human Nature can arrive at; a Coward has often fought, a Coward has often conquer'd, but *a Coward never forgave.* The power of doing that flows from a Strength of Soul conscious of its own Force, whence it draws a certain Safety which its Enemy is not of Consideration enough to interrupt . . . .

had convinced him we were all in another's power by turns, and stand in need of one another's pity and compassion:—and that to restrain the cruelties, and stop the insolences of men's resentments, God has so ordered it in the course of his providence, that very often in this world—our revenges return upon our own heads, and men's violent dealings upon their own pates.

That besides these considerations,—that in generously forgiving an enemy; he was the truest friend to his own character, and should gain more to it by such an instance of subduing his spirit, than if he had taken a city.[3]—The brave know only how to forgive;—it is the most refined and generous pitch of virtue,[4] human nature can arrive at.—Cowards have done good and kind actions,—cowards have even fought—nay sometimes even conquered;—but a coward never forgave. —It is not in his nature;—the power of doing it flows only from a strength and greatness of soul, conscious of its own force and security, and above the little temptations of resenting every fruitless attempt to interrupt its happiness.

From many another sermon further illustrations could be cited wherein Yorick drew upon two or more of his predecessors and combined them to illustrate an idea;[5] but the quotations already presented should be sufficient to show that this practice was the rule rather than the exception. And the implication seems plain: Sterne must have kept and made constant use of some sort of "commonplace book," into which he either copied such extracts from his reading as particularly appealed to him or else entered, under appropriate and efficiently devised headings, volume and page references to facilitate finding his way back to an author when the occasion demanded. The practice of compiling classified collections of quotations was not uncommon; and with such a document before him Yorick could utilize at a moment's notice the results of his acquaintance with literature of all sorts.

Additional supplementary evidence, tending to substantiate this conjecture, is afforded by Sterne's use of Bishop Hall. Unquestionably the Bishop's contemplation on "The Levite's Concubine" sug-

3. Cf. Proverbs 16.32.
4. Sterne acknowledged his indebtedness at this point in a footnote.
5. Borrowings from Tillotson and Wollaston are thus pieced together in *Sermons,* I, 5, pp. 137–9, and II, 13, pp. 184–7; from Tillotson, Norris, and Clarke in *idem,* v, 2 (29), pp. 38–42; from Tillotson and Stillingfleet in *idem,* v, 6 (33), pp. 150–6; from Wollaston and Leightonhouse in *idem,* VII, 17 (44), pp. 124–5. There are many additional examples.

gested to Yorick the possibilities of composing a sermon upon the same subject; four short but verbatim transcripts establish a relationship between the two accounts. But the choice of details, treatment of the characters, management of the story, and the spirit in which the whole was conceived differ so radically in the two narratives that Hall's contemplation could almost be taken as an illustration of that very attitude against which Sterne was pleading. As the Bishop tells it, the history is a warning that God's just retribution will inevitably fall upon the heads of sinners; in Yorick's hands, it illustrates the dangers and cruelty of forming hasty judgments, especially on slight evidence, and is used to support his exhortation for greater tolerance and leniency in our thinking and treatment of others. In like manner, "Joseph's History Considered," which Ferriar unjustly described as "merely a dilated commentary on the beautiful conclusion of the *Contemplation* 'of Joseph,' "[6] is no further indebted to Hall than for minor verbal similarities in a dozen or so lines. In the earlier account Sterne found four short observations, which he transferred to his larger narrative; in other respects the two interpretations of the common biblical story are contrastingly different. So different, in fact, was Yorick's handling of the stories of the Levite and Joseph that one is forced to believe the passages taken from Hall had been transcribed into a commonplace book at least a year before use was made of them. Had Sterne gone directly to the *Contemplations* during the composition of his discourse, would not the Bishop's interpretation have had greater influence?

Again, the same passages from Young's "Sermon Concerning Nature and Grace" were utilized upon three different occasions: twice in posthumously published discourses and once in a discourse which Sterne himself prepared for the press.[7] It is quite possible, of course, that on the later occasions when Yorick decided to avail himself once more of this material he recollected his earlier transcripts and turned back to that discourse in which the appropriations from Young first appeared; there is a stronger possibility, however, that a commonplace book made his task still easier.

Against the arguments for believing that Yorick employed some such labor-saving device, there must be cited his humorous acknowledgment of indebtedness, from the *Fragment in the Manner of Rabelais*. In this posthumous publication, generally assumed to have been a "discarded digression originally written for the fourth volume of Tristram Shandy," Sterne drew a picture of his supposed methods of sermon composition.

6. Ferriar, *Illustrations of Sterne*, I, 126. Cf. *Life*, p. 243.

7. *Sermons*, V, 4 (31), pp. 94–6, 101–04, and 108–11; VI, 11 (38), pp. 118–19, 131–6; II, 8, pp. 35–6.

Homenas who had to preach next Sunday (before God knows whom) knowing nothing at all of the matter—was all this while at it as hard as he could drive in the very next room:—for having fouled two clean sheets of his own, and being quite stuck fast in the entrance upon his third general *division,* and finding himself unable to get either forwards or backwards with any grace—"Curse it," says he . . . "why may not a man lawfully call in for help in this, as well as any other human emergency?"—So without any more argumentation, except starting up and nimming down from the top shelf but one, the second volume of Clark—tho' without any felonious intention in so doing, he had begun to clap me in . . . five whole pages, nine round paragraphs, and a dozen and a half of good thoughts all of a row; and . . . was transcribing it away like a little devil.—Now—quoth Homenas to himself "tho' I hold all this to be fair and square, yet, if I am found out, there will be the duce and all to pay."—*Why are the bells ringing backwards, you lad? what is all that crowd about, honest man?* Homenas *was got upon Dr. Clark's back, sir—and what of that, my lad? Why an please you, he has broke his neck, and fractured his skull, and befouled himself into the bargain, by a fall from the pulpit two stories high.* Alas! poor Homenas! Homenas has done his business!—Homenas will never preach more while breath is in his body.—[8]

Had the borrowings in the *Sermons* been less varied, had Yorick contented himself with making extracts from one source only in any given discourse, it would be easier to accept this explanation as a true picture of how his homilies came into being. Three or four of the posthumously published discourses might have been composed after some such fashion: "The Sin of Murder," based exclusively upon extracts from Clarke; "Trust in God" which, excepting one short passage from Tillotson, was derived solely from Leightonhouse; or "St. Peter's Character," where Young supplied the outline and all that was of importance to the argument.[9] For the rest, however, the method suggested by the *Fragment* is much too simplified to be taken seriously or accepted as Yorick's general rule of procedure when writing his sermons—though it is a significant illustration of his nonchalant manner.

Were such a hypothetical commonplace book still in existence and available for inspection, it would probably bring to light new and interesting information about the extent of Sterne's reading. As it is, from the appropriations already discovered embedded in the discourses, certain suppositions may now be deduced; but there were doubtless many additional passages, sufficiently suggestive and tempting to Yorick at first sight to prompt a recording of them (even though they were not utilized later), which would make the account

8. The *Fragment* was first published in 1775 by Sterne's daughter Mrs. Medalle in the third of a three-volume edition of *Letters of the Late Rev. Mr. Laurence Sterne* (London, 1775), pp. 170–3. Cf. *Life*, p. 522.

9. *Sermons,* VI, 8 (35); VI, 7 (34); and V, 4 (31).

more complete. Based on the evidence at hand, Sterne's acquaintance with theological writings must be characterized as more varied than might be supposed but, on the whole, rather superficial; the implications suggested by his plagiarisms from John Norris, Rector of Bemerton, are representative.

That Norris' name should appear at all in the list of predecessors to whom Yorick was indebted is surprising, for the two men could have had little in common; this acquaintance with the mystic, Platonist, and poet of Bemerton stands as another illustration of how impossible it is to predict from whom Yorick was likely to borrow. Perhaps it was because Norris' voluminous publications included one of the earliest criticisms of Locke that Sterne's attention was first directed to him; at the end of his *Practical Discourses upon the Beatitudes,* Norris had inserted a little monograph entitled: "Cursory Reflections upon a Book Call'd *An Essay Concerning Human Understanding* . . . In a Letter to a Friend." At all events, use was made of two different publications: one sermon from the *Beatitudes* volume; two, possibly three, additional sermons from *Practical Discourses upon Several Divine Subjects.* What was taken from these discourses has been discussed elsewhere; the point worth remarking now is what Yorick overlooked: in "A Practical Treatise Concerning Humility" there were many excellent and suitable observations which could have been fitted easily into sermons; a wealth of illustrative material on all sorts of congenial topics lay ready to hand in the *Treatises upon Several Subjects* or *A Collection of Miscellanies; Letters Concerning the Love of God,* from its very title, might conceivably have impressed Yorick as being too specialized and limited in scope to bother with; but the "Treatise Concerning Christian Prudence" and other individual discourses in the two volumes from which he had already helped himself were filled with just that sort of quotation Sterne had found so much to his liking elsewhere. Why was Sterne's use of Norris so very limited? Had he read, or looked through, the volumes just mentioned and been deterred from making further appropriations because he feared the increased chances of detection that additional transcripts would render possible? The extent to which he indebted himself to Tillotson and Clarke, clergymen enjoying a much more widespread popularity than Norris, makes such an explanation unlikely.

An unavoidable suspicion arises that Yorick's acquaintance with Norris' writings may have been limited strictly to those three or four sermons which he had ransacked; that, instead of having read the *Beatitudes* volume or the *Practical Discourses upon Several Divine Subjects* from cover to cover, he may have found the homilies in question in some collection of miscellaneous sermons, so common in the

seventeenth and eighteenth centuries. The Todd and Sotheran catalogue, which included Sterne's entire library, lists many such compilations.

Item 678   Sermons (18) by Bentley, Sharpe, Bishop of Worcester, &c. *in Boards,* 2s

679   ———(23) by Patrick, Clagget, Lake, Lardner, Trimnel, Grove, &c. *in Boards,* 2s 6d

680   ———(30) by Hicks, Fleetwood, Scot, &c. *in Boards,* 2s 6d

681   ———(15) by Lloyd, Fleetwood, Mead, Hooper, Fisher, Fynch, &c. *half bound,* 2s

And on the last page of the catalogue there appeared this item: "A large Collection of single Sermons at one Shilling per Dozen."

The same suspicion regarding the extent and degree of Yorick's acquaintance with Norris similarly invests most of the other predecessors from whom he chose to borrow. Joseph Butler, for instance, won
his greatest contemporary renown from the weighty *Analogy of Religion;* his discourses, in comparison, were of minor importance. Yet
it was to these discourses, and to but one of them—not to the length-
ier and more complex *Analogy*—that Sterne was indebted; there is
no evidence to show that the *Analogy* had been of any influence or
that it had even been consulted. Nor is there any reason for believing
that Yorick's reading of Leightonhouse, Rogers, Stillingfleet, or Wise
carried him further than to the single sermon of each from whom appropriations were made. Demonstrable acquaintanceship with Swift
and Blair is limited to two discourses apiece; with Bentley and Foster,
to three; and with Young, to four. The increased indebtedness to the
last three clergymen suggests that here, at any rate, Yorick's reading
may have been more extensive than usual; but it is well within the
realm of possibility that the library at Sutton contained a single volume of miscellaneous sermons, including all the specific discourses
to which reference has just been made, and that someone eventually
may stumble upon that very copy which proved so useful to Sterne;
such a volume would very probably have been described by Todd
and Sotheran as: "Sermons (22) by Swift, Butler, Foster, Bentley,
Blair, Young, Rogers, Leightonhouse, Norris, Stillingfleet, &c. . . ."

One or two of Tillotson's and Clarke's discourses might also have
found their way into this hypothetical volume, for these two churchmen were widely read and discussed during the first half of the
eighteenth century. Yorick's obligation to them, however, was of so
fundamental and widespread a nature that such inclusions would
not be sufficient to account for his many appropriations. There were,
to be sure, no indebtednesses to Clarke's erudite miscellaneous writings—*A Demonstration of the Being and Attributes of God* or *A Dis-*

course Concerning the Unchangeable Obligations of Natural Religion, and the Truth and Certainty of the Christian Revelation, Boyle Lectures for 1704 and 1705; to the controversial *Scripture Doctrine of the Trinity* or *Some Reflections on That Part of a Book Called Amyntor, or a Defence of Milton's Life, Which Relates to the Writings of the Primitive Fathers, and the Canon of the New Testament;* or to his *Paraphrase on the Four Evangelists;* but the discourses which influenced Sterne were so numerous and distributed so evenly throughout the ten volumes of the 1730–31 edition of Clarke's sermons as to leave little doubt about Sterne's familiarity with all of them. Even more profoundly than to Clarke was Yorick obligated to Tillotson; as it will be pointed out in the next chapter, the Archbishop was his "chief model" and must have been a constant companion. The imprint of Tillotson is clearly discernible throughout all seven of Mr. Yorick's volumes; not even Locke, who colored so much of the thinking in *Tristram Shandy,* exercised a greater ascendancy; here, unquestionably, was a writer whom Sterne had studied.

To the three additional writers from whom it has been shown that Yorick took extracts for his discourses, the indebtedness was limited to one publication each: Hall's *Contemplations on the Historical Passages of the Old and New Testaments,* Steele's *Christian Hero,* and Wollaston's *Religion of Nature Delineated.* Available evidence suggests that Sterne perused these books from cover to cover; but there is no reason for believing that the acquaintanceship with these writers was further extended.

However widespread and diversified his reading may have been in other fields, this résumé of Yorick's soundings in theology is not impressive. Despite the presence of those volumes of divinity which stood on the shelves in his study[1]—despite the factual evidence that he had, from time to time, withdrawn certain tomes from the York Minster Library[2]—the belief grows on one that Sterne was rather inclined to seek the easy way out. Obviously he must have read more sermons than the ones from which he borrowed; his use of Clarke and Tillotson demonstrates that; but in general, it is to be feared, his preparatory reading in theology was determined quite considerably by the length and titles of those discourses which chance brought in his way. It would be a waste of time here to elaborate upon a list of "writings examined, showing no evidence of Sterne's having made use of them in his sermons." Two significant facts, however, underscored by such a list, must be stated: first, Yorick's name never appeared in the list of subscribers for any of the volumes examined in connection with this study; and, secondly, no transcripts were ever made (Tillotson and Clarke again excepted) from any

1. *Life,* p. 153.   2. See above, p. 9.

sequence of discourses upon a single topic, so commonly to be met with in the volumes of seventeenth- and eighteenth-century clergymen; such sequences, for example, as Samuel Ogden's twenty-two sermons "On the Ten Commandments";[3] or Francis Bragge's series of twenty-five "Practical Observations upon Our Saviour's Miracles" or his twenty-six "Practical Discourses upon the Parables of Our Blessed Saviour."[4] Nor, indeed, is there any evidence to show that Yorick was ever influenced by any of the longer, more detailed treatises, even when they dealt with his favorite topics; why should he bother himself with so extended a work as Richard Lucas' three-volume edition of *An Enquiry after Happiness* when there were available so many short, less complicated homilies on the same subject? A thousand-page discussion of any one topic by an obscure author was too much of a good thing. Likewise, and probably for much the same reason, use was never made of any of the better-known manuals of devotion: Richard Allestree's *Whole Duty of Man*, Robert Nelson's *Companion for the Festivals and Feasts of the Church of England*, or Richard Baxter's *Saints' Everlasting Rest*.

If further instances of plagiarism are forthcoming, they will most likely appear not in the multi-volumed collected editions of discourses, in any of the sermon sequences—such as Thomas Manton's one hundred ninety sermons on Psalm XIX—or in the more formal and philosophical discussions of the period but rather in modest little books like Rogers' *Twelve Sermons Preached upon Several Occasions* and Leightonhouse's *Twelve Sermons, Preached at the Cathedral of Lincoln,* in one of the miscellanies, similar to the hypothetical one that the Vicar of Sutton may have possessed, or in separately printed homilies. But the conscientious investigator cannot ignore those less likely, ponderous theological writings; his must be the arduous and time-consuming task of scrutinizing authors of whose existence Sterne was perhaps not even aware. Fitting retribution, indeed, for anyone meddlesome enough to wish to expose him in his thefts; and how delighted Mr. Yorick would have been, could he have foreseen such a possibility.

3. Samuel Ogden, *Sermons* (4th ed. Dublin, 1788, 1 vol.).
4. Francis Bragge, *The Works of Francis Bragge, A New Edition* (Oxford, 1833, 5 vols.), Vols. I–III.

IV

In Extenuation

IN the foregoing chapters, attention has been directed almost exclusively to an examination of Sterne's use of appropriated material, his self-emancipation from a dependence upon others, and the conclusions which may be drawn, in the light of his changing practice, as to when and in what order the sermons were probably written; certain conjectures have also been advanced about his reading habits and those books he found most useful. These aspects of the subject, significant in themselves and fundamental to an understanding of the problem, warranted undivided attention. But they do not comprise the whole story. Individualistic and eccentric as he may later have become, Yorick was also an eighteenth-century Englishman; no appraisal of his achievements which does not take contemporary currents and modes into account can possibly be either adequate or fair. The matter of his plagiarisms is a case in point. What was the attitude of his century in such matters? May anything be said in extenuation of a practice which we have come to look upon as fraudulent and dishonest?

That twentieth-century attitudes and customs have not always been in vogue is clearly brought out by Mr. H. M. Paull in the opening paragraph of his illuminating study of the history of literary ethics: "It is a commonplace in ethics that practices once deemed innocent become gradually to be regarded as crimes as civilization advances. Infanticide, polygamy and slavery may be cited as examples. The standard of morality changes with the ages. In no branch of human activity is the change more marked than in that of literature, which is, after all, a reflection of life."[1] We know, for example, that at the end of the sixteenth century collections of homilies were provided by royal edict for the use of preachers; and that Queen Elizabeth tried to repress free speech in the pulpit by limiting clergymen to the reading of such homilies.[2] More than a half-century later, when publishing some sermons of his father's, the younger John Donne observed in his prefatory remarks "To the Reader":

1. H. M. Paull, *Literary Ethics. A Study in the Growth of the Literary Conscience* (London, 1928), p. 13.
2. A. E. Garvie, *The Christian Preacher* (New York, 1921), pp. 147–8. For this and several additional references to follow, I am primarily indebted to Mr. Paull's chapter, "Piracy. Sermons."

Upon the Death of my Father Dr. *Donne* . . . I was sent to, by his *Majesty of Blessed Memory,* to recollect and publish his Sermons; I was encouraged by many of the Nobility, both *Spiritual* and *Temporal* . . . telling me, what a publick good I should confer upon the *Church,* and, that by this means I should not only preach to all the Parishes of *England,* but to those, whose Affairs carried them into Forraigne Countries. . . . our most Honorable *Lord Chancellor* . . . is not only content, that the *Churches* should be furnished with good *Preachers,* but that those *Preachers* should have good Sermons . . . .[3]

John Earle's "Character" of "A young rawe Preacher" would tend to show that such a practice was widespread; following a generalized description of the typical clergyman, Earle observes: "His small standing and time hath made him a proficient onely in boldness, out of which and his Table booke he is furnisht for a Preacher. His Collections of Studie are the notes of Sermons, which taken up at St. *Maries,* hee utters in the Country. . . . The pace of his Sermon is a ful careere. . . . The labour of it is chiefly in his lungs. And the onely thing hee ha's made of it himselfe, is the faces."[4]

At the beginning of the eighteenth century, Pope and Walsh discussed the general question of literary borrowing, and the poet declared that ". . . it seems not so much the perfection of sense, to say things that had never been said before, as to express those best that have been said oftenest; and that writers, in the case of borrowing from others, are like trees which of themselves would produce only one sort of fruit, but by being grafted upon others may yield variety . . . . like merchants, [they] should repay with something of their own what they take from others; not like pyrates, make prize of all they meet."[5] Dealing more specifically with the question in hand was the advice given by Bishop George Bull (*circa* 1708) to young clergymen

. . . not to trust at first to their own compositions, but to furnish themselves with a provision of the best sermons, which the learned divines of our church have published; that by reading them often, and by endeavouring to imitate them, they may acquire a habit of good preaching themselves. And where, through poverty, or any other impediment, ministers are incapable of discharging this duty as they ought, he directed them to use the Homilies of the church, and sometimes to read a chapter to the people, out of that excellent book, called *The Whole Duty of Man.*[6]

3. *XXVI Sermons* (London, 1660).
4. John Earle, *Micro-cosmographie,* Arber, E., ed. (London, 1869).
5. Alexander Pope, letter to Walsh, July 2, 1706, reprinted in *The Works of Pope,* Warburton, ed. (London, 1751, 9 vols.), VII, 62–3.
6. *The Works of George Bull, with a Life by Robert Nelson,* Burton, E., ed. (Oxford, 1827, 7 vols.), VII, 358–9.

Addison, as is well known from the recommendation he has Sir Roger make to his chaplain,[7] was in full sympathy with such sentiments; so also was Dr. Johnson—at least by implication; for in a letter to Charles Laurence, August 30, 1780, he observed: "Your present method of making your sermons seems very judicious. . . . Take care to register, somewhere or other, the authors from whom your several discourses are borrowed; and do not imagine that you will always remember, even what perhaps you now think it impossible to forget.

"My advice, however, is, that you attempt, from time to time, an original sermon. . . ."[8] Of even greater significance is this statement of Boswell's: "We shall in vain endeavour to know with exact precision every production of Johnson's pen. He owned to me, that he had written about forty sermons; but as I understood that he had given or sold them to different persons, who were to preach them as their own, he did not consider himself at liberty to acknowledge them."[9] One is reminded of the comment Goldsmith put into the mouth of a Grub Street hack: "Would you think it, gentlemen . . . I have actually written last week sixteen prayers, twelve bawdy jests and three sermons, all at the rate of sixpence a-piece."[1] And indeed, as these two quotations might imply, the trade of supplying model sermons to young or lazy clergymen in the middle years of the eighteenth century approached wholesale proportions. In 1769, within a year of Sterne's death, Dr. John Trusler "sent circulars to every parish in England and Ireland proposing to print in script type, in imitation of handwriting, about a hundred and fifty sermons at the price of one shilling each, in order to save the clergy both study and the trouble of transcribing. This ingenious scheme appears to have met with considerable success."[2]

The practice of using the sermons of another as one's own sometimes brought the preacher into difficulties and was not without its amusing aspects, as the two following anecdotes will testify.

A clergyman having picked up a homily composed when the plague was raging in London, unconsciously took the choice document with him, one Sunday, to church, and read it to his congregation. Towards the close, after having sharply reproved vice, he added, "for these vices it is that God has visited you and your families with that cruel scourge, the plague, which is now spreading everywhere in this town!" Hearing this astounding announcement, the people were all so thunderstruck that the chief magistrate was obliged to go to the pulpit, and to ask him, "For God's sake, sir, where is the plague, that I may instantly take measures to prevent its spreading."

---

7. *The Spectator*, July 2, 1711, No. 106.   8. Boswell, *Life of Johnson*, III, 437.
9. *Idem*, IV, 383.   1. *The Citizen of the World*, Letter 30.
2. *D.N.B.*, under John Trusler (art. by Thomas Cooper).

"The plague, sir?" replied the preacher, "I know nothing about the plague; but whether it is in the town or not, it is in my homily." [3]

And, on another occasion, we are told, when it came the turn of the Reverend Ozias Linley, a minor canon in Norwich Cathedral, to preach before the congregation, he "copied verbatim from Bishop Hoadly, whom the Dean and Chapter looked upon as an execrable heretic, but who was an especial favourite of the Bishop, Dr. Bathurst. After the service (the anecdote was related by Ozias Linley, himself), as we were going in procession to the vestry, the Bishop turned to me with a gracious smile, 'Mr. Linley, I am much obliged to you for the excellent sermon you *selected.*'" [4]

Mr. Paull cites ample proof that clergymen continued to avail themselves of the sermons of older writers and that the practice of buying collections of model discourses has continued to the present day. [5] But what more concerns us here is the attitude of Sterne's contemporaries toward plagiarism in sermons. Most of the correspondents who pointed out similarities between Yorick's discourses and those of his predecessors were inclined to make light of what they had found. "Eboracensis" might feel that, because of their many indebtednesses and borrowings, Sterne's writings "are debased to the level of the lowest of all literary larcenies" and are found "to shine with reflected light, to strut in borrowed plumes"; [6] but "Eboracensis" was the exception. Much more representative of the century's view on the matter was Dr. Ferriar's judgment. Despite the presence in the *Sermons* of unacknowledged indebtednesses, Yorick, he felt, was left "in possession of every praise, but that of curious erudition, to which he had no great pretence, and of unparalleled originality, which ignorance only can ascribe to any polished writer. It would be enjoining an impossible task, to exact much knowledge on subjects frequently treated, and yet to prohibit the use of thoughts and expressions rendered familiar by study, merely because they had been occupied by former authors." [7] And again, "Charges of Plagiarism in his Sermons have been brought against Sterne, which I have not been anxious to investigate, as in that species of composition, the principal matter must consist of repetitions." [8] It is worthy of note that Dr. Ferriar's attitude was given prominent endorsement on both sides of the Atlantic. During the course of a controversy occasioned by the

3. Related, without any indication of the source, by Frederick Saunders, *Salad for the Social* (New York, 1856), p. 335.

4. John Sinclair, *Sketches of Old Times and Distant Places* (London, 1875), pp. 155-6. The anecdote is also repeated by Clementia Black, *The Linleys of Bath* (London, 1911), pp. 211-12.

5. Paull, *op. cit.*, pp. 95-101.

6. *The Gentleman's Magazine*, Vol. LXIV, Pt. 1, 406.

7. *The Annual Register*, 1793, pp. 397-8.   8. *Illustrations of Sterne*, I, 123.

arrival of the Reverend Mr. Hemphill in Philadelphia in 1734, Benjamin Franklin sided with the clergyman and in a revealing passage from the *Autobiography* made the following observation.

One of our adversaries having heard him [Hemphill] preach a sermon that was much admired, thought he had somewhere read the sermon before, or at least a part of it. On search, he found that part quoted at length, in one of the British Reviews, from a discourse of Dr. Foster's. This detection gave many of our party disgust, who accordingly abandoned his cause, and occasion'd our more speedy discomfiture in the synod. I stuck by him, however, as I rather approved his giving us good sermons compos'd by others, than bad ones of his own manufacture, tho' the latter was the practice of our common teachers. He afterwards acknowledg'd to me that none of those he preached were his own; adding, that his memory was such as enabled him to retain and repeat any sermon after one reading only.[9]

One may object at this point that the evidence presented, though applicable to oral discourses delivered from the pulpit, cannot be used in justification of what a clergyman prints as his own; that, precisely as a speaker is not expected to acknowledge every quotation during a lecture, the case is altered if he decides to prepare those lectures for publication. Or, to rephrase the objection: even granting that differences in standards between Sterne's era and ours might mitigate the degree of culpability, does not the fact remain that Yorick was nonetheless guilty of attempting to impose conscious literary deception upon his contemporaries? A partial answer to this question—and carrying with it explicit exoneration—may be found by examining the list of writers Sterne chose to borrow from.

Of the numerous English divines to whom Yorick was unquestionably indebted, no one was better known and more admired in the eighteenth century than Dr. John Tillotson (1630–94), Archbishop of Canterbury and leader of the Latitudinarian section of the Church of England.[1] Dryden had already "owned with pleasure, that if he had any talent for English prose . . . it was owing to his having often read his Grace's writings";[2] Addison listed him with the half-dozen "great masters" whom Sir Roger de Coverley recommended to his country chaplain;[3] Swift called him "that excellent Prelate";[4] and Dr. Johnson, on the authority of Mr. Wickins of Lichfield, comparing the Archbishop's sermons to those of Sterne, observed, "*there*

9. Franklin, *Autobiography*, Modern Library ed. (1944), p. 111.
1. *The Cambridge History of English Literature* (New York, 1932), VIII, 333.
2. *The Works of Dr. John Tillotson*, Birch, ed. (London, 1820, 10 vols.), I, ccxxxv It is to this edition that subsequent references to Tillotson are made.
3. *The Spectator*, No. 106.
4. "A Letter to a Young Gentleman Lately Enter'd into Holy Orders."

you drink the cup of salvation to the bottom; here you have merely the froth from the surface."[5]

Sterne himself was well aware of his obligations to Tillotson: not only did he twice acknowledge the Archbishop by name as a source, and in at least two other instances distinguish his borrowings by including them within rarely used quotation marks, attributing them to "a great man" and "one of our divines," respectively;[6] but Tillotson's influence predominated in all four of the discourses known to have been written before 1751; and as late as 1762, when making up a box of books to be sent to his friend Diderot, Sterne requested Thomas Becket to include a set of Tillotson's sermons.[7] The Archbishop was, indeed, as Cross asserts, Sterne's "chief model"[8] and the indebtedness was much more profound than the list of parallel passages assembled in the Appendix might suggest—imposing as that list is. For if Yorick's familiarity with Tillotson was as deep and long continued as there is every reason to believe it was, it would be only natural to find many thoughts reflected in the sermons even though not quoted literally; conceivably there must have been many occasions when Sterne preferred to trust his memory rather than take the trouble of referring to an actual passage. Again, Yorick's sermons were invariably shorter than Tillotson's; the Archbishop's three discourses on "The Parable of the Rich Man and Lazarus" suggested several things to our preacher; but when, content to summarize, he disposed of an idea in a page and a half, to which the Archbishop had devoted an entire sermon,[9] it is virtually impossible to prove the existence of the obligation. In like manner, the relatively few passages from Tillotson's "Success Not Always Answerable to the Probability of Second Causes" which have been reprinted to illustrate Sterne's "Time and Chance" can but faintly reflect the conviction which a reader must have, fresh from a comparison of both in their entirety, that Sterne's homily was largely—and could have been wholly—derived from the Archbishop's.[1] At least one third of *The Sermons of Mr. Yorick* stand in similar relationship to Tillotson's published discourses; the influence of the older upon the younger clergyman was as far-reaching as it was deep-rooted. Had Sterne been attempting to impose conscious literary deception upon his con-

5. George B. Hill, *Johnsonian Miscellanies* (New York, 1897, 2 vols.), II, 429. Bishop Beveridge and Dean Sherlock were also included with Tillotson in Dr. Johnson's comparison.

6. *Sermons*, II, 8, p. 35, and II, 11, p. 135. See also *idem*, II, 11, p. 134, and III, 3 (18), p. 90.

7. *Letters*, p. 166.   8. *Life*, pp. 241–2.

9. Tillotson, *Works*, VI, Nos. 125–7. Compare Tillotson's sermon No. 125 with *Sermons*, IV, 8 (23), pp. 36–7.

1. Tillotson, *Works*, III, No. 36. Cf. *Sermons*, II, 8.

temporaries, would he have taken Tillotson for his "chief model"—
a preacher whose writings had gone through innumerable editions,
were so extensively known, and were admitted to have "been a very
important element in directing the religious thought" of the period?[2]

Second only to Tillotson in the extent and degree to which the
indebtednesses reached, the churchman who exercised the greatest
influence upon Sterne was Dr. Samuel Clarke (1675–1729).[3] At the
head of the Latitudinarian party and an active controversialist, Dr.
Clarke was also interested in classical research, experimental physics,
and philosophy, coming to occupy a prominent position among the
intellectual leaders of his generation.[4] Twice in "The Sin of Murder"
Yorick made partial acknowledgment of his obligations, mentioning
Clarke by name, and once again, elsewhere, under the veiled reference to "a great reasoner."[5] Nor were these appropriations any
secret to Sterne's contemporaries; witness James Boswell's *Poetical
Epistle to Dr. Sterne, Parson Yorick and Tristram Shandy.*

> He had of books a chosen few;
> He read as Humour bid him do.
> If Metaphysics seemed too dark,
> Shifted to Gay from Dr. Clark[e].[6]

There was more reason for including this theologian's name than
merely to satisfy the demands of rhyme; Dr. Clarke was one of the
few churchmen whose writings Yorick must have studied. As might
be expected, no evidence exists to indicate perusal either of the controversial publications or of the more scholarly and doctrinal of the
homilies; but the discourses from which Sterne did plagiarize are
to be found scattered throughout the whole of the ten-volume edition
of the *Sermons,* which the Sutton vicarage library probably contained.[7] This fact is worth stressing because in practically all other
instances where Yorick helped himself to the discourses of another
—Tillotson, Locke, and Bishop Hall excepted—the borrowings, as
we have seen, were limited to one or two sermons only; and these,
most likely, had been found in one of the innumerable collections
of miscellaneous writers which our ancestors were so fond of binding
together rather than in any complete edition of the individual preachers concerned.[8] As one reads through Clarke, looking for traces of

2. C. J. Abbey and J. H. Overton, *The English Church in the Eighteenth Century*
(London, 1878, 2 vols.), I, 283.

3. *Life,* p. 242. As the evidence presented in the Appendix will show, Mr. Cross's
estimate of Sterne's indebtedness to Dr. Clarke must be substantially increased.

4. *The Cambridge History of English Literature* (New York, 1932), IX, 332.

5. *Sermons,* VI, 8 (35), pp. 51–2; and II, 8, p. 41.

6. Written 1761–62. Douce Ms. 193, Bodleian Library, Oxford.

7. Todd and Sotheran, *Catalogue,* item 1061.

8. *Idem,* items 678–94 and 1101–11.

anything which might have attracted Sterne's attention, a shrewd suspicion arises that these pages were more carefully consulted than any list of parallel passages can indicate; and that what it is worth while to quote, in proof of definite indebtednesses, by no means takes into account the full measure of what Sterne appropriated.

As has already been intimated, "the learned Bishop Hall . . . who was Bishop of Exeter in King James the First's reign"[9] stands third among those to whom Yorick was most indebted. That several unacknowledged quotations in the *Sermons* had been taken from the *Contemplations on the Historical Passages of the Old and New Testaments* was one of the earliest charges of plagiarism to be brought against Sterne; the literary detective, of course, was Dr. John Ferriar, whose *Illustrations of Sterne* had appeared in 1798. Ferriar's interest, designed rather to illustrate a favorite author than to convict him of literary felony, was chiefly *Tristram Shandy;* borrowings in the sermons he was not anxious to investigate, "as in that species of composition, the principal matter must consist of repetitions."[1] One source, however, he did look into sufficiently to venture a generalization: ". . . it has long been my opinion, that the manner, the style, and the selection of subjects for those *Sermons,* were derived from the excellent *Contemplations* of Bishop Hall. There is a delicacy of thought, and tenderness of expression in the good Bishop's compositions, from the transfusion of which Sterne looked for immortality."[2] From a casual reading of those examples which Ferriar quoted, it would seem that his opinion was well founded; but a study of the *Contemplations* serves chiefly to convince one of how painstaking Ferriar must have been in his investigation; the most striking and significant resemblances are the ones he detected; what remained is negligible. Sterne probably read all the *Contemplations,* took notes on passages that appealed to him, and later wove some of the Bishop's observations into seven of his own discourses. It is further possible that Hall's sermon, "The Mourner in Sion," may have suggested the outline of and general development for "The House of Feasting and the House of Mourning Described";[3] but nothing from the *Characters,* the *Satires,* or the *Epistles*—those writings by which the Bishop is best remembered—found their way into Mr. Yorick's *Sermons.* Here, it must be admitted, Sterne was poaching upon a preserve where detection was unlikely; the *Contemplations* were not well known in the eighteenth century. In view of the more numerous and extended indebtednesses to Tillotson and Clarke, however, the com-

9. *Tristram Shandy,* Bk. I, chap. xxii; see also Bk. VIII, chap. xii. Joseph Hall was born in 1574 and died 1656.
1. *Loc. cit.*   2. *Ibid.*
3. *The Remaining Works of That Incomparable Prelate Joseph Hall, D.D.* (London, 1660), pp. 181–2. Cf. *Sermons,* I, 2.

parative obscurity of Hall, alone, could hardly have been the reason for the use that was made of him.

Quite the contrary. More often than not, it was to so prominent a figure as William Wollaston (1660–1724), clergyman and moral philosopher, that Sterne turned when in quest of homiletic material. Another Latitudinarian and friend of Dr. Clarke, Wollaston's rationalistic theories met with considerable favor from his contemporaries and led him to write *The Religion of Nature Delineated*. This book, which has been described as "a version of the 'intellectual' theory of morality of which Samuel Clarke was the chief . . . representative,"[4] was long and widely read. First printed in 1722, ten thousand copies were sold within a few years and a sixth edition had been called for by 1738. Sterne must have read *The Religion of Nature* with care; parts of it appear in eight of his discourses. In a footnote, toward the end of "Job's Account of the Shortness and Troubles of Life," acknowledgment was made that "Most of these reflections upon the miseries of life, are taken from Woollaston";[5] an additional admission of indebtedness appeared upon the manuscript (unfortunately now lost) for "The Ways of Providence Justified to Man."[6] As this was one of the posthumously published discourses, Yorick can hardly be blamed for having failed to include the admission in the printed text.

Certainly, in helping himself to material from John Locke (1632–1704) Sterne cannot be accused of plundering an obscure writer; it is difficult to conceive of any available source more open to speedy detection. The influence which the philosopher exerted upon the clergyman was frequently acknowledged but never more generously than when, in answer to Suard, who asked him if he could explain his extraordinary personality, Yorick replied that, in addition to his natural endowments, there were

certain acquired traits affecting mind and style, which had come from "the daily reading of the Old and New Testaments, books which were to his liking as well as necessary to his profession"; and from a prolonged study of Locke, "which he had begun in youth and continued through life." Anyone, he told Suard, who was acquainted with Locke might discover the philosopher's directing hand "in all his pages, in all his lines, in all his expressions."[7]

Comparatively easy to detect in *Tristram Shandy*, these indebtednesses are somewhat obscured in the *Sermons* from the fact that

4. *D.N.B.*, under William Wollaston (art. by Leslie Stephen).

5. *Sermons*, ii, 10, p. 102.

6. *Idem*, vii, 17 (44). See *Life*, p. 243, n., and p. 506. Roughly, about one sixth of the sermon was derived from Wollaston.

7. D. J. Garat, *Mémoires historiques sur le* xviiie *siècle, et sur M. Suard* (2d ed. Paris, 1821, 2 vols.), ii, 149. Cf. *Life*, pp. 301–02.

Sterne must often have obtained them at second-hand. For example, in his study of Locke's influence upon eighteenth-century English literature, MacLean quotes a passage from "The Pharisee and the Publican," in which, he says, "we are urged to distinguish carefully between the primary and secondary qualities of religion lest we yield to the general tendency to construe pomp, or appearance, for inner worth or substance."[8] The idea is Locke's; but the particular passage to which MacLean refers resembles more nearly a paragraph in one of Clarke's discourses;[9] Sterne's familiarity with Locke undoubtedly caused him to notice Clarke's embodiment of the idea and suggested this particular appropriation. In like manner, Yorick's analysis of Herod's character in the light of his "ruling passion," or his comment that "we live amongst mysteries and riddles,"[1] though obvious reflections of Locke's general influence, do not echo the philosopher's phraseology with sufficient conclusiveness to eliminate the possibility that these passages may have been derived through some intermediary, not yet identified. This uncertainty will account for the comparatively few passages from Locke included in the Appendix; the last two groups of quotations illustrate the difficulties attending the making of any such selections.

Jonathan Swift (1667–1745) is another well-known writer whom Sterne was not deterred from laying under contribution. In his *Illustrations of Sterne*, Dr. Ferriar established a connection between *A Tale of a Tub* and *Tristram Shandy;*[2] and it wasn't long before an open letter appeared in the *Gentleman's Magazine*, wherein correspondent "B," after referring to Ferriar's observations, enlarged the scope of Yorick's indebtedness by suggesting "that Sterne, when he wrote his Sermon on Conscience, published in his Tristram Shandy, had in his eye Dean Swift's Discourse on the same subject."[3] What Sterne took from Swift, however, at least in the *Sermons*, was of such relative insignificance that, were there no worse instances of plagiarism than these, the whole subject could justifiably be dismissed.[4]

8. Kenneth MacLean, *John Locke and English Literature of the Eighteenth Century* (New Haven, 1936), p. 95. Cf. *Sermons,* i, 6, p. 174.

9. *Sermons,* i, 6, pp. 174–5. See below, p. 112.

1. *Sermons,* ii, 9, pp. 60 ff., and MacLean, *op. cit.,* p. 48; *Sermons,* iii, 4 (19), p. 118, and MacLean, *op. cit.,* p. 137.

2. Ferriar, *Illustrations of Sterne,* i, 70.

3. *The Gentleman's Magazine,* Vol. lxxvi, Pt. 1, 407–08.

4. Several years earlier, for example, at the conclusion of a communication to *The European Magazine,* in which "O.P.Q." first pointed out similarities between Sterne's *Sermons* and those of Dr. Edward Young (*The Gentleman's Magazine,* xvi, 119), the anonymous correspondent wrote: "I will not trouble you or myself further by the accumulated instances that follow of imitation. Should you, however, think there is a striking similitude in the expression of Sterne in his 11th Sermon, and a passage of Swift, be pleased to insert it. The sentiment is similar. Sterne [*Sermons,* ii, 11, pp. 132–3]: 'Could it be established as a law in our ceremonial, that whenever characters

Answering to much the same description was the use made of Richard Steele (1672–1729). From *The Christian Hero* two, possibly three, short passages were incorporated into "Joseph's History Considered" and "Job's Expostulation with His Wife"; the borrowings were of comparatively minor significance and Sterne himself admitted the most important of them in a footnote.[5] Steele's "little manual of meditations," popular throughout the century with religiously minded readers (about twenty editions had been called for by 1820), would not have been a good source for unacknowledged quotations had Yorick desired to pose as the author of what he appropriated.[6]

When we come to consider those churchmen to whom Sterne was indebted for material contained in three sermons or less and where the probability becomes stronger that Yorick found them separately printed rather than in collected editions, the count is evenly balanced between those who were well known and those who were obscure. Sterne's appropriation of nearly all of the twelfth of Walter Leightonhouse's *Twelve Sermons, Preached at the Cathedral Church of Lincoln* (1697) has long been cited as the "most daring" and "the most flagrant" of his many plagiarisms.[7] From this one discourse Yorick supplied himself with the outline, main heads, and several solid paragraphs for "Trust in God," as well as extracts that reappeared in four additional sermons.[8] Little is known about Leightonhouse save what the title page to his volume of *Sermons* informs us: that he was "late Fellow of Lincoln College, Oxon.," before becoming a Prebendary of Lincoln Cathedral.[9] Equally obscure was Dr. Thomas Wise, "one of the Six Preachers at Christ-Church in Canterbury," in whose *Fourteen Discourses on Some of the Most Important Heads in Divinity and Morality* (1717) Yorick found one short paragraph which he inserted in "Follow Peace."

---

in either sex were become notorious, it should be deemed infamous either to pay or receive a visit from them, and the door were to be shut against them in all public places.' Swift: 'That women of tainted reputations find not the same countenance and reception in public places with those of the nicest virtue, who pay and receive visits from them.' " This "similitude in the expression" did not seem sufficiently striking to warrant its inclusion in the Appendix.

5. *Sermons*, II, 12, p. 157.

6. *The Cambridge History of English Literature*, IX, 32.

7. The earliest reference to this indebtedness of Sterne's is contained in William Jackson's *The Four Ages; Together with Essays on Various Subjects* (London, 1798), pp. 249–53. See also Frederick Saunders, *op. cit.*, p. 378; Fitzgerald, *Life*, II, 425; *Life*, p. 505.

8. *Sermons*, VI, 7 (34); comments from Leightonhouse are to be found embodied in *Sermons*, II, 12; II, 15; III, 5 (20); and IV, 8 (23). As might be expected, in those volumes which Sterne himself prepared for publication the indebtedness to Leightonhouse is slight.

9. There are no accounts of either Leightonhouse or Wise in the *D.N.B.*, in Abbey and Overton's *History of the English Church in the Eighteenth Century*, or in any of the other better-known church histories of tne period.

Dr. Edward Young (1642?–1705), Dean of Salisbury, father of the celebrated author of *Night Thoughts* and writer of two volumes of *Sermons on Several Occasions* (1702), was another of the few comparatively unknown clergymen to whom Sterne was indebted. References to Dean Young's only publication are scarce, though John Wesley admired the *Sermons* for their elegance and plain style. Yorick also found them so much to his liking that, in helping himself quite generously to three, he considered it unnecessary to make many changes; only from Leightonhouse's "Twelfth Sermon" did he copy so extensively and take so little pains to alter what he took.[1]

The name of Dr. John Rogers (1679–1729) brings us back again to that group of churchmen who occupied positions of prominence during the first half of the eighteenth century. As lecturer of St. Clement Danes in the Strand for more than a dozen years and later chaplain-in-ordinary to George II when he was Prince of Wales, Dr. Rogers was an active controversialist who attracted to himself considerable attention.[2] From the last of his *Twelve Sermons Preached upon Several Occasions* (1730) Sterne made several extracts which he utilized in his discourse on "Humility."[3]

Nothing can more convincingly illustrate the wide range of Sterne's reading or the catholicity of his tastes than that there should be found included among those clergymen from whom he plagiarized Dr. James Blair (1656–1743), founder and first president of William and Mary College in Virginia, and John Norris (1657–1711), one of the "Cambridge Platonists." Blair also served as Rector of Bruton Church in Williamsburg and from the homilies prepared for his congregation selected one hundred seventeen discourses which in 1722 were published in London under the title of *Our Saviour's Divine Sermon on the Mount.*[4] The sermons attracted considerable attention on both sides of the Atlantic and a second edition was printed in 1732. Paragraphs from two of these discourses reappear in two of Yorick's.[5] Norris was a more voluminous writer than Blair; his publications included poems and one of the earliest criticisms of Locke,[6] as well as theological treatises. The existence of resemblances between Norris and Sterne was first pointed out in a communication to the *Gentleman's Magazine* in 1800: "I was astonished to find, on looking into

1. An anonymous quotation in *The European Magazine*, XVI, 118–19, first called attention to Sterne's indebtedness to Young. Material from Young appears in *Sermons*, II, 8; III, 2 (17); IV, 9 (24); V, 1 (28); V, 4 (31); and VI, 11 (38).

2. *D.N.B.*, under John Rogers (art. by E. C. Marchant).

3. *Sermons*, IV, 10 (25).

4. D. E. Motley, *Life of Commissary James Blair*, Johns Hopkins University Studies in Historical and Political Science, Ser. XIX, No. 10 (Baltimore, 1901), pp. 9–14.

5. *Sermons*, IV, 10 (25), and V, 1 (28).

6. *D.N.B.*, under John Norris (art. by Leslie Stephen). See also Abbey and Overton, *op. cit.*, II, 236.

Sterne's Sermons the other day, whole passages copied from those of John Norris, M.A., rector of Newton St. Loo, Somersetshire, and Bemerton, Wilts., and of All Souls college, Oxford. . . . Perhaps some of your correspondents could point out the parallel passages in Sterne and Norris."[7] Sterne's acquaintance with Norris, as might be expected, extended only to the published sermons but included the popular *Practical Discourses upon the Beatitudes* (1690)—by 1728 this volume had passed through a fifteenth edition—as well as the lesser-known *Practical Discourses upon Several Divine Subjects*. The borrowings, though few in number, were transcribed with little change into the framework of three of Mr. Yorick's *Sermons*.[8]

It is not surprising that Sterne's discourses should also betray the influence of Joseph Butler (1692–1752), philosopher and theologian, who had served successively as Dean of St. Paul's and Bishop of Bristol before his translation to Durham in 1750. Butler's was "the greatest name both in the theology and in the ethical thought of the period," a reputation gained largely through his *Fifteen Sermons Preached at the Rolls Chapel, London* (1726), and the weighty *Analogy of Religion, Natural and Revealed, to the Constitution and Course of Nature* (1736).[9] Though no use was made of the *Analogy*, Butler's tenth sermon—"Upon Self-Deceit"—suggested much that later found its way into "Self Knowledge."[1] The *Rolls Sermons* were certainly more thought provoking than stylistic and Sterne's use of them tended to the incorporation of ideas rather than an echoing of phraseology. The Bishop's emphasis upon active benevolence and self-love as influential factors contributing to virtuous conduct and his stressing of the role of conscience in controlling a man's actions would naturally appeal to Yorick.

Two additional predecessors who exerted an influence upon Sterne were of sufficient prominence to attract the attention of Alexander Pope: Richard Bentley (1662–1742) and James Foster (1697–1753). The full-length caricature of the former in the fourth book of *The Dunciad* is too well known to need repetition; less familiar, perhaps, is the graceful couplet from the *Epilogue to the Satires*.

> Let modest Foster, if he will, excell
> Ten Metropolitans in preaching well.[2]

In the fame which came to Dr. Bentley as classical scholar, editor, and founder of the modern English school of textual criticism, it is often forgotten that he was also a clergyman; that, in addition to his many

7. *The Gentleman's Magazine*, Vol. LXX, Pt. 2, 741.
8. *Sermons*, IV, 11 (26); V, 1 (28); and V, 2 (29).
9. *The Cambridge History of English Literature*, IX, 338. See also *D.N.B.*, under Joseph Butler (art. by Leslie Stephen).
1. *Sermons*, I, 4.   2. *Epilogue to the Satires*, I, 132–3.

and demanding secular pursuits, he delivered the first Boyle Lectures in 1692, served as Master of Trinity College, Cambridge, and wrote occasional sermons.[3] An article entitled "Various Supposed Plagiarisms of Sterne Detected and Pointed Out," appearing in the issue of the *European Magazine* for March, 1792, first called attention to the fact that Yorick was not unacquainted with Bentley and that "the celebrated Sermon on Conscience" contained ideas and expressions reminiscent of the famous scholar's "Sermon Preached November 5, 1715."[4] More striking was Sterne's use of another of Bentley's discourses, not mentioned in the article—"A Sermon Preached before King George I, on February the 3rd, 1716/7"[5]—though the total indebtedness is not very great. Neither were the appropriations from Dr. Foster of special importance. In obligating himself to this eloquent dissenting preacher, Yorick was again ransacking a widely read source; a later, two-volume edition of *Discourses on All the Principal Branches of Natural Religion and Social Virtue* (1749 and 1752) contained the names of more than two thousand subscribers; Yorick felt he had done well to collect six hundred ninety-three for his third and fourth volumes.[6]

And finally, in the long list of predecessors to whom Sterne was indebted, comes Edward Stillingfleet (1635–99), Dean of St. Paul's and afterward Bishop of Worcester. No preacher during the second half of the seventeenth century enjoyed a higher reputation or was more universally admired.[7] Pepys, no unworthy judge in such matters, records the enthusiasm of his contemporaries.

Thence to the Chapell and heard the famous young Stillingfleet, whom I knew at Cambridge, and is now newly admitted one of the King's chaplains; and was presented, they say, to my Lord Treasurer . . . with these words: that . . . he is the ablest young man to preach the gospel of any since the Apostles. He did make the most plain, honest, good, grave sermon, in the most unconcerned and easy yet substantial manner, that ever I heard in my life.[8]

A Latitudinarian and controversialist, Stillingfleet also devoted himself to classical study; Gilbert Burnet recommended him to William III as "the learnedst man of his age in all respects."[9] But the reputation did not last. In print Stillingfleet's words seemed to lose their eloquence and appeal; his style was rather ponderous and suffers in comparison with the naturalness and simplicity of his more

---

3. *D.N.B.*, under Richard Bentley (art. by R. C. Jebb).
4. *The European Magazine, XXI*, 167–9.
5. Appropriations from Bentley appear in *Sermons*, II, 7; II, 10; and IV, 12 (27).
6. *D.N.B.*, under James Foster (art. by Leslie Stephen). See also *Life*, p. 370.
7. *D.N.B.*, under Edward Stillingfleet (art. by W. H. Hutton).
8. *Diary*, entry for April 23, 1665.
9. *The Cambridge History of English Literature*, VIII, 344 (art. also by W. H. Hutton).

enduring contemporary, Tillotson. Sterne's acquaintance with Stillingfleet was limited to one discourse on "The Danger and Deceitfulness of Sin" which, together with material collected from Tillotson, accounts for most of his unnamed sermon, later called "God's Forbearance Abused."[1]

When a roll call, thus, has been taken of those churchmen and scholars from whose writings Yorick was wont to gather ideas and illustrative material and an appraisal made of the varying degrees and extent of his obligations, the results show that an overwhelming majority of indebtednesses were to men of prominence and popularity. Were Sterne attempting to practice conscious literary deception, would he have chosen to plagiarize from what may be considered the "best sellers" of his day—from those sources where detection would have been the most likely? No real reason exists—in the light of these findings—for not taking at face value what Yorick himself had to say on the subject, in the Preface to his first volume of *Sermons*.

I have nothing to add, but that the reader, upon old and beaten subjects, must not look for many new thoughts,—'tis well if he has new language; in three or four passages, where he has neither the one or the other, I have quoted the author I made free with—there are some other passages, where I suspect I may have taken the same liberty,—but 'tis only suspicion, for I do not remember it so, otherwise I should have restored them to their proper owners, so that I put it in here more as a general saving, than from a consciousness of having much to answer for upon that score: in this however, and every thing else, which I offer, or shall offer to the world, I rest, with a heart much at ease, upon the protection of the humane and candid . . . .[2]

The reader is again reminded, on the one hand, of Dr. Johnson's advice to Charles Laurence: "Take care to register, somewhere or other, the authors from whom your several discourses are borrowed; and do not imagine that you will always remember, even what perhaps you now think it impossible to forget."[3] On the other hand, there are the similar pleas for tolerance in judgment from many another clergyman who had succumbed to the temptation of going into print. Compare with the quotation from Yorick's Preface this admission by Philip Doddridge, in the Advertisement to his *Religious Education of Children*.

. . . when I came to look over Dr. Tillotson's sermons, and some other treatises on this subject, I found many of the thoughts I had before inserted in my plan. They seemed so obvious to every considerate person, that I did not think myself obliged to mention them as quotations. What I have expressly taken from others, I have cited as theirs in the margin; and

---

1. *Sermons*, v, 6 (33).   2. *Sermons*, I, Preface, pp. ix–xi.
3. See above, p. 76.

if I have been obliged to any for other thoughts or expressions, which is very possible, though I do not particularly remember it, I hope this general acknowledgment may suffice.[4]

A second extenuating consideration, which the new understanding of how Sterne used his sources now permits advancing for the first time, is of equal relevancy. As has been shown in the earlier chapters of this study, Yorick's borrowings were many and, at times, brazen; but practically without exception the glaring instances are to be met with only in the three posthumous volumes, which were not prepared for publication by the author. In other words, the last group of eighteen sermons, as Yorick left them, were nothing more than ordinary homilies, composed for immediate parish use and without design for future publication; they may, therefore, be considered in the light of oral discourses. These are the sermons in which nearly all the verbatim copying is to be found; and it was upon quotations from these that most of the earlier critics based their charges of plagiarism. So that however the reader may feel disposed to regard the sincerity and pertinency of Sterne's general apology, if extended so as to include all the sermons, there should be little objection to accepting, quite literally, the assurance that no offence was intended, when that assurance is restricted to the first four volumes. What Yorick published he made his own and, despite the suggestions he took from others, no one but him could have written the first twenty-seven discourses. It was solely to these that his Preface had reference; and here he may be absolved completely from having attempted conscious literary deception.

4. *The Works of Philip Doddridge* (London, 1804, 5 vols.), III, 4.

V

Yorick's Christianity

NO reader already familiar with *Tristram Shandy* or *A Sentimental Journey* needs to be forewarned about the type of discourse Yorick would be likely to compose or the aspects of the Christian religion he would choose to expound. The majority of critics dealing with Sterne have felt called upon to censure him on one or both of these counts and to point out his obvious limitations. To Walter Bagehot, "Sterne was a pagan. He went into the Church; but Mr. Thackeray, no bad judge, said most justly that his sermons 'have not a single Christian sentiment.' They are well expressed, vigorous moral essays, but they are no more."[1] Mr. Peter Quennell's less violent and, therefore, fairer estimate may be taken as representative of the most recent comments; the *Sermons,* he feels, are a "curious and, from a mystical point of view, not very consolatory compilation of religious essays in which the Second Person of the Trinity is but rarely represented, and the First and Third as Abstract Benevolence or Deified Common Sense."[2] Mr. Yorick's discourses are, it must be admitted, rather earthly in concept; they contain little which might even remotely resemble the poetical meditations on the awful mysteries of life and death characteristic of a Jeremy Taylor, the practicality and intensity of a William Law, or the exuberant devotion and fire of a John Wesley; nor should one be surprised by the complete absence of any attempt in them to "beget a spiritual palsy or soul-quake in the Christian sinner."[3] Though a priest of the Established Church of England, Sterne was too much the man of his day to lend countenance to what he and most of his contemporaries would have considered such evidences of "enthusiasm"—or, as one would now say, fanaticism.[4] A respectable moderation in one's living, a com-

1. Walter Bagehot, *Literary Studies,* II, 110–11.
2. Peter Quennell, *The Profane Virtues,* pp. 153–4.
3. Henry Hammond, *Thirty-one Sermons Preached on Several Occasions,* reprinted by The Library of Anglo-Catholic Theology (Oxford, 1849, 2 parts), Pt. 1, 151.
4. Cf. James Foster, *Sermons* (London, 1744, 4 vols.), III, 280: "*Enthusiasm,* in the general notion of it, is an ungrounded and wrong pretence to *divine illumination* and *influence:* Which, every one must see, may lead to *various degrees* of error, according to the *nature,* and in proportion to the *languidness,* or *force,* of the inward *impression* which is supposed to proceed from God."
See also Thomas Secker, *The Works of Thomas Secker,* I, 85: "The general reasonableness of his [Christ's] doctrine, the coolness of his temper, the composedness and familiarity of his whole conversation prove he was no enthusiast. . . ."

bination of good sense, good taste and, therefore, good morality, was the conventional goal sought by the ordinary Englishman living during the middle years of the eighteenth century.

Christianity was the name given to this commonplace code of ethics but almost any other appellation would have been equally pertinent; it characterized Christian and Deist alike. Indeed, as Mr. Root succinctly observes,

Except in the heat of controversy, it is not easy to distinguish between the religion of an orthodox divine such as Swift and the free-thinking deists whom he despised. The creed of deism, or "natural" religion, was that to which, so men thought, one is inevitably driven by innate human reason; its articles—a God who is seen in nature, and is nature's great "first cause"; charity and justice as the most acceptable worship; a future life of rewards and punishments—are those which are common to all respectable religions the world over, including that of Pope's "poor Indian." Christian revelation constitutes, no doubt, a desirable supplement to natural religion, but one will emphasize its reasonableness rather than its supernatural character. And so religion becomes for nearly everyone . . . an impersonal affair, whose chief concern is decent living.[5]

Though Sterne was somewhat influenced by this fashionable heresy,[6] he was a Christian, as may be shown by quoting various assertions from the *Sermons*. For example, in the discourse on "St. Peter's Character," we are told

—That our Saviour had the words of eternal life,—Peter was able to deduce from principles of natural reason; because reason was able to judge from the internal marks of his doctrine, that it was worthy God, and accommodated properly to advance human nature and human happiness.—But for all this,—reason could not infallibly determine that the messenger of this doctrine was the Messias, the eternal son of the living God:—to know this required an illumination;—and this illumination, I say, seems to have been vouchsafed . . . .[7]

The paragraph, it is true, was copied from one of Young's discourses;[8] but, if there be any justification for judging a man by the society he frequents or the books he reads, certainly the things he chooses to quote should also be considered. Borrowing once more from Young, Yorick at least implies his concurrence with the belief that ". . . education, precepts, examples, pious inclinations and practical diligence, are great and meritorious advances towards a religious state;—yet

5. Robert Kilburn Root, *The Poetical Career of Alexander Pope* (Princeton, 1938), p. 181.
6. For further professions of orthodoxy, see *Sermons*, IV, 11 (26), pp. 145–6, 150; V, 2 (29), p. 37; VII, 14 (41), p. 43; II, 8, p. 36; and I, 3, pp. 72–4.
7. *Idem*, V, 4 (31), pp. 110–11.   8. See below, p. 187.

the state itself is got and finished by God's grace . . . ."[9] He accepts miracles as "extraordinary gifts, in the most literal sense of the words," and Christianity as a "mystery" of "divine original"; no doubt is left in a reader's mind about the preacher's conviction that the Bible is the inspired word of God: "—As the infinite wise Being has condescended to stoop to our language, thereby to convey to us the light of revelation, so has he been pleased graciously to accommodate it to us with the most natural and graceful plainness it would admit of."[1] These and other similar assertions indicate an acceptance of certain fundamental Christian principles to which no advocate of a purely "natural" religion would be willing to subscribe. Certainly Yorick did not consider himself a member of that heretical body; upon two different occasions he went out of his way to cast slurring aspersions upon the Deists.[2]

Though Sterne may thus be absolved from the charges of heresy, there is not a great deal of evidence to show that he was particularly concerned with the doctrines peculiar to or distinctive of the Christian religion; his precepts tend to make of Christianity a moral philosophy rather than a religion—even on a basis comparative with the general laxity in standards betrayed by so many of his contemporaries and immediate predecessors. For "theology and more abstracted points"[3] he had no interest. Most of the collections of homilies available to Sterne, as we have seen, contained sets of discourses devoted to a consideration of such subjects as "The Attributes of God,"[4] the "two positive institutions in the Christian Church, as of necessity *generally* to Salvation; Baptism and the Lord's Supper," or "Principles, without which a man cannot so much as *begin* to be a Christian."[5] Other clergymen could expatiate upon these matters but not Yorick; he preferred simpler topics lending themselves to short, homely treatment. Occasionally he might give half-line résumés of the conclusions that some illustrious theologian had arrived at: "God is merciful, loving and righteous,"[6] for instance, summarizes three of Tillotson's sermons. At other times he begged the question with such evasive comments as the following: "Thank God, the truth of our holy religion is established with such strong evidence, that it rests upon a foundation never to be overthrown, either by the open assaults or cunning devices of wicked and designing men.—"[7] or,

9. *Sermons*, VI, 11 (38), p. 136. See below, p. 191.
1. *Sermons*, VI, 11 (38), p. 124; VI, 9 (36), p. 76; V, 6 (33), p. 153; and VII, 15 (42), pp. 64–5.
2. *Idem*, V, 6 (33), p. 170, and VI, 12 (39), p. 171.
3. *Idem*, IV, 11 (26), p. 158.
4. Tillotson, *Works*. Cf. Sermons 133–42 in Vol. IV and 145–52 in Vol. VII.
5. Clarke, *Sermons*. In Vol. IV, sermons 1–4 concern Baptism; 5–8, Holy Communion. See also Vol. IX, Sermon 98.
6. *Sermons*, III, 3 (18), p. 95.　　　　7. *Idem*, VII, 15 (42), pp. 77–8.

. . . the shortness and uncertainty of life,—the unalterable event hanging over our heads, . . . the certainty of this,—the uncertainty of the time when,—the immortality of the soul,—the doubtful and momentous issues of eternity,—the terrors of damnation, and the glorious things which are spoken of the city of God, are meditations so obvious . . . so very interesting, and, above all, so unavoidable,—that it is astonishing how it was possible, at any time, for mortal man to have his head full of any thing else.[8]

Yet in no extant discourse did Yorick attempt to enlarge upon these considerations which he found "so very interesting" as generalizations; it was sufficient for his purposes to repeat, in the words of the Evangelist, that "God is a spirit—and must be worshipped suitable to his nature,"[9] without attempting to define more closely what the words implied. Nowhere in the sermons is there so much as an allusion either to Holy Communion or to Baptism. In like manner, the great festival days of the Church were skipped over; footnotes, it is true, inform the reader that two of the discourses were "Preached in Lent";[1] there would have been little reason to suspect it otherwise. "The Case of Elijah and the Widow of Zerephath," for example, may be associated with the occasion upon which it was delivered by an apostrophe to Christ, ". . . to accomplish our salvation [thou] *becamest obedient unto death*, suffering thyself, as on this day, *to be led like a lamb to the slaughter!*"[2] but here the account ended, with nothing to imply the triumph of the Resurrection.

Doctrinal Christianity, quite obviously, held no charms for Sterne; nor was he much more concerned with expounding the traditional educational duties of his calling. Despite the implications contained in Yorick's answers to Archbishop Herring's questionnaire and the obvious pains he had taken to insure the spiritual well-being of his parishioners,[3] the *Sermons* contain no counterpart to Tillotson's discourses "Concerning Family Religion," with their emphasis that homes should be made "the first seminaries" of virtuous living, or to Clarke's enumeration of the domestic responsibilities incumbent upon fathers.[4] It was advisable, Sterne felt, that youth should be given "an early tincture of religion"; just what he meant by that phrase, however, is not clear.[5]

8. *Idem*, VI, 12 (39), pp. 166–7.   9. *Idem*, I, 6, p. 175. Cf. John 4.24.

1. *Sermons*, I, 2, p. 39, and I, 6, p. 159.

2. *Idem*, I, 5, pp. 141–2. Cf. Philippians 2.8 and Isaiah 53.7.

3. See above, pp. 55–6.

4. Tillotson, *Works*, III, 479 ff.; and Clarke, *Sermons*, III, 90 ff.

5. The *N.E.D.* lists two meanings for Tincture: either "to imbue or impregnate with a quality" or "to have a smattering of." The word appears frequently in early eighteenth-century theological writings and is used in both senses. Thus, in Jeremiah Seed's *Discourses on Several Important Subjects* (4th ed. London, 1751, 2 vols.), II, 35: "The Author of the Psalm had a Mind deeply tinctured with Piety." Again, in John Norris' *Practical Treatise Concerning Humility* (London, 1707), p. 60: "A slight superficial Tincture of Knowledge, a smattering as we call it . . . ." In one of Zachariah Mudge's

Though in one or two instances Mr. Yorick did touch lightly upon what he called "historical Christianity," his pages are amazingly free of the contemporary language of polemics—of "joining issue with our adversaries" or "here we fix our foot." There is never any marshaling of authorities, with copious quotations from Bellarmine, Suarez, Vasquez, Scotus, Durandus, Petrus ab Alliaco, or Cardinal Contarenus, to show whether or not the doctrine of Transubstantiation was known before the Council of Nicaea;[6] no mention of Solifidians, Marcionites, Manichees, or the gnosticism of Simon Magus; nothing to indicate that there had ever been such matters as sins of omission and commission, regeneration and irresistible grace, or Trinitarian controversies to trouble the heads of churchmen. Mention was made, it is true, of certain doctrines of the Church of Rome; but instead of arguing the matter soberly, as so many others had done, pointing out the errors and inconsistencies contained in such dogmas, Sterne contented himself with denunciation and abuse.[7]

If the doctrinal, educational, historical, and polemic aspects of Christianity found no expression in Mr. Yorick's *Sermons*, with what subjects, then, did he concern himself when the necessity for preaching arose? Two passages from the novels furnish us with the answer. The text, " 'Cappadosia, Pontus and Asia, Phrygia and Pamphillia'— is as good as any one in the Bible," Sterne confessed in the *Sentimental Journey*;[8] and, as Uncle Toby, in enumerating the perfections of Mrs. Wadman, bade Corporal Trim begin the list by writing down the word "HUMANITY—thus,"[9] so these two quotations, taken together, symbolize what Sterne found interesting in life and wanted to talk about from the pulpit: the social virtues and vices; man in his public relationships, particularly when his appetites were "gently stirred" or various emotions were in conflict—but not to such an extent as to "ferment the blood and set the desires in a flame."[1] Nothing could be more characteristic than that a discourse entitled "The Ways of Providence Justified to Man" should, immediately after a reading of the text, resolve itself into a series of illustrations designed to show "the difficulties of coming . . . at the true characters of men";[2] or

---

Sermons on Different Subjects (London, 1739), p. 25, the word is used in much the same way that Sterne uses it here: "There is therefore no way of making a thorough Conversion but by beginning at a Season when the whole is yet to come, by tincturing them very early with good Principles and good Manners."

6. Tillotson, *Works*, ii, 26 ff.

7. *Sermons*, ii, 9, pp. 50–1; v, 4 (31), p. 114; and vi, 10 (37), pp. 96–7, for example, mention by name some of the doctrines of the "Romish dreamers" to which Yorick's contemporaries took special exception. The discourses in which Sterne does nothing more than revile are mostly to be found in the posthumously published volumes.

8. Vol. ii, p. 148. 9. *Tristram Shandy*, Bk. ix, chap. xxxi.

1. *Sermons*, i, 2, p. 18. 2. *Idem*, vii, 17 (44), p. 117.

that one of the principal reasons advanced for urging people to a better attendance at divine worship was that no other social relationship so effectively united men together.[3] *"It is not good for man to be alone . . .* the best parts of our blood, and the purest of our spirits suffer most under the destitution";[4] the invariable application of the majority of texts is, "Let us see if some social virtue may not be extracted . . . ."[5] In keeping with such a conception, it is not surprising that the preacher should urge an avoidance of sin, not so much because all sin is in violation of God's commandments—though this consideration was not ignored—but because it acts against the common interests of mankind.[6] Similarly pride is condemned for "the natural connection it has with vices of an unsocial aspect"; it is "inconvenient . . . in a social light."[7] To overcome pride effectually, Sterne reminded his auditors, "we must add the arguments of religion, without which, the best moral discourse may prove little better than a cold political lecture"; these "arguments," however, turn out to be little more than a series of dramatized appeals: "Send forth your imagination, I beseech you, to view the last scene of the greatest and proudest who ever awed and governed the world—see the empty vapour disappearing . . . . —Approach his bed of state—lift up the curtain—regard a moment with silence—"[8] "HUMANITY—thus" was written too large upon Yorick's heart to permit his doing otherwise. Time and time again throughout the *Sermons* he reverts, obviously with the best of intentions, to the tenet that morality alone is insufficient as a motivating factor in human behavior; but invariably the naturalistic implications, not the teleological, are the ones he lingers over and illustrates.

The scope of the discourses, one has to admit, is limited; in addition, it had the disadvantage of tempting Yorick, occasionally, to wander a bit further from the beaten paths than a clergyman perhaps should. Yet, despite these qualifications, there is reason for believing that Sterne's choice of subject matter resulted more from a seriously conceived and sincere desire to help his listeners than might be apparent at first sight. Like William Wishart, he must have felt that there were already in existence a sufficient number of printed homilies and manuals dealing with the great truths and doctrines of Christianity amply to take care of any in need of such instruction and comfort: "Such

3. *Idem,* VII, 16 (43), p. 97.   4. *Idem,* III, 2 (18), p. 73.
5. *Idem,* III, 2 (17), p. 46. See, further, *idem,* III, 1 (16), p. 5; III, 4 (19), p. 116, etc.
6. *Idem,* V, 6 (33), pp. 151, 156–8. This indifference to or deliberate avoidance of the burden and danger of sin and his failure so much as to mention the redemptive work of Christ as one who bore the sins of the world upon the cross is the most noticeable lack in Sterne as a Christian preacher.
7. *Idem,* IV, 9 (24), pp. 89–90.
8. *Idem,* IV, 9 (24), pp. 92–3. Cf. *Life,* pp. 247–8.

weighty considerations as these have already employed the discourses
and pens of the best preachers and writers upon religious subjects;
who appear to me to have so much exhausted the matter of these arguments, that scarce anything remains to be said upon them . . . ."[9]
What had not been sufficiently stressed, and indeed never can be,
were the less striking, homelier virtues which count for so much in
everyday living: toleration and kindliness, patience and understanding, thoughtfulness and sympathy, modesty and sincerity. Most
clergymen, Yorick felt, had occupied themselves too exclusively with
matters of only the greatest moment; from his observations he had
discovered that "In the lesser evils of life we seem to stand unguarded
—and our peace and contentment are overthrown, and our happiness
broke in upon by . . . the cross and untoward accidents we meet
with.—These stand unprovided for, and we neglect them as we do
the slighter indispositions of the body—which we think not worth
treating seriously—and so leave them to nature."[1]

This humbler province was the one he chose for himself; and in it
Sterne had few peers. His keen powers of observation and ready sympathy made him quick to discover those sources of friction which have
embittered so many lives; his good nature and lively imagination suggested ways and means for their alleviation. Obviously, one would
not turn to Mr. Yorick for guidance and strength in moments of great
crisis; it was never his intention that one should. The *Sermons* do,
however, contain many helpful precepts and recommendations not
unworthy of a Christian clergyman and which, if followed, would go
far toward making this world a pleasanter and happier place to live
in. Upon more than one occasion, during the past few years, I have
suddenly found myself thinking of something Mr. Yorick had said,
and feel I have profited from the recollection. As a result of such an
experience, even making full allowance for differences in personal
opinion, it is impossible at times not to wonder how intimate was the
acquaintance of some of Sterne's commentators with those writings
of his which they have not hesitated to appraise. Mr. Desmond Mac-
Carthy, for example, in his review of Robert W. Jackson's *Jonathan
Swift, Dean and Pastor*, has this to say of Yorick's *Sermons*.

There have been other very queer clergymen—Laurence Sterne for one.
But there is an enormous difference between the seriousness with which
those two eighteenth-century divines took their calling. There is an airy not
to say worldly elegance about Sterne's sermons which bridges the gap
between the clerical and secular writer. The Christianity Sterne preached
was at bottom that of Uncle Toby, and it was doubtless also in his spirit
Sterne went about (whenever he did) his pastoral duties, dispensing

9. William Wishart, *Discourses on Several Subjects* (London, 1753, 1 vol.), p. 7.
1. *Sermons*, II, 15, p. 233.

among his flock a whimsical sympathy and an intermittent charity that brought tears to his own eyes.[2]

That there is an atmosphere of worldly elegance about some of the *Sermons* or that Sterne and Uncle Toby shared many ideas in common no one would wish to deny; but in revoicing what has become the traditional estimate of Yorick's discourses as a whole, Mr. Mac-Carthy leaves the reader with a somewhat erroneous impression. Perhaps Paul Stapfer went too far in the opposite direction when he wrote:

Sterne was short and substantial; but he possessed a virtue still more rare: I mean the *sincerity* of his preaching. He understood what he was saying and believed it. I don't say he practised what he preached; that's a different matter; but he knew what he was doing and put trust in it. What the English call *cant*, and the French, *patois de Chanaan*—that unintelligible gibberish, made up of obscure biblical metaphors, badly interpreted—never came to darken either his thoughts or his delivery. There was nothing of the hypocrite in him; and however peculiar this clergyman may have been nothing could be falser than to represent him as a Tartufe. It is scarcely just to represent him simply as a buffoon.[3]

It is my personal conviction, however, that M. Stapfer's appraisal comes closer to the truth.

Illustrations of the homely, practical matters Yorick preferred to expound may be found in nearly all the discourses. Consider once more the imagined soliloquy of the Good Samaritan, as he gazes at the Jew whom thieves had robbed and left half-dead by the roadside.

. . . he is a Jew and I a Samaritan.—But are we not still both men? partakers of the same nature—and subject to the same evils?—let me change conditions with him for a moment and consider, had his lot befallen me as I journeyed in the way, what measure I should have expected at his hands— Should I wish when he beheld me wounded and half-dead, that he should shut up his bowels of compassion from me, and double the weight of my miseries by passing by and leaving them unpitied?—But I am a stranger to the man—be it so,—but I am no stranger to his condition . . . . Besides, though I am a stranger—'tis no fault of his that I do not know him . . . . Had I known him, possibly I should have had cause to love and pity him the more . . . .[4]

Or this observation, made during the analysis of "St. Peter's Character."

---

2. Desmond MacCarthy's review appeared in the issue of the London *Times* for Sunday, August 30, 1939.

3. Paul Stapfer, *Laurence Sterne, Étude biographique et littéraire*, pp. 104–05. The translation is mine. See also *Life*, p. 246, for an endorsement of this opinion.

4. *Sermons*, 1, 3, pp. 67–8.

. . . the truth and regularity of a character is not, in justice, to be looked upon as broken, from any one single act or omission which may seem a contradiction to it:—the best of men appear sometimes to be strange compounds of contradictory qualities: and were the accidental oversights and folly of the wisest man,—the failings and imperfections of a religious man, —the hasty acts and passionate words of a meek man;—were they to rise up in judgment against them,—and an ill-natured judge be suffered to mark in this manner what has been done amiss,—what character so unexceptionable as to be able to stand before him?[5]

And, again, the reflections inspired by Yorick's retelling of the story of "The Levite and his Concubine."

. . . the world talks of everything: give but the outlines of a story,—let *spleen* or *prudery* snatch the pencil, and they will finish it with so many hard strokes, and with so dirty a coloring, that *candour* and *courtesy* will sit in torture as they look at it.—

. . . How often must ye repeat it, "That such a one's doing so or so,"— is not sufficient evidence by itself to overthrow the accused? That our actions stand surrounded with a thousand circumstances which do not present themselves at first sight;—that the first springs and motives which impell'd the unfortunate lie deeper still . . . .

. . . we should all of us, I believe, be more forgiving than we are, would the world but give us leave . . . . the truth is, it has it's laws, to which the heart is not always a party; and acts so like an unfeeling engine in all cases without distinction, that it requires all the firmness of the most settled humanity to bear up against it.[6]

These and similar comments, in all probability, will not impress the modern reader as being either novel or striking—any more than would the old adage about a burned child dreading the fire; we have become surfeited with a plethora of popularized textbooks on psychology. This, of course, was not the situation during the middle years of the eighteenth century; fully as much as *A Sentimental Journey* differed from the average guidebook of the period did Mr. Yorick's discourses depart from the usual run; and to the audience for whose benefit his observations were designed their directness and simplicity, as well as their concern with the ordinary incidents of everyday life, must have been as helpful as they were refreshing.

Sterne's conception of what constituted a good sermon and the form he adopted for the transmission of his ideas were quite in keeping with the message he chose to preach. Walter Shandy had expressed pleasure in hearing "The Abuses of Conscience" read aloud, because of its dramatic qualities—"there is something in that way of writing, when skilfully managed, which catches the attention";[7] and

5. *Idem*, v, 4 (31), pp. 106–07.　　6. *Idem*, iii, 3 (18), pp. 65–7, 75–6.
7. *Tristram Shandy*, Bk. ii, chap. xvii.

for much the same reason a well-known Parisian preacher won Yorick's approval.

I have been three mornings together to hear a celebrated pulpit orator near me, one Père Clement, who delights me much . . . most excellent indeed! his matter solid, and to the purpose; his manner, more than theatrical, and greater, both in his action and delivery, than Madame Clarion, who, you must know, is the Garrick of the stage here; he has infinite variety, and keeps up the attention by it wonderfully; his pulpit, oblong, with three seats in it, into which he occasionally casts himself; goes on, then rises, by a gradation of four steps, each of which he profits by, as his discourse inclines him: in short, 'tis a stage, and the variety of his tones would make you imagine there were no less than five or six actors on it together.[8]

Nearly every critic who has written about Sterne has called attention to the dramatic qualities inherent in the *Sermons;* but no one with more discrimination and understanding than Cross. It is a pleasure to recall some of these comments.

Sterne was more than an actor. His best sermons are embryonic dramas, in which an effort is made to visualize scene and character, as though he were writing for the stage. Everywhere a lively imagination is at work on the Biblical narrative. If the preacher wishes to vindicate human nature against the charge of selfishness, he simply portrays the life of an average man, like scores in his congregation, from boyhood through youth, and through manhood on to old age, and lets the proof of his thesis rest with the portrait. No one who has read or heard the sermon is disposed to doubt the text that "none of us liveth to himself" . . . . The statement may be a commonplace to everyone in his congregation; but the commonplace is forgotten in Sterne's illustration of it . . . from his own experience and observation . . . . For setting forth the character of . . . men in Scripture, Sterne frequently impersonated them, spoke as he fancied they must have spoken, giving their points of view, their reasons for their conduct, in conversation or in monologue . . . . Everywhere Sterne thus lets his imagination play upon the few details furnished him by Scripture, building up scenes and character just as Shakespeare knew how to do from an incident or two out of Holinshed.[9]

Yorick had a simple explanation for all this; he was able to achieve what he did for much the same reason that Père Clement scored such successes with his preaching; in both cases, what was said proceeded "more from the heart than from the head."[1]

I have undergone such unspeakable torments, in bringing forth this sermon, quoth *Yorick,* upon this occasion,—that I declare, *Didius,* I would suffer martyrdom . . . a thousand times over, before I would sit down and make such another: I was delivered of it at the wrong end of me—it came from

8. *Letters,* pp. 154–5 (March 16, 1762).   9. *Life,* pp. 247–8.
1. *Sermons,* I, *Preface,* p. ix.

my head instead of my heart . . . . To preach, to shew the extent of our reading, or the subtleties of our wit—to parade it in the eyes of the vulgar with the beggarly accounts of a little learning, tinseled over with a few words which glitter, but convey little light and less warmth—is a dishonest use of the poor single half hour in a week which is put into our hands— 'Tis not preaching the gospel—but ourselves—For my own part, continued *Yorick*, I had rather direct five words point blank to the heart.[2]

From comments made in a letter to George Whatley, arranging for a promised appearance at the Foundling Hospital in London, we are given additional insight into Sterne's theory of sermon writing and another reason, undoubtedly, for the favorable contemporary reception which the discourses received.

On April the 5th, 1761 [Sterne wrote], and sure as the day comes, and as sure as the Foundling Hospital stands, will I—(that is, in case I stand myself) discharge my conscience of my promise in giving you, not a half hour (not a poor half hour), for I could never preach so long without fatiguing both myself and my flock to death—but I will give you a short sermon, and *flap* you in my turn:—preaching (you must know) is a theological flap upon the heart, as the dunning for a promise is a political flap upon the memory:—both the one and the other is useless where men have *wit enough* to be honest.[3]

Who but Yorick would have conceived of preaching as the administering of short "theological flaps upon the heart"?[4] The description, of course, perfectly characterizes his own offerings: short, dramatized flaps, as contrasted with the lengthy and ponderous blows which regularly descended from most eighteenth-century pulpits. Mr. Yorick's sermons are short—refreshingly so; the longest of them can be read in twenty minutes, the shortest in ten; only Samuel Ogden's discourses exceed them in brevity.[5]

2. *Tristram Shandy*, Bk. IV, chap. xxvi.   3. *Letters*, p. 134; cf. p. 135, n. 4.
4. Sterne's "definition" of preaching was doubtless suggested to him by a passage in the third book of Swift's *Gulliver's Travels* [chap. ii]. While being conducted up the stairway of the King of Laputa's palace, Gulliver noticed that his guides "forgot several Times what they were about . . . till their Memories were again rouzed by their *Flappers* . . . ." And a few lines later: "There stood by him [the King] on either Side, a young Page, with Flaps in their Hands; and when they saw he was at Leisure, one of them gently struck his Mouth, and the other his Right Ear; at which he started like one awaked on the sudden, and looking towards me, and the Company I was in, recollected the Occasion of our coming, whereof he had been informed before."
5. The following table will best illustrate how much shorter Sterne's discourses are than those of his predecessors and most of his contemporaries. The basis of comparison is the number of words contained in a sermon of average length.

	Words
Ofspring Blackall	11,850
Edward Stillingfleet	9,500
Thomas Sprat	8,300
John Sharp	7,500
Francis Atterbury	7,000

It is probable that the weakness of Sterne's lungs had no small share in preventing more sustained efforts; the first hemorrhage occurred during his undergraduate days at Cambridge and thereafter he was never free from the danger of fresh seizures. A letter of inquiry concerning his health early in 1762 called forth this characteristic reply: "Indeed I am very ill, having broke a vessel in my lungs—hard writing in the summer, together with preaching, which I have not the strength for, is ever fatal to me. . . ."[6] Such an admission was all too often necessary.

However restricting these limitations imposed by a bodily infirmity may have been, they alone are not sufficient to account for the brevity of Mr. Yorick's sermons. The preacher's easy-going temperament, compounded of a happy-go-lucky disposition inherited from his father, and that sense of optimism which so frequently colors the outlook of those afflicted with tuberculosis must also be taken into consideration. Let others, if they so desire, engage in "a warfare, wherein we must *not only fight,* but so *fight* as to overcome"; or stress the need for "going on from strength to strength, and pressing forward continually towards the mark of . . . our high calling."[7] Yorick's Christianity was of a less strenuous, more agreeable nature; he preached what he liked to believe, always emphasizing the pleasantness of his creed: God's commandments are not grievous; Christ calls upon us to give up "no rational pleasure—or natural endearments."[8] How could anyone fail to be attracted to "a religion so courteous ———so good temper'd———that every precept of it carries a balm . . . and sweeten[s] our spirits . . . ."[9] which, "when rightly explained and practised, is all meekness and candour, and love and courtesy"—"so kindly calculated for the ease and tranquility of man . . . ."[1] The demands of this religion were all so "reasonable": "—We have nothing to do for Christ's sake—but what is most for our own;—that is, to be temperate, and chaste, and just,—and peaceable,—and charitable,—and kind to one another." "Of all duties,

	Words
Jeremy Taylor	6,000
Edward Young	5,900
John Tillotson	5,600
Samuel Clarke	4,400
Daniel Waterland	4,340
James Blair	4,130
Jonathan Swift	3,750
Laurence Sterne	3,160
Samuel Ogden	1,850

6. *Letters,* p. 150. See also p. 164 and *Life,* p. 35.
7. Clarke, *Sermons,* II, 115, and IX, 72.
8. *Sermons,* VI, 10 (37), p. 85, and VI, 9 (36), p. 78.
9. *Idem,* III, 3 (18), pp. 95–6.
1. *Idem,* IV, 10 (25), p. 123, and VI, 10 (37), p. 90.

prayer certainly is the sweetest and most easy." ". . . a little time for reflection . . . is all that most of us want to make us wiser and better men." "If there is an evil in this world, 'tis sorrow and heaviness of heart."[2] The most pressing concern is not with what we usually think of as being the problem of evil, or suffering, in the world but the methods by which happiness may be most surely attained. Such an inquiry occupied Sterne's attention in the first of his printed sermons and, were an index to be made of the subjects discussed throughout the seven volumes, "Happiness" would have by far the largest number of entries.

Appropriate to such a conception, Mr. Yorick's discourses were short and, in form, simple—entirely freed from the paraphernalia of outlines, headings and subheadings, capital letters and Roman numerals, anticipating paragraphs and lengthy recapitulations, footnotes and documentary proofs, which so frequently encumbered the weightier, more argumentative, and certainly more profound disquisitions of the period. But it is neither accurate nor just to dismiss the sermons as "mere moral essays." Sterne was a Christian clergyman and the doctrine he preached is not unworthy of that high calling. If he preferred to stress "philanthropy, and those kindred virtues to it, upon which hang all the law and the prophets,"[3] even to the exclusion of the fundamental dogmas of his religion, was he doing much more than anticipating, though perhaps to a somewhat greater degree, the practice of many twentieth-century preachers? Like them he was content to refer to, rather than expound, the great truths of Christianity; but his acceptance of those truths is clear.

2. *Idem*, vi, 9 (36), p. 78; vii, 16 (43), p. 86; i, 2, p. 28; and iv, 7 (22), p. 30.
3. *Idem*, i, Preface, pp. viii–ix.

APPENDIX

SOURCES FOR THE SERMONS OF MR. YORICK,
LISTED ALPHABETICALLY BY AUTHOR

RICHARD BENTLEY (1662–1742)

BENTLEY

"A Sermon upon Popery," pp. 258–9[1]

Dreadful indeed it [i.e., the Gunpowder plot] was, astonishing to the imagination . . . . Yet . . . who would not choose and prefer a short and despatching death, quick as that by thunder and lightning, which prevents pain and perception, BEFORE THE ANGUISH OF MOCK TRIALS,[2] before the legal accomodations of goals and dungeons . . . ? Who would not rather be placed direct above the infernal mine than pass through the pitiless mercies, the salutary torments of a popish inquisition, that last accursed contrivance of atheistical and devilish politic? . . . Hither are haled poor creatures . . . without any accuser, without allegation of any fault. They must inform against themselves, and make confession of something heretical; or else undergo the discipline of the various tortures; a REGULAR SYSTEM OF INGENIOUS CRUELTY, COMPOSED BY THE UNITED SKILL AND LONG SUCCESSIVE EXPERIENCE OF THE BEST ENGINEERS AND ARTIFICERS OF TORMENT. . . . The force, the effect of every rack, every agony, are exactly understood: THIS STRETCH, that strangulation, is THE UTMOST NATURE CAN BEAR, the least addition will overpower it; THIS POSTURE KEEPS THE WEARY SOUL HANGING UPON THE LIP, READY TO LEAVE THE CARCASS, AND YET NOT SUFFERED TO TAKE ITS WING; this extends and prolongs the very moment of expiration, continues the pangs of dying without the ease and benefit of death. O pious and proper methods for the propagation of faith! O true and genuine vicar of Christ, the God of mercy, and the Lord of peace![3]

STERNE

Sermons IV, 12 (27), pp. 201–03

To be convinced of this, go with me for a moment into the prisons of the inquisition.————Behold *religion* with mercy and justice chain'd down under her feet,————there sitting ghastly upon a black tribunal, propp'd up with racks and instruments of torment.————Hark! ————What a piteous groan!————See the melancholy wretch who utter'd it, just brought forth to undergo the anguish of a mock trial, and endure the utmost pains that a studied system of *religious cruelty* has been able to invent. Behold this helpless victim delivered up to his tormentors. His body so wasted with sorrow and long confinement, you'll see every nerve and muscle as it suffers.————Observe the last movement of that horrid engine. ————What convulsions it has thrown him into.————Consider the nature of the posture in which he now lies stretch'd. ————What exquisite torture he endures by it.—'Tis all nature can bear.———— Good God! See how it keeps his weary soul hanging upon his trembling lips, willing to take its leave,————but not suffer'd to depart. Behold the unhappy wretch led back to his cell,————dragg'd out of it again to meet the flames,———— and the insults in his last agonies, which this principle————this principle that there *can* be religion without morality, has prepared for him.

1. Page references are to *The Works of Richard Bentley*, Dyce, A., ed. (London, 1838, 3 vols.), III.

2. Capital letters indicate the similarities noted by the correspondent to *The European Magazine;* see above, p. 2.

3. Cf. Wollaston, *The Religion of Nature, Delineated*, Sec. IX, Pt. 8, quoted below, pp. 181–2.

"A Sermon Preached before King George
I, on February the 3rd, 1716/7," p. 263

Sermons, II, 7, pp. 1–2⁴

Our apostle having in this chapter and
before discoursed of the mutual duties
and obligations in human life, concludes
the whole with the words . . . *That no
one liveth to himself, and no one dieth to
himself.* Which without doubt must seem
a harsh paradox to a narrow-minded person, that is wholly involved and contracted within his own little self, and
makes his private pleasure or profit the
sole centre of his designs, and the circum-
ference of all his actions.

There is not a sentence in scripture,
which strikes a narrow soul with greater
astonishment—and one might as easily
engage to clear up the darkest problem
in geometry to an ignorant mind, as make
a sordid one comprehend the truth and
reasonableness of this plain proposition.
—No man liveth to himself! Why—Does
any man live to anything else?—In the
whole compass of human life can a prudent man steer to a safer point? . . . Can
any interests or concerns which are foreign to a man's self have such a claim over
him, that he must serve under them—sus-
pend his own pursuits—step out of his
right course, till others have pass'd by
him, and attain'd the several ends and
purposes of living before him?

p. 267

pp. 8–9

Our Creator has implanted in mankind
such appetites and inclinations, such natural wants and exigencies, that they lead
him spontaneously to the love of society
and friendship, to the desire of government and community. Without society
and government, man would be found in
a worse condition than the very beasts of
the field.

We know that our creator, like an all-wise
contriver in this, as in all other of his
works has implanted in mankind such appetites and inclinations as were suitable
for their state; that is, such as would naturally lead him to the love of society and
friendship, without which he would have
been found in a worse condition than the
very beasts of the field.

p. 268

p. 9

No one, therefore, that lives in society,
and expects his share in the benefits of it,
can be said to live to himself. No, he lives
to his prince and his country; he lives to
his parents and his family; he lives to his
friends and to all under his trust; he lives
even to foreigners . . . nay, he lives to
the whole race of mankind: whatsoever
has the character of man, and wears the
same image of God that he does, is truly
his brother, and, on account of that natural consanguinity, has a just claim to his
kindness and benevolence.

No one therefore who lives in society, can
be said to live to himself,—he lives to his
God,—to his king, and his country.—He
lives to his family, to his friends, to all
under his trust, and in a word, he lives to
the whole race of mankind; whatsoever
has the character of man, and wears the
same image of God that he does, is truly
his brother, and has a just claim to his
kindness.

p. 271

p. 8

. . . there is no station or condition of
life, no office or relation, or circumstance,
but there arises from it such special obligation, that he [man] may truly be said
to live to others rather than to himself.

In whatsoever light we view him [man],
we shall see evidently, that there is no station or condition of his life,—no office or
relation, or circumstance, but there arises
from it so many ties, so many indispen-
sable claims upon him, as must perpetually
carry him beyond any selfish considera-

4. In the later editions this sermon is included in the first volume, the second volume
commencing with No. 8.

p. 269

And he that has given his mind a contrary turn and bias . . . Whilst he foolishly designs *to live to himself alone,* he loses that very thing which makes life itself desirable.

p. 272

. . . let such a one consider, that even in the most private life there are various relations and duties thence arising; as a husband, as a father, a master, a neighbor, a member of the community . . . .

p. 274

. . . does not daily experience teach us, that intemperance, temerity, and violence, cut men off in the flower of their age, in the very meridian of life? And again, how many are daily reprieved and rescued from the very jaws of impending death by the saving care and skill of the physician! But then withal, though the space of life may be thus *shortened,* and the thread of it broken by such accidents . . . yet perhaps it can never be *lengthened* by all the power and wisdom of man. A flower or fruit may be plucked off by force before the time of their maturity; but they cannot be made to outgrow the fixed period when they are to fade and drop of themselves. The hand of nature then plucks them off, and all human art cannot withhold it. And as God has so appointed and determined the several growths and periods of the vegetable race, so he seems to have prescribed the same law to the various kinds of living creatures. In the first formation and rudiments of every organical body, there are contained the specific powers both of its stature and duration. And when the evolution of those animal powers is all exhausted and run out, the creature expires and dies of itself, as ripe fruit falls from the tree.

tion, and shew plainly, that was a man foolishly wicked enough to design to live to himself alone, he would either find it impracticable, or he would lose, at least, the very thing which made life itself desirable.

pp. 10–14

To illustrate this, let us take a short survey of the life of any one man . . . and try how far it will answer such a representation. . . . begin with him in that early age . . . . Follow him, I pray you . . . where he has enter'd into engagements and appears as the father of a family . . . . Take a short view of him in this light, as acting under the many tender claims which that relation lays upon him . . . .

Sermons II, 10, pp. 88–9

If he [man] escapes the dangers which threaten his tender years, he is soon got into the full maturity and strength of life; and if he is so fortunate as not to be hurried out of it then by accidents, by his own folly or intemperance————if he escapes these, he naturally decays of himself;————a period comes fast upon him, beyond which he was not made to last. ————Like a flower or fruit which may be plucked up by force before the time of their maturity, yet cannot be made to outgrow the period when they are to fade and drop of themselves; when that comes, the hand of nature then plucks them both off, and no art of the botanist can uphold the one, or skill of the physician preserve the other, beyond the periods to which their original frames and constitutions were made to extend. As God has appointed and determined the several growths and decays of the vegetable race, so he seems as evidently to have prescribed the same laws to man, as well as all living creatures, in the first rudiments of which, there are contained the specifick powers of their growth, duration and extinction; and when the evolutions of those animal powers are exhausted and run down, the creature expires and dies of itself, as ripe fruit falls from the tree, or a flower preserved beyond its bloom droops and perishes upon the stalk.

JAMES BLAIR (1656–1743)

BLAIR

STERNE

Sermon 6, pp. 119–20[5]

Sermons, IV, 10 (25), pp. 112–14

. . . the Virtue of *Meekness;* a Virtue which of all other seems to expose a Man the most to Oppression and Injuries of all Sorts from their insolent Neighbours.

When we reflect upon the character of Humility,—we are apt to think it stands the most naked and defenceless of all virtues whatever,—the least able to support it's claims against the insolent antagonist who seems ready to bear him down . . . .

p. 120

It is worth our Consideration that tho' the Meek Man, if we consider him as standing alone, seems to be very much overmatched by the Proud and Fierce Oppressor; yet if we will consider him as he is commonly fenced and guarded with the Countenance and Protection of Laws and Government; and with the Friendship and Love of his Neighbours; and the General good Opinion of all Men; (whereas the Oppressor is as much discountenanced and hated) we shall find the Meek Man is not so much Overmatched, as at first Sight he would seem to be.

Now, if we consider him as standing alone,—no doubt, in such a case he will be overpowered and trampled upon by his opposer;—but if we consider the meek and lowly man, as he is—fenced and guarded by the love, the friendship and wishes of all mankind,—that the other stands alone, hated, discountenanced, without one true friend . . .—when this is balanced, we shall have reason to change our opinion, and be convinced that the humble man, strengthened with such an alliance, is far from being so overmatched as at first sight he may appear . . . .

Sermon 8, p. 157

Sermons, v, 1 (28), pp. 13–15

. . . *Justice* and *Honesty* in our Dealings is the surest way to guard against Want . . . . For the better imprinting of which Truth in your Minds and Memories, there are these few things I would briefly offer to your Consideration.

    1. The *First* is, That *Justice* and *Honesty* contribute very much towards the Improvement of all the Faculties of the Soul; I mean, that it clears up the Understanding from that Mist, which crooked dark Designs are apt to raise in it: That it preserves the Rectitude of the Will . . . and that it keeps up a regularity in the Affections, by suffering no sinister Design of Lusts or By-ends to disorder them. It likewise preserves the Conscience from all Damps of Grief and Melancholy, which are the Natural and Infallible Consequences of Unjust Designs and Actions. And by this Improvement of the Faculties, it makes a Man so much the Abler to discern, and so much the more Chearful, Active, and Diligent to Mind his Business.

For the better imprinting of which truth [i.e., that an uncorrupted life is the most effectual means of attaining happiness] in your memories, give me leave to offer a few things to your consideration.

    The first is,—that justice and honesty contribute very much towards all the faculties of the mind: I mean, that it clears up the understanding from that mist, which dark and crooked designs are apt to raise in it,—and that it keeps up a regularity in the affections, by suffering no lusts or *by-ends* to disorder them.—That it likewise preserves the mind from all damps of grief and melancholy, which are the sure consequences of unjust actions; and that by such an improvement of the faculties, it makes a man so much the abler to discern, and so much the more chearful, active and diligent to mind his business.—Light is sown for the righteous, says the prophet, and gladness for the upright in heart.—

5. Page references are to *Our Savior's Divine Sermon on the Mount . . . Explained . . . in Diverse Sermons and Discourses,* I.

Light is sown for the Righteous, says the
Psalmist, *and Gladness for the upright in
Heart . . . .*

p. 158

. . . being conscious to himself of his sincere upright Intentions, he [the honest
man] can with good Assurance recommend his Affairs to Gods Blessing and Direction; whereas the Dishonest Fraudulent Man dares not call for Gods Blessing
upon his Wicked Designs, or if he does,
he knows it is in vain to expect it. Now a
Man who believes that he has God on his
side, acts with another sort of Life and
Chearfulness, and with another Vigour
and Resolution, than he who knows he is
alone in what he does . . . . *The Eyes
of the Lord,* says the Psalmist, *are upon
the Righteous, and his Ears are open unto
their Cry. The Face of the Lord is against
them that do Evil . . . .*

. . . The Honest Man is most likely to
be kept in Business and Employ; For all
Men, whatever they may be themselves,
love to find Honesty in those they deal
with; and hate to be tricked and cheated.
This is so true an Observation, that the
greatest Knaves and Cheats have no other
way to get into Business, but by Counterfeiting Honesty, and pretending to be
what they are not. And if they happen to
be discovered, as it is a thousand to one
but that they will, they are presently
blown upon, and discountenanced; and
every one is cautious of having any further
Dealings with such a Person.

p. 159

. . . In all good Governments, such as
understand their own Interest, the Upright Honest Man stands much fairer for
Preferment than the Knave. . . .

The Honest Man has this great Advantage, that the more and the longer he
is known, so much the better is he Liked,
and Trusted; so that his Reputation and
his Wealth have a gradual Increase, as he
comes to be better acquainted with Mankind, and they with him . . . .

p. 160

. . . all Men are apt to pity an Honest
Man, if he falls into Troubles thro' Misfortune . . . .

pp. 17–18

Consider, in the third place, that . . .
the religious and moral man . . . being
conscious of upright intentions . . . can
look towards heaven, and with some assurance recommend his affairs to God's
blessing and direction:—whereas the
fraudulent and dishonest Man, dares not
call for God's blessing upon his designs,—
or if he does, he knows it is in vain to expect it.—Now a man who believes that
he has God on his side, acts with another
sort of life and courage, than he who
knows he stands alone;—like Esau, with
his hand against every man, and every
man's hand against his.

The eyes of the Lord are upon the
righteous, and his ears are open to their
cry,—but the face of the Lord is against
them that do evil.

pp. 18–20

Consider, in the fourth place, that in
all good governments who understand
their own interest, the upright and honest
man stands much fairer for preferment,—
and much more likely to be employed in
all things when fidelity is wanted:—for
all men, however the case stands with
themselves, they love at least to find honesty in those they trust; nor is there any
usage we more hardly digest, than that of
being outwitted and deceived.—This is so
true an observation, that the greatest
knaves have no other way to get into business, but by counterfeiting honesty, and
pretending to be what they are not; and
when the imposture is discovered, as it is
a thousand to one but it will, I have just
said, what must be the certain consequence:—for when such a one falls,—he
has none to help him,—so he seldom rises
again.—

p. 20

This brings us to a fifth particular in
vindication of the text,—That a virtuous
man has this strong advantage on his side
(the reverse of the last) that the more and
the longer he is known, so much the better
is he loved,—so much the more trusted;—
so that his reputation and his fortune have
a gradual increase:—and if calamities or
cross accidents should bear him down,—
. . . if he should fall, who would not pity
his distress,—who would not stretch forth
his hand to raise him from the ground!—

JOSEPH BUTLER, BISHOP OF DURHAM (1692–1752)

BUTLER

"Upon Self-Deceit," p. 169[6]

David passes sentence, not only that there should be a fourfold restitution made; but he proceeds to the rigour of justice, *the man that hath done this thing shall die:* and this judgment is pronounced with the utmost indignation against such an act of inhumanity . . . .

Near a year must have passed, between the time of the commission of his crimes, and the time of the Prophet's coming to him; and it does not appear from the story, that he had in all this while the least remorse or contrition.

. . . many men seem perfect strangers to their own characters.

They think, and reason, and judge quite differently upon any matter relating to themselves, from what they do in cases of others where they are not interested. Hence it is one hears people exposing follies, which they themselves are eminent for; and talking with great severity against particular vices, which, if all the world be not mistaken, they themselves are notoriously guilty of.

p. 170

This . . . was the reason why that precept, *Know thyself,* was so frequently inculcated by the philosophers of old. For if it were not for that partial and fond regard to ourselves, it would certainly be no great difficulty to know our own character . . . .

STERNE

Sermons, I, 4, pp. 90–1

It can scarce be doubted here, but that David's anger was *real* . . . and, indeed, his sentence . . . proves he was so above measure. For to punish the man with death, and oblige him to restore fourfold besides, was highly unequitable, and not only disproportioned to the offence, but far above the utmost rigour and severity of the law . . . .

p. 96

—A whole year had almost passed from the first commission of that injustice, to the time the prophet was sent to reprove him—and we read not once of any remorse or compunction of heart for what he had done . . . .

p. 80

. . . who, you'll say, can be truly ignorant of himself and the true disposition of his own heart. If a man thinks at all, he cannot be a stranger to what passes there— . . . .

p. 94

What other man speaks so often and vehemently against the vice of pride, sets the weakness of it in a more odious light, or is more hurt with it in another, than the proud man himself?

p. 84

So that however easy this knowledge of one's-self may appear at first sight . . . we find it one of the hardest and most painful lessons. Some of the earliest instructors of mankind, no doubt, found it so too, and for that reason, soon saw the necessity of laying such a stress upon this great precept of self knowledge . . . .

6. Page references are to the *Sermons of Joseph Butler,* Gladstone, W. E., ed. (Oxford, 1896). Sterne made use of only one sermon (No. 10) and incorporated all he took into his discourse on "Self Knowledge."

pp. 172-3

In some there is to be observed a general ignorance of themselves . . . in everything relating to themselves . . . everything in which self can come in . . . . In others this partiality is not so general . . . but is confined to some particular favourite passion, interest, or pursuit . . . . And these persons may probably judge and determine what is perfectly just and proper, even in things in which they themselves are concerned, if these things have no relation to their particular favourite passion or pursuit.

p. 178

And whilst men are under the power of this temper . . . they are fortified on every side against conviction: and when they hear the vice and folly of what is in truth their own course of life, exposed in the justest and strongest manner, they will often assent to it, and even carry the matter further; persuading themselves . . . that they are out of the case, and that it hath no relation to them.

pp. 94-5

Next to these instances of self deceit and utter ignorance of our true disposition and character, which appears in not seeing *that* in ourselves which shocks us in another man, there is another species still more dangerous and delusive, and which the more guarded perpetually fall into from the judgments they make of different vices, according to their age and complexion, and the various ebbs and flows of their passions and desires.

p. 92

. . . a man may be guilty of very bad and dishonest actions, and yet reflect so little, or so partially, upon what he has done, as to keep his conscience free, not only from guilt, but even the remotest suspicions, that he is the man which in truth he is, and what the tenor and evidence of his life demonstrate.

SAMUEL CLARKE (1675–1729)

CLARKE

Vol. I, Sermon 6, pp. 122–5[7]

. . . our consequent *Duty* is . . . worshipping him accordingly *in Spirit and in
Truth* . . . after such a *manner* as is
worthy of God and suitable to his Nature
. . . in opposition to merely *ritual and
ceremonial Forms* . . . .

. . . 'tis his Will and Pleasure that all
reasonable Creatures . . . should con-
form themselves to his Likeness . . . .

. . . These Dispositions of Mind, are
. . . the Great *End and Design,* for the
promoting of which, all religious Institutions were intended; and no external Per-
formances whatsoever, are any otherwise
of any Value, than as *Means* to promote
these Great *Ends.* When therefore Men
invert this natural Order of Things, and
separate the *Means* from the *End;* when
they take up wholly with those external
Observances . . . their religion . . . [is]
like a Shadow without a Substance, is
vain . . . .

The *antient Jews* . . . mistaking the
Design of their own Law . . . neglected
the *End* . . . and contented themselves
with the bare *Means* . . . an Error . . .
affecting even the very Essence of Religion . . . .

Vol. II, Sermon 8, pp. 180–1

. . . the *Mercy* of God is . . . as an Example to excite us to Charity . . . . As
if *Perfection,* and *Mercy* or *Charity,* were
one and the same thing; and as if he that
was truly indued with this virtue of *Charity,* might *consequently* be supposed to be
perfect in all *other* virtues likewise.

Vol. III, Sermon 10, pp. 207–08

Pride grows upon Men insensibly by im-
perceptible degrees, and creeps in un-
taken notice of upon innumerable Occasions, and veils itself often under an affected Appearance even of *Humility* itself.

7. Page references are to Clarke, *Sermons.*

STERNE

Sermons, I, 6, pp. 174–6

. . . weak minds . . . are ever apt to be
caught by the pomp of . . . external
parts of religion. . . . we see thousands
who every day mistake the shadow for
the substance . . . .

. . . this was almost universally the case
of the Jewish church—where, for want of
proper guard and distinction betwixt the
means of religion and religion itself,
the ceremonial part in time eat away the
moral part, and left nothing but a shadow
behind. . . . What then remains, but
that we rectify these gross and pernicious
notions of religion . . . by always re-
membering that God is a spirit—and must
be worshipped suitable to his nature, *i.e.*
in spirit and in truth— . . . and however
necessary it is, not to leave the ceremonial
and positive parts of religion undone—
yet not . . . omit the weightier matters,
but keep this in view perpetually, that
though the instrumental duties are duties
of unquestionable obligation to us—yet
they are still but Instrumental Duties, conducive to the great end of all religion—
which is to purify our hearts—and conquer our passions—and in a word, to make
us wiser and better men— . . . and better servants to God.

Sermons, II, 13, pp. 174–5

She [the woman of Shunem] considered
that charity and compassion was so leading a virtue, and had such an influence
upon every other part of a man's character, as to be a sufficient proof by itself
of the inward disposition and goodness of
the heart . . .

Sermons, IV, 9 (24), pp. 84–5

. . . so much may be allowed to the observation, That Pride is a vice which
grows up in society so insensibly;—steals
in unobserved upon the heart upon so
many occasions;—forms itself upon such

strange pretensions, and when it has done, veils itself under such a variety of unsuspected appearances,—sometimes even under that of Humility itself . . . that upon the whole, there is no one weakness into which the heart of man is more easily betray'd . . . .

Vol. vi, Sermon 10, pp. 238–9

. . . consider that there is a God, a Powerful and Just, a Wise and Good Being, that governs the World: By whose Wisdom and Goodness all things are designed, by whose Providence all things are conducted, to bring about the greatest and best Ends . . . . without whose direction no Evil can befal us, without whose permission no Power can hurt us . . . .

Sermons, ii, 15, pp. 229–30

Consider then . . . . That there is a God, a powerful, a wise and good being, who first made the world and continues to govern it;—by whose goodness all things are designed—and by whose providence all things are conducted to bring about the greatest and best ends. . . . without his direction I know that no evil can befall me,—without his permission that no power can hurt me . . . .

Vol. vi, Sermon 11, p. 269

. . . It is to be considered, that . . . if virtuous and good men be sometimes involved [in "God's publick judgments upon the World"], it ought to be a sufficient satisfaction to them to consider, that *this* is not the proper time for Rewards and Punishments . . . . [That] God has reserved to *another state* the final and equitable distribution of justice according to every man's desert; wherein . . . every inequality shall be exactly set right, and every circumstance of each person's case be considered and adjusted; when God will perfectly justify himself in all his Proceedings, and *every mouth shall be stopped before him* . . . .

Sermons, vii, 17 (44), pp. 112–13

To this it is answered,—that therefore there is a future state of rewards and punishments to take place after this life,—wherein all these inequalities shall be made even, where the circumstances of every man's case shall be considered, and where God shall be justified in all his ways, and every mouth shall be stopt.

Vol. vi, Sermon 13, p. 307

Not only *piously* therefore, but even with the *strictest and most philosophical Truth of expression,* does the Scripture tell us, that God *commandeth the Ravens* . . . that they are *His* directions, which *even the Winds and the Seas obey* . . . .

Sermons, ii, 8, pp. 41–2

So that as a great reasoner justly distinguishes, upon this point,—"It is not only religiously speaking, but with the strictest and most philosophical truth of expression, that the scripture tells us, *that* God *commandeth* the ravens,—that they are his directions, which *the winds and the seas obey.*[8]

pp. 308–09

. . . the *Providence of God,* by means of *natural Causes,* which are all entirely of *His* appointment, and *Instruments only* in *His* hand; does often, for wise reasons in his government of the World, disappoint the most probable expectations. Ridiculous therefore is the Arguing of the

p. 41

And though the fatalist may urge, that every event in this life, is brought about by the ministry and chain of natural causes,—yet, in answer,—let him go one step higher—and consider,—whose

8. The rest of this paragraph, which Sterne included in quotation marks, I have been unable to find, either in Clarke or in any other volume of sermons.

Infidels and Irreligious . . . . For, *what* are *Natural* Causes? Nothing but those *Laws* and *Powers*, which God merely of his *own good pleasure* has implanted in the several parts of Matter, in order to make them Instruments of fulfilling his supreme Will.

Vol. vi, Sermon 14, p. 327[9]

Did not therefore the Passions, the Ambition, the Covetousness, and other the like unnatural Vices of corrupt Minds, hinder this *Reason* and *Moral Understanding*, which is the peculiar Excellency and Glory of Mankind, from producing its natural and proper Effect in the world; the Earth would even in this present time . . . be that Scene of universal Happiness, which God hath promised shall take place hereafter . . . .

Vol. vi, Sermon 17, pp. 404–05[1]

This ["Mercy and compassion towards our *Brethren*,"] he has expresly commanded us by our Saviour and his Apostles, and it fills almost every page both of the Old and New Testament . . . . Concerning *This,* the great Enquiry will be made at the day of Judgment; and according to our behaviour in *this* particular, will the final Sentence, as our Saviour himself has described to us the Solemnity of that great day, be principally determined: *I was an hungred, and ye gave me meat: I was thirsty, and ye gave me drink: I was a stranger, and ye took me in: Naked, and ye clothed me: I was sick, and ye visited me: I was in prison, and ye came unto me.* Not as if any *other* good or evil Action should then be over-looked by the eye of the All-seeing Judge; but to intimate to us, that a charitable or uncharitable disposition, is a principal and *ruling* part of a man's character; the most considerable Test of the whole frame and temper of his Mind; with which all other Virtues or Vices respectively, will almost necessarily be connected.

pp. 406–07

With respect to our *Neighbour.* . . . We are all partakers of the same common nature, and are therefore under the same

power it is, that enables these causes to work,—whose knowledge it is, that foresees what will be their effects,—whose goodness it is, that is invisibly conducting them forwards to the best and greatest ends for the happiness of his creatures.

Sermons, vii, 14 (41), pp. 34–5

Could christianity persuade . . . us . . . to go on and exalt our natures, and, after the subduction of the most unfriendly of our passions, to plant, in the room of them, all those . . . humane and benevolent inclinations, which . . . should dispose us to extend our love and goodness to our fellow creatures . . . could this be accomplished,—the world would be worth living in;—and might be considered by us as a foretaste of what we should enter upon hereafter.

Sermons, i, 3, pp. 72–4

. . . 'Tis observable in many places of scripture, that our blessed Saviour in describing the day of judgment does it in such a manner, as if the great enquiry then, was to relate principally to this one virtue of compassion—and as if our final sentence at that solemnity was to be pronounced exactly according to the degrees of it. I was a hungred and ye gave me meat—thirsty and ye gave me drink—naked and ye cloathed me—I was sick and ye visited me—in prison and ye came unto me. Not that we are to imagine from thence, as if any other good or evil action should then be overlooked by the eye of the All-seeing Judge, but barely to intimate to us, that a charitable and benevolent disposition is so principal and ruling a part of a man's character, as to be a considerable test by itself of the whole frame and temper of his mind, with which all other virtues and vices respectively rise and fall, and will almost necessarily be connected.—

Sermons, vii, 14 (41), pp. 45–7

This debt [i.e., of maintaining a "benevolent frame of mind towards all our fellow creatures"] christianity has highly exalted; though it is a debt that we were sensible of before, and acknowledged to

9. Cf. Tillotson's "The Advantages of Religion to Societies," *Sermons,* Vol. i, No. 3, quoted below, p. 155.

1. Cf. Tillotson's *Sermons,* Vol. vi, No. 125, quoted below, p. 172.

ties of common humanity. God *has made of one blood,* as St. *Paul* expresses it, *all nations of men, for to dwell on all the face of the Earth* . . . . All subject to the same Infirmities, All liable to fall under the same misfortunes . . . and therefore have All of us reason to exercise that compassion, which no man knows but he may stand in need of himself. *The merciful man,* saith *Solomon, doth good to his own Soul; but he that is cruel, troubleth his own Flesh* . . . . God is equally the common Father of us all; and in his Government of the World, *accepteth not the persons of Princes, nor regardeth the rich more than the poor; for they are all the work of his hands.* . . . So *we* in like manner, are to make no distinction of Persons **. . . .**

be owed to human nature,—which, as we all partake of,—so ought we to pay it in a suitable respect.—For, as men, we are allied together in the natural bond of brotherhood . . . . We have the same Father in heaven . . . . Our earthly extraction too is nearer alike, than the pride of the world cares to be reminded of . . . . The prince and the beggar sprung from the same stocks . . . . We are all formed too of the same mould . . . . So that, to love our neighbour, and live quietly with him, is to live at peace with ourselves.—He is but self-multiplied, and enlarged into another form; and to be unkind or cruel to him, is but, as Solomon observes of the unmerciful, to be cruel to our own flesh.—As a farther motive and engagement to this . . . God has placed us all in one another's power by turns,— in a condition of mutual need and dependence.

pp. 413–14

. . . such is the instability of all temporal things, that, as the wise man elegantly expresses it, *Riches make themselves wings, and fly away, as an eagle towards Heaven;* that is, we cannot . . . secure them to ourselves for any certain time . . . . We know not how soon they may be snatch'd from *Us,* by numberless unforseen Accidents . . . . That which has been well laid out in doing Good to Mankind, has a greater Probability of turning to our Advantage even *here;* (considering the variety of Accidents all human Affairs are subject to.) . . . .

p. 49

. . . there is a great portion of mutability in all human affairs, to make benignity of temper not only our duty, but our interest and wisdom.—There is no condition in life so fixed and permanent as to be out of danger . . . of change:— . . . we shall take our turns of wanting and desiring.— By how many unforseen causes may riches take wing!—

Sermons, I, 5, pp. 130–1

. . . so many surprising revolutions do every day happen . . . that many a man has lived to enjoy the benefit of that charity which his own piety projected.

p. 419

. . . there is one comprehensive method of Charity, which in its extent and effects is a compendium of all the instances of beneficence in one; and That is the education of poor children, to which your contribution is now desired. . . . This is early sowing the Seeds of virtue and piety, and preventing the first beginnings of those habits of wickedness, which afterwards perhaps no Zeal for Reformation of manners would ever be able to root out; This is . . . making those to be useful members of the publick, who otherwise might be a burden and a hindrance to it.

pp. 143–5

The proper education of poor children . . . [is] the ground-work of almost every other kind of charity . . . .
    Without this foundation first laid, how much kindness in the progress of a benevolent man's life is unavoidably cast away? . . . I said, therefore, this was the foundation of almost every kind of charity,— and might not one have added, of all policy too? since the many ill consequences which attend the want of it . . . are [felt] . . . by the community of which they are members; and moreover, of all mischiefs seem the hardest to be redressed.

Vol. vii, Sermon 5, pp. 111–12[2]

I will not presume to affirm, (though some have done it, not without appearance of reason,) that if God should transplant such [wicked] persons into Heaven, he *could* not make them happy there . . . .

Sermons, v, 2 (29), p. 42

The consideration of this has led some writers so far, as to say, with some degree of irreverence in the expression,—that it was not in the power of God to make a wicked man happy, if the soul was separated from the body, with all its vicious habits and inclinations unreformed . . . .

Vol. vii, Sermon 12, pp. 261–2

. . . what *Abraham's* Reply directly *charges* him [the Rich Man] with, does not obviously and at first sight appear to be *Criminal* . . . that he was *cloathed in Purple and fine linnen, and fared sumptuously every day.* And as his Quality or Station in the World may be supposed to have been, there is no impossibility but he might be conceived to have done this, without the imputation of any Scandalous Excesses. Differences of Station, there must be in the World. . . . and . . . they should be supported with proper Marks of Distinction. Luxury does not consist in the innocent enjoyment of any of the good things, which God has created to be received with Thankfulness; but in the wastful Abuse of them to vicious Purposes, in ways inconsistent with Sobriety, Justice, or Charity. The exceeding plenty in which *Solomon* is described to have lived, I *Kings* iv. 22. is not laid to his charge as a *Sin,* but remarked as an Instance of God's Blessing upon him . . . .[3]

Sermons, iv, 8 (23), pp. 51–3

—That he [the Rich Man] had received his good things,—'twas from heaven,—and could be no reproach; with what severity soever the scripture speaks against riches, it does not appear, that the living or faring sumptuously every day, was the crime objected to the rich man; or that it is a real part of a vicious character: the case might be then, as now: his quality and station in the world might be supposed to be such, as not only to have justified his doing this, but, in general, to have required it without any imputation of doing wrong; for differences of stations there must be in the world, which must be supported by such marks of distinction as custom imposes. The exceeding great plenty and magnificence, in which Solomon is described to have lived, who had ten fat oxen, and twenty oxen out of the pastures, and a hundred sheep, besides harts, and roebucks, and fallow deer, and fatted fowl, with thirty measures of fine flower, and three score measures of meal, for the daily provision of his table; [4]—all this is not laid to him as a sin, but rather remarked as an instance of God's blessing to him;—and whenever these things are otherwise, 'tis from a wastful and dishonest perversion of them to pernicious ends, —and oft times, to the very opposite ones for which they were granted . . . .

pp. 265–6

'Tis probable . . . that our Saviour intended to give an intimation of the Dangers of the Sin of *Uncharitableness,* when he represents *Lazarus* lying in a very miserable condition at the Rich man's door, and *desiring to be fed with the Crumbs that fell from his Table.* For though he

pp. 47–8

In this state he [Lazarus] is described as desiring to be fed with the crumbs which fell from the rich man's table; and tho' the case is not expressly put, that he was refused, yet as the contrary is not affirmed in the historical part of the parable,—or pleaded after by the other, that

2. Cf. Norris' "Discourse the Sixth," quoted below, p. 142.
3. Cf. Tillotson's "The Parable of the Rich Man and Lazarus," *Sermons,* Vol. vi, No. 125, quoted below, p. 171.
4. Cf. I Kings 4.22–3.

does not *expressly* put the case, that the *Poor man* found *no relief* in those circumstances; yet since, on the contrary, 'tis neither expressed in the Historical part of the Parable, nor pleaded by the Rich man in his Own behalf, that there was any Relief given, 'tis reasonable to suppose that our Lord intended to be understood, as making *Uncharitableness* a part of the *Character* represented under this Parable.

Vol. VIII, Sermon 13, pp. 268–9

Solomon, to whom God gave a wise and understanding heart . . . who had carefully considered and thoroughly examined all things under the Sun; and was therefore most likely to give a true judgment of them; gives us *his* opinion of this whole matter in that affectionate conclusion of his book of *Ecclesiastes . . . Fear God and keep his Commandments . . . .*

pp. 279–80

As the upright man is well assured that the way he intends to walk in, will lead him right to his designed end; so he is very certain that he shall not mistake that way. The paths of Virtue and Righteousness are plain and straight; so that the Blind, *i.e.* persons of the meanest capacity . . . shall not err therein. The ways of iniquity and injustice, of fraud and deceit, are infinitely various and uncertain; full of intricate mazes, perplexity, and obscurity: It requires great skill and industry to find out such methods of overreaching our neighbours, as will have any probability of success . . . and it cannot but cause much sollicitude of mind, to be always in fear of being disappointed by a discovery. How many do we meet with in the world, who (out of a greedy desire of a little greater gain) endeavouring to overreach and deceive their neighbours, have for want of laying their contrivances cunningly enough, and managing them with secrecy and advantage, fallen short of that gain which they might without farther trouble have gotten in the plain way of Honesty and Uprightness? The upright man lays no projects which it is the interest of his neighbour to hinder from suc-

he shewed mercy to the miserable, we may conclude his request was unsuccessful,—like too many others in the world, either so high lifted up in it, that they cannot look down distinctly enough upon the sufferings of their fellow creatures,—or by long surfeiting in a continual course of banqueting and good cheer, they forget there is such a distemper as hunger, in the catalogue of human infirmities.

Sermons, I, 1, p. 23

Never did the busy brain of a lean and hectick chemist search for the philosopher's stone with more pains and ardour than this great man [Solomon] did after happiness.—He was one of the wisest enquirers into nature—had tried all her powers and capacities, and after a thousand vain speculations and vile experiments . . . the conclusion of the whole matter was this—that he advises every man who would be happy, to fear God and keep his commandments.[5]

Sermons, v, 1 (28), pp. 15–16

The paths of virtue are plain and strait, so that the blind, persons of the meanest capacity, shall not err.—Dishonesty requires skill to conduct it, and as great art to conceal—what 'tis every one's interest to detect.

p. 16

And I think I need not remind you how oft it happens in attempts of this kind—where worldly men, in haste to be rich, have over-run the only means to it,—and for want of laying their contrivances with proper cunning, or managing them with proper secrecy and advantage, have lost for ever, what they might have certainly secured by honesty and plain-dealing.

p. 15

. . . honesty is in its own nature the freest from danger.

First, because such a one lays no proj-

5. Cf. Tillotson's "The Prejudices against Jesus and His Religion Considered," *Sermons,* Vol. VI, No. 118, quoted below, p. 170.

ceeding; and therefore he needs no indirect methods, no fraudulent and deceitful practices, to secure his own Interest by
undermining his neighbour's . . . .

ects, which it is the interest of another
to blast, and therefore needs no indirect
methods or deceitful practices to secure
his interest by undermining others.

p. 281

. . . In the *continuance* and whole
course of his affairs, he has the greatest
probability not to fall into any considerable disappointment or calamity. . . .
1st, Because the way of Uprightness is
in itself freest from danger. . . . *2dly*,
Because it is moreover guarded and protected, by the peculiar favour and providence of God.

Secondly, let it be observed,—that in
the continuance and course of a virtuous
man's affairs, there is little probability
of his falling into considerable disappointments or calamities;—not only because guarded by the providence of God,
but that honesty is in its own nature the
freest from danger.[6]

pp. 282–3

Then is Uprightness undeniably the securest and least dangerous course.

p. 284

But farther; as uprightness is *in itself*
the safest and least dangerous course; so
is it moreover guarded by the peculiar
favour and providence of God.

pp. 16–17

The general causes of the disappointments
in their business, or of unhappiness in
their lives, lying but too manifestly in
their own disorderly passions, which by
attempting to carry them a shorter way
to riches and honour, disappoint them
of both for ever . . . .

p. 282

. . . the general causes of mens misfortunes and disappointments, lie manifestly
in their own Irregularities and Disorders;
and the ruine of most men be evidently
owing, to their own deceitful and indirect practices . . . .

Sermons, I, 1, p. 1

The great pursuit of man is after happiness: it is the first and strongest desire
of his nature— . . . he searches for it
. . . and though perpetually disappointed,—still persists— . . . asks every
passenger who comes in his way—Who
will shew him any good?

Vol. IX, Sermon 15, pp. 343–4[7]

There is nothing wherein all mankind
so naturally and universally agree, as in
desiring and searching after their own
Happiness; and yet nothing wherein they
differ more, than in their several means
of pursuing it. All men naturally enquire,
and search after what may make them
happy; *There be many that say, Who will
shew us any good?*

pp. 7–8

In this uncertain and perplexed state—
. . . so often abused and deceived by
the many who pretend . . . to shew us
any good—Lord! says the psalmist, Lift
up the light of thy countenance upon
us. . . . let us not wander for ever without a guide in this dark region in endless
pursuit of our mistaken good, but . . .

p. 344

But while vicious and debauched persons
. . . weary themselves in vain, about
things wherein is no Profit; the Psalmist
determines, that true, solid and lasting

6. In the Ms. of this sermon Sterne has crossed out a sentence originally inserted
here: "1st Because [the Paths of] Virtue is a strait Road & Plain, so that the blind—
i.e. Persons of the meanest Capacity shall not err therein—"
7. Cf. Tillotson, *Sermons*, Vol. VI, No. 131, quoted below, pp. 172–3.

Happiness, is to be found only in the Knowledge and in the Favour of God; in the practice of Virtue and true Religion. *Lord, lift Thou up the light of thy countenance upon us.*

From the words therefore we may observe these three things;

1st; That there is necessarily implanted in the very Nature of Man, a Desire of promoting his own Happiness. 2dly; That wicked and corrupt men seek this Happiness in the sinful Enjoyments of the present Life; and that their chusing so to do, is their great Errour and Folly. 3dly; That righteous and good men, believe their chief Happiness, to consist in the Knowledge and in the Favour of God . . . .

Vol. ix, Sermon 19, pp. 436–7

. . . the Duty of Prayer . . . is upon Earth the Primary . . . part of Divine Worship, as *Thanksgiving* is the Chief . . . part . . . in *Heaven. Obedience itself,* or the Practice of Virtue and Righteousness . . . is indeed still more *excellent* than either of these . . . . Behold, *to Obey is better than sacrifice and to hearken than the Fat of Rams. . . .* Nevertheless, as the *One* ought above all things to be *Done,* so the *Other* ought not by any means to be left *Undone.* As God is to be *Obeyed,* so he is to be *Worshipped* also . . . .

pp. 441–2

Nor can it here reasonably be objected, that God, by reason of his Omniscience, *knows already* what we want . . . . We do not ask of God, in order to *acquaint* Him, what things we stand in need of; but to express the Sense *we ourselves* have, of his being alone able to supply our Wants . . . .

Vol. x, Sermon 9, pp. 206–07

Now of *all* crimes that a man is capable of committing, that which is condemned in . . . the Text, is the most enormous; because 'tis, in the nature of the thing, irreparable; and which no after-act can make any Amends for. For, what recompence can be given a man in exchange for his Life? Or what satisfaction can *He* make for destroying the

make us know the joy and satisfaction of living in the true faith and fear of thee, which only can carry us to . . . that sure haven, where true joys are to be found . . . .

pp. 8–9

The words thus opened, naturally reduce the remaining part of the discourse under two heads—The first part of the verse—there be many that say, who will shew us any good—To make some reflections upon the insufficiency of most of our enjoyments towards the attainment of happiness, upon some of the most received plans on which 'tis generally sought.

The examination of which will lead us up to the . . . true secret of all happiness . . . that there can be no real happiness without religion and virtue, and the assistance of God's grace and Holy Spirit to direct our lives in the true pursuit of it.

Sermons, vii, 16 (43), p. 94

And, no doubt, though a virtuous and a good life are more acceptable in the sight of God, than either prayer or thanksgiving;—for, behold, to obey is better than sacrifice, and to hearken than the fat of rams;—nevertheless, as the one ought to be done, so the other ought not, by any means, to be left undone.—As God is to be obeyed,—so he is to be worshipped also.—

pp. 95–6

And though God is all-wise, and therefore understands our thoughts afar off . . . yet God himself has . . . command[ed] us to pray to him . . . that we might testify the sense we have of all his mercies and loving kindness to us,— and confess that he has the propriety of every thing we enjoy . . . .

Sermons, vi, 8 (35), pp. 33–4

Of all . . . attacks which can be made against us,—that of a man's life . . . is . . . the greatest . . . the most heinous . . . .

pp. 36–7

. . . the injury [is] irreparable.—No after-act could make amends for it.—

Image of God . . . ? By the Law of *Nature* therefore, this Crime was always pursued with the most extreme vengeance: Which made the Barbarians to judge . . . when they saw St. *Paul* upon the point, as they thought, of dying a sudden and unnatural Death: *No doubt this man is a* Murderer, *whom, though he has escaped the Sea, yet Vengeance suffereth not to live.*

What recompence can he give to a man in exchange for his life?—What satisfaction to the widow,—the fatherless,—to the family,— . . . cut off from his protection,—and rendered perhaps destitute,—perhaps miserable forever!—

No wonder, that, by the law of nature, —this crime was always pursued with the most extreme vengeance;—which made the barbarians to judge, when they saw St. Paul upon the point of dying a sudden and terrifying death,—No doubt this man is a murderer; who, though he has escaped the sea, yet vengeance suffereth not to live.

pp. 207–08

By the Laws of *all civilized Nations* in all parts of the World, it has always been punished with Death. And by the Law of *God himself*, it is of All Offences declared to be the most unpardonable. (*Gen.* ix.5; and *Num.* xxxv.31;) *At the hand of every man's Brother, will I require the life of Man: Whoso sheddeth man's Blood, by man shall his Blood be Shed. Ye shall take no satisfaction for the life of a Murderer:—he shall surely be put to Death.—So ye shall not pollute the Land wherein ye are: For blood defileth the Land; and the Land cannot be cleansed of the blood that is shed therein, but by the Blood of him that shed it.*

pp. 34–5

. . . the offence, in God's dispensation to the Jews, was . . . represented as most unpardonable.—At the hand of every man's brother will I require the life of man.—Whoso sheddeth man's blood, by man shall his blood be shed.—Ye shall take no satisfaction for the life of a murderer;—he shall surely be put to death.—So ye shall not pollute the land wherein ye are,—for blood defileth the land;—and the land cannot be cleansed of blood that is shed therein, but by the blood of him that shed it.—For this reason, by the laws of all civilized nations, in all parts of the globe, it has been punished with death.—

pp. 208–10

It has been a very ancient imagination in persons guilty of the most *crying Immoralities,* that the Regard men are apt to have for the relative Sacredness of Places dedicated to the most solemn part of God's Worship, should be a sort of *Refuge* to them, and *Protection from Justice.* . . . But . . . God was pleased . . . expressly to declare . . . that no . . . Sacredness of Place or Thing, no Worship or Sacrifice at His Altar, should upon any account be a *Cover* or *Protection* to any Vice or Immorality whatsoever. How much more absurd therefore is it . . . to set up, as the Church of *Rome* has done in innumerable Instances, —a Protection to Criminals of the Highest kind . . . .

pp. 45–6

The text says,—Thou shalt take him from my altar that he may die.—It had been a very ancient imagination, that for men guilty of this and other horrid crimes, —a place held sacred, as dedicated to God, was a refuge and protection to them from the hands of justice.—The law of God cuts the transgressor off from all delusive hopes of this kind;—and I think the Romish church has very little to boast of in the sanctuaries which she leaves open, for this and other crimes and irregularities.—

p. 210

What Scripture and Nature and Reason teach, concerning the Crime of at-

p. 47

What Scripture and all civilized nations teach concerning the crime of taking away another man's life,—is applicable to the wickedness of a man's attempting to bereave himself of his own.—He has no more right over it,—than over that of others:—

tempting *another man's* life; is applicable in proportion to the Folly of a man's . . . bereaving himself of his own life. . . . no man has a Right to remove himself therefrom [this present World] . . . .

pp. 211–12

. . . there are very many Degrees, in which the Command given in the *Law* . . . may in different manners be transgressed.

p. 213

. . . How much *more* reasonable is it, that Transports of *Passion* and even of the most *sudden* Provocation, should not be allowed in excuse of an irreparable Damage! a Damage, not only irreparable in *This* World, but of unspeakable ill consequence with regard also to that which *is to come;* For persons in these Circumstances generally leave the World, without any real *Forgiveness* of *each other,* and without any possibility of effectual *Repentance and Amendment* towards God.

pp. 213–14

. . . The Laws of God, relating to the Life of our Neighbour; taking them according to their real Design, and in their true Extent; are transgressed by all real *Mischiefs* and *Injuries* whatsoever, done by One man to Another . . . . They are transgressed by all wilful *Frauds,* and deliberate *Adulterations,* of things made use of either in *Food* or *Medicines;* and, in a word, by *every* thing . . . in consequence whereof any man receives detriment in his Person. . . . For, though no man is answerable for any accidental ill Consequences, which he may possibly be the occasion of in the Performance of his Duty; yet whenever any man does any *unlawful* Action, he is undoubtedly *answerable* . . . not only for the Evil he *directly intended,* but also for the *accidental* ill Consequences of That Action . . . .

p. 49

. . . I shall . . . proceed to consider some other cases, in which the law . . . is transgressed in different degrees.—

pp. 39–40

That it [murder] is the highest act of injustice to man, and which will admit of no compensation,—I have said.—But the depriving a man of life, does not comprehend the whole of his suffering;—he may be cut off in an unprovided or disordered condition, with regard to the great account betwixt himself and his Maker.— He may be under the power of irregular passions and desires.—The best of men are not always upon their guard.—And I am sure we have all reason to join in that affecting part of our Litany,—That . . . God would deliver us from sudden death;—that we may have some fore-sight of that period to compose our spirits,— prepare our accounts,—and put ourselves in the best posture we can to meet it . . . .

pp. 49–50

. . . our Saviour . . . has explained in how many slighter and unsuspected ways and degrees,—the command in the law,— Thou shalt do no murder, may be opposed, if not broken.—All real mischiefs and injuries maliciously brought upon a man . . . are this sin in disguise . . . .

pp. 54–7

There is another species of this crime which is seldom taken notice of in discourses upon the subject,—and yet can be reduced to no other class:— And that is, where the life of our neighbor is shortened,—and often taken away as directly as by a weapon, by the empirical sale of nostrums and quack medicines,—which ignorance and avarice blend. . . . the best medicines, administered with the wisest heads,—shall often do the mischief they were intended to prevent.— These are misfortunes to which we are subject . . . . but when men . . . make merchandize of the miserable,—and from a dishonest principle—trifle with the pains of the unfortunate . . . . It is murder in the true sense . . . .

In doing what is wrong,—we stand chargeable with all the bad consequences

which arise from the action, whether forseen or not.

p. 49

St. John says, Whosoever hateth his
brother is a murderer;—it is the first step
to this sin . . . .

pp. 215–17

. . . The Precept of the *old Law* . . .
as explained in the *Gospel-sense* by our
Saviour . . . is transgressed by all *Wrath,
Malice, Strife, Contentiousness,* and Hatred towards our Brethren. I Joh.iii.15;
*Whosoever hateth his Brother, is a Mur-
derer* . . . . The *Ground* of the Apostles
expressing himself after this manner, is;
not only because the Beginnings of wrath
and animosities, in event often extend to
great and unforseen Effects; as *Cain's*
causeless Anger against his Brother, which
the Apostle alludes to in the foregoing
verses, ended at length in taking away his
Life . . . . For which reason our Saviour, in the *place before referred to,* explaining the Ancient Law upon this head,
enlarges it Thus. *Ye have heard that it
was said by them of old time, Thou shalt
not kill:—But I say unto you, Whosoever
is Angry with his Brother without a cause,
shall be in danger of the Judgment; And
whosoever shall say to his Brother, Raca,
shall be in danger of the Council; But
whosoever shall say, Thou Fool, shall be
in danger of Hell-fire.* The words are an
allusion to three different degrees of Punishment, in three several Courts of Judicature among the *Jews.* And the Sense of
them is, that every degree of *Hatred,
Malice,* and *Uncharitableness* towards our
Brethren, shall finally receive from God
a proportionable Punishment . . . to
each degree of the Offence; whereas the
Old Law (according to the *Jews* interpretation of it,) extended not to these
things at all, but forbad only *Murder* and
outward Injuries. *Whosoever shall say,
Thou Fool, shall be in danger of Hell-
Fire:* The Meaning is; not that, in the
strict and literal sense, every such rash
and passionate expression shall be punished with eternal damnation: (For who
then should be saved?) But that at the
exact Account in the judgment of the
Great Day . . . every secret Thought
and Intent of the Heart, shall have its
just Estimation and Weight, in determining the *degrees* of Happiness or Punishment, which shall be assigned to every
man in his final and eternal State.

pp. 50–1

. . . and the grounds of the Scripture
expressing it with such severity, is,—that
the beginnings of wrath and malice,—in
event, often extend to such great and unforseen effects, as, were we fortold them,
—we should give . . . little credit to
. . . . As Cain's causeless anger (as Dr.
Clark observes) against his brother,—to
which the apostle alludes—ended in taking away his life . . . .

pp. 52–4

Ye have heard . . . says our Saviour,
that it was said by them of old time,—
Thou shalt not kill;—but I say unto you,
—whosoever is angry with his brother
without a cause, shall be in danger of the
judgment;—and whosoever shall say to
his brother, Raca,—shall be in danger of
the council:—but whosoever shall say,
"thou fool,"—shall be in danger of hell-
fire.—The interpretation of which I shall
give you in the words of a great scriptur-
ist, Dr. Clark,—and is as follows:—That
the three gradations of crimes are an allusion to the three different degrees of punishment, in the three courts of judicature
amongst the Jews.—And our Saviour's
meaning was,—That every degree of sin,
from its first conception to its outrage,—
every degree of malice and hatred, shall
receive from God a punishment proportionable to the offence.—Whereas the old
law, according to the jewish interpretation, extended not to these things at all,—
forbade only murder and outward injuries.
—Whosoever shall say, "thou fool," shall
be in danger of hell-fire.—The sense of
which is not that, in the strict and literal
acceptation, every rash and passionate expression shall be punished with eternal
damnation;—(for who then would be
saved?)—but that at the exact account
in the judgment of the great day, every
secret thought and intent of the heart
shall have its just estimation and weight
in the degrees of punishment, which shall
be assigned to every one in his final state.

JAMES FOSTER (1697–1753)

FOSTER	STERNE

FOSTER

Sermon 1, pp. 2–3[8]

Felix, by the confession of *Tacitus* the *Roman* historian, governed the *Jews* in a very arbitrary manner, and committed the grossest acts of *oppression* and *tyranny*. And *Drusilla* his wife, without any good reason to justify a divorce, had left her former husband, and given herself to him; and consequently was an *adultress:* When St. *Paul*, therefore, was sent for to explain to them the nature of the Christian Religion, which was then newly published, and, upon that account, a matter of *curiosity;* and in discoursing on the morality of the gospel . . . took occasion to inculcate the eternal laws of justice, and the immutable obligations of temperance and chastity; the conscience of the governour was alarmed and terrified, and a sense of his crime, and dread of the righteous and awful judgment of God upon all such notorious offenders against the rules of *righteousness* and *humanity,* filled him with the utmost confusion. *Drusilla* indeed does not appear to have discovered any remorse; perhaps she was naturally, of a more hard, insensible, unrelenting temper; or confided in her *Jewish* priviledges, and expected to be saved, as a daughter of *Abraham*, notwithstanding the immorality and wickedness of her life. However this be, as 'tis not my business to make conjectures, I shall proceed to consider what is directly related by the historian . . . .

STERNE

Sermons, III, 4 (19), pp. 106–09

It seems that Drusilla, whose curiosity, upon a double account, had led her to hear Paul,———(for she was a daughter of Abraham———as well as of Eve) ———was a character, which might have figured very well even in our own times; for as Josephus tells us, she had left the Jew her husband, and without any pretence in their law to justify a divorce, had given herself up without ceremony to Felix; for which cause, tho' she is here called his wife, she was in reason and justice the wife of another man,—and consequently lived in an open state of adultery. So that when Paul, in explaining the faith of Christ, took occasion to argue upon the morality of the gospel, ———and urged the eternal laws of Justice,—the unchangeable obligations to temperance, of which chastity was a branch,———it was scarce possible to frame his discourse so, (had he wished to temporize) but that either her interest or her love must have taken offence: and tho' we do not read, like Felix, that she trembled at the account, 'tis yet natural to imagine she was affected with other passions, of which the apostle might feel the effects . . . .
But this by the way,———for as the text seems only to acknowledge one of these motives, it is not our business to assign the other.

FOSTER

Sermon 4, pp. 81–5

I am to show wherein the image of the Deity, in man, consists; and that not only the *first parents* of the human race, but *all mankind* since, notwithstanding the corrupt and degenerate state of the world, were originally formed after the image of God. . . .
Man is a being partly *sensitive,* and partly *rational.* There can be no resemblance of his great Creator in the sensi-

STERNE

Sermons, II, 7, pp. 4–5

The scripture tells, That God made man in his own image,—not surely in the sensitive and corporeal part of him, that could bear no resemblance with a pure and infinite spirit,—but what resemblance he bore was undoubtedly in the moral rectitude, and the kind and benevolent affections of his nature. And tho' the brightness of this image has been sullied greatly by the fall of man, in our first parents,

8. Page references are to James Foster's one-volume edition of *Sermons* (3d ed. London, 1736).

tive part of his frame, because HE is a
pure and infinite spirit. . . . The image
of God, in man, has a respect, farther, to
the *moral rectitude* in which he was created . . . and the exercise of benevolence, one of the brightest characters of
the Deity . . . . This was the first happy
state of man. And in consequence of . . .
the kind and benevolent affections of his
nature, (in which consisted his more immediate resemblance to his maker) he
was appointed to exercise dominion . . .
in all these respects, not only the *first
parents* of mankind, but their *descendants,*
were originally formed after the divine
image.

Sermon 8, pp. 191–4

. . . in an affluent prosperity, when every
thing about us is gay, and has a smiling
aspect, we are too apt to contract an habit-
ual *levity* of mind, and neglect all *grave*
and *serious* reflections. . . . For there are
too many, to whom a time of affliction is a
season of *some sort* of piety, because, then
their *sufferings* put them in mind of their
sins . . . .—What a *perverse* creature
is man! he wishes not to be *miserable,* and
yet forgets the author of his happiness,
because he has not allotted him some
mixtures of *evil* and *misery* with it!

and the characters of it rendered still
less legible, by the many super-inductions
of his own depraved appetites since—yet
'tis a laudable pride . . . to cherish a belief, that there is so much of that glorious
image still left upon it, as shall restrain
him from base and disgraceful actions . . . .

Sermons, I, 2, p. 34

. . . the gay and smiling aspect of
things . . . .

pp. 28–9

. . . . a season of affliction is in some sort
a season of piety—not only because our
sufferings are apt to put us in mind of
our sins, but . . . they allow us . . . a
little time for reflection . . . .
So strange and unaccountable a creature
is man! he is so framed, that he cannot
but pursue happiness—and yet unless he
is made sometimes miserable, how apt is
he to mistake the way which can only
lead him to the accomplishment of his
own wishes!

JOSEPH HALL, BISHOP OF EXETER (1574–1656)

HALL	STERNE

HALL

Vol. i, Bk. iii, Contemplation 2, p. 35[9]

Not long after, Rachel, the comfort of his life, dieth. And when? but in her travel, and in his travel to his father. When he had now before digested in his thoughts the joy and gratulation of his aged father, for so welcome a burden, his children (the staff of his age) wound his soul to the death. Reuben proves incestuous, Judah adulterous, Dinah ravished, Simeon and Levi murderous, Er and Onan stricken dead, Joseph lost . . . himself driven by famine, in his old age, to die amongst the Egyptians, a people that held it abomination to eat with him.

Vol. i, Bk. iii, Contemplation 5, p. 41

How much is servitude, to an ingenuous nature, worse than death! for this is common to all; that, to none but the miserable.

p. 46*[1]

The guilty conscience can never think itself safe: so many years' experience of Joseph's love could not secure his brethren of remission. Those that know they have deserved ill, are wont to misinterpret favours, and think they cannot be beloved. All that while, his goodness seemed but concealed and sleeping malice, which they feared in their father's last sleep would awake, and bewray itself in revenge . . . .

STERNE

Sermons, iv, 7 (22), pp. 9–10

Scarce had he recovered from these evils, when the ill conduct and vices of his children, wound his soul to death.— Reuben proves incestuous, Judah adulterous,—his daughter Dinah is dishonoured,—Simeon and Levi dishonour themselves by treachery,—two of his grandchildren are stricken with sudden death,— Rachael his beloved wife perishes, and in circumstances which embitter'd his loss,— his son Joseph, a most promising youth, is torn from him . . . and to close all, himself driven by famine in his old age to die amongst the Egyptians, a people who held it an abomination to eat bread with him.

Sermons, ii, 12, pp. 147–8

. . . they [Joseph's brothers] had changed the sentence for one no less cruel in itself, and what to an ingenuous nature was worse than death, to be sold for a slave.—The one was common to all,— the other only to the unfortunate.

pp. 142–3

. . . they had had so many years experience of his love and kindness. And yet it is plain all this did not clear his motive from suspicion . . . . But does not a guilty conscience often do so?—and though it has the grounds, yet wants the power to think itself safe.

pp. 150–1

—A series of benefits and kindnesses from the man they [Joseph's brothers] had injured, gradually heightened the idea of their own guilt, till at length they could not conceive, how the trespass could be forgiven them . . . they were convinced

---

9. Page references are to the *Contemplations on the Historical Passages of the Old and New Testaments*, Wardlaw, ed. (Glasgow, 1834, 2 vols.).

1. Passages marked with an asterisk (*) indicate those which Ferriar had already noted as having been used by Sterne.

his resentment slept, yet they thought it only slept, and was likely some time or other to awake, and most probably then, that their father was dead, when the consideration of involving him in his revenge had ceased . . . .

Vol. I, Bk. XI, Contemplation 1, pp. 201–02°

The law of God allowed the Levite a wife; human connivance, a concubine: neither did the Jewish concubine differ from a wife, but in some outward compliments; both might challenge all the true essence of marriage.

Sermons, III, 3 (18), p. 72

Our annotators tell us, that in Jewish *aeconomicks*, these [concubines] differ'd little from the wife, except in some outward ceremonies and stipulations, but agreed with her in all the true essences of marriage . . . .

p. 202°

What husband would not have said, She is gone, let shame and grief go with her! I shall find one no less pleasing, and more faithful.

p. 64

—Then shame and grief go with her, and wherever she seeks a shelter, may the hand of justice shut the door against her.

p. 202°

Mercy becomes well the heart of any man, but most of a Levite. He that had helped to offer so many sacrifices to God, for the multitude of every Israelite's sins, saw how proportionable it was, that man should not hold one sin unpardonable. He had served at the altar to no purpose, if he, whose trade was to sue for mercy, had not at all learned to practise it.[2]

pp. 80–1

"Mercy well becomes the heart of all thy creatures,————but most of thy servant, a Levite, who offers up so many daily sacrifices to thee, for the transgressions of thy people.————
————But to little purpose, he would add, have I served at thy altar, where my business was to sue for mercy, had I not learn'd to practise it."

p. 203

Great is the power of love, which can in a sort undo evils past; if not for the act, yet for the remembrance.

p. 83

. . . great—great is it's [love's] power in cementing what has been broken, and wiping out wrongs even from the memory itself . . . .

Vol. I, Book XVI, Contemplation 1, p. 338°

There is no small cruelty in the picking out of a time for mischief; that word would scarce gall at one season, which at another killeth. The same shaft flying with the wind pierces deep, which against it can hardly find strength to stick upright.

Sermons, III, 1 (16), pp. 7–8

There is no small degree of malicious craft in fixing upon a season to give a mark of enmity and ill will: a word,—a look, which at one time would make no impression—at another time wounds the heart; and like a shaft flying with the wind, pierces deep, which, with its own natural force, would scarce have reached the object aimed at.

2. Ferriar comments here, "It were needless to pursue the parallel." (*Illustrations of Sterne*, p. 125.) The implication that other parallels existed is without justification. Excepting the single additional passage which I have quoted, there is no reason to believe that Sterne was any further indebted to this "Contemplation" of Bishop Hall's than he was to the common source, in the biblical account.

p. 338

In all the time of David's prosperity, we heard no news of Shimei; his silence and colourable obedience made him pass for a good subject . . . .

p. 340

David's patients draws on the insolence of Shimei. Evil natures grow presumptuous upon forbearance. In good dispositions, injury unanswered grows weary of itself, and dies in a voluntary remorse; but in those dogged stomachs, which are only capable of the restraints of fear, the silent digestion of a former wrong provokes a second.

O the base minds of inconstant time-servers! Stay but a while, till the wheel be a little turned, you shall see humble Shimei fall down on his face before David, in his return over Jordan . . . .

Vol. i, Bk. xviii, Contemplation 6, p. 411*

The prophet follows the call of his God; the same hand that brought him to the gate of Sarepta, led also this poor widow out of her doors . . . .[3]

p. 413

The dearth thus overcome, the mother looks hopefully upon her only son, promising herself much joy in his life and prosperity . . . .

p. 411

Many widows were in Israel in the days of Elijah, when the heaven was shut up three years and six months, when great famine was throughout all the land; but unto none of them was Elijah sent, save unto this Sarepta . . . unto a woman that was a widow.[4]

p. 413

. . . and in all these [aspects of his prayer], implying the scandal that must

p. 11

. . . in all David's prosperity, there is no mention made of him—he thrust himself forward into the circle, and possibly was number'd amongst friends and well-wishers.

p. 9

An injury unanswered in course grows weary of itself, and dies away in a voluntary remorse.
In bad dispositions capable of no restraint but fear———it has a different effect———the silent digestion of one wrong provokes a second.

p. 10

The insolence of base minds in success is boundless . . . .

p. 12

The wheel turns round once more . . . David returns in peace—Shimei suits his behaviour to the occasion, and is the first man . . . who hastes to greet him . . . .

Sermons, I, 5, p. 116

The prophet follows the call of his God:—the same hand which brought him to the gate of the city, had led also the poor widow out of her doors, oppressed with sorrow.

pp. 122–3

. . . it is natural to suppose, the danger of the famine being thus unexpectedly got over, that the mother began to look hopefully forwards upon the rest of her days. There were many widows in Israel at that time, when the heavens were shut up for three years and six months, yet, as St. Luke observes, *to none of them was the prophet sent, save to this widow of Sarepta* . . . .

pp. 126–7

He was moreover involved in the success of his prayer himself;—honest minds are most hurt by scandal.—And he was afraid, lest so foul a one, so unworthy of

3. Ferriar comments (*idem*, p. 127), "The succeeding passages which correspond, are too long for insertion." This, again, is misleading. I have included all the passages which bore the least resemblance; certainly they are neither numerous nor striking.
4. Cf. Luke 4.25–6. Note that neither Hall nor Sterne use quotation marks.

needs arise from this event, wherever it should be noised, to the name of his God, to his own; when it should be said, Lo! how Elijah's entertainment is rewarded: surely the prophet is either impotent, or unthankful.

Vol. II, Bk. XIX, Contemplation 7, pp. 36-7

The Shunamite . . . finding his [Elisha's] occasions to call him to a frequent passage that way, moves her husband to fit up, and furnish a lodging for the man of God: it was his holiness that made her desirous of such a guest . . . .

p. 37

The good Shunamite . . . solicits her husband to build him a chamber on the wall apart; she knew the tumult of a large family unfit for the quiet meditations of a prophet.

p. 38

The good matron needs no shelter of the great: "I dwell among mine own people;" as if she said, The courtesy is not small in itself, but not useful to me: I live here quietly, in a contented obscurity, out of the reach either of the glories or cares of a court; free from wrongs, free from envies. Not so high as to provoke an evil eye, not so low as to be trodden on . . . . If the world afford any perfect contentment, it is in a middle estate . . . .

Vol. II, Bk. XX, Contemplation 10, p. 101

I do not hear Hezekiah rage, and fret at the message . . . but he meekly turns his face to the wall, and weeps, and prays. Why to the wall? was it for the greater secrecy of his devotion? was it for the more freedom from distraction? . . . or, was it for that this wall looked towards the temple, which his heart and eyes still moved unto, though his feet could not?

his character, might arise amongst the heathen, who would report with pleasure, "Lo! the widow of Zerephath took the messenger of the God of Israel under her roof, and kindly entertained him, and see how she is rewarded; surely the prophet was ungrateful, he wanted power, or what is worse, he wanted pity!"

Sermons, II, 13, pp. 170-1

. . . finding his occasions called him to a frequent passage that way;—she moves her husband to set up and furnish a lodging for him . . . . She perceived he was a holy man . . . .

pp. 175-6

It is observable she does not sollicit her husband to assign him an apartment in her own house, but to build him a chamber in the wall apart;—she considered . . . that the tumult and distraction of a large family were not fit for the silent meditations of so holy a man . . . .

pp. 183-4

. . . the Shunamite . . . declines the offer . . . "I *dwell* amongst my own *people;*" as if she had said, "The intended kindness is far from being small, but it is not useful to me; I live here, as thou art a witness, in peace, in a contented obscurity;—not so high as to provoke envy, nor so low as to be trodden down and despised. In this safe and middle state, as I have lived amongst my own people, so let me die out of the reach, both of the cares and glories of the world.—

Sermons, III, 2 (17), pp. 33-4

. . . upon the delivery of the message he wept sore . . . he turned his face towards the wall,—perhaps for the greater secrecy of his devotion, and that, by withdrawing himself thus from all external objects, he might offer up his prayer unto his God, with greater and more fervent attention.

p. 36

. . . if we suppose, as some have done, that he turned his face towards the wall, because that part of his chamber looked towards the temple, the care of whose preservation lay next his heart, we may consistently enough give this sense to his prayer.

p. 101

Couldst thou fear, O Hezekiah, that God had forgotten thine integrity? . . . or dost thou therefore doubt of his remembrance of thy faithfulness, because he summons thee to receive the crown of thy faithfulness . . . ?

p. 34

O Hezekiah! How couldst thou fear that God had forgotten thee? or, How couldst thou doubt of his remembrance of thy integrity, when he called thee to receive it's recompence?

p. 102

Certainly the best man cannot strip himself of some flesh; and, while nature hath an undeniable share in him, he cannot but retain some smatch of the sweetness of life, of the horror of dissolution . . . .

pp. 34-5

But here it appears of what materials man is made: he pursues happiness—and yet is so content with misery, that he would wander for ever in this dark vale of it, . . . and so long as we are cloathed with flesh, and nature has so great a share within us, it is no wonder if that part claims it's right, and pleads for the sweetness of life, notwithstanding all it's care and disappointments.

p. 102

His very tears said, O God, thou knowest that the eyes of the world are bent upon me, as one that hath abandoned their idolatry, and restored thy sincere worship; I stand alone in the midst of a wicked and idolatrous generation, that looks through all my actions, all my events; if now they shall see me, snatched away in the midst of my days, what will these heathens say; how can thy great name but suffer in this mine untimely extinction?

pp. 36-7

"O God! . . . thou knowest that the eyes of the world are fixed upon me, as one that hath forsaken their idolatry, and restored thy worship;—that I stand in the midst of a crooked and corrupt generation, which looks thro' all my actions, and watches all events which happen to me: if now they shall see me snatched away in the midst of my days and service, How will thy great name suffer in my extinction?"

pp. 104-05

The fame of Hezekiah's sickness, recovery, form, and assurance of cure, have drawn thither messengers and presents from Berodachbaldan, king of Babylon.

The Chaldees were curious searchers into the secrets of nature, especially into the motions of the celestial bodies; though there had been no politic relations, this very astronomical miracle had been enough to fetch them to Jerusalem, that they might see the man, for whose sake the sun forsook his place, or the shadow forsook the sun.

pp. 39-40

. . . Baradock-baladan, son of Baladine king of Babylon, sent letters and a present unto Hezekiah: he had heard the fame of his sickness and recovery; for as the Chaldeans were great searchers into the secrets of nature, especially into the motions of the celestial bodies, in all probability they had taken notice at that distance, of the strange appearance of the shadow's returning ten degrees backwards upon their dials, and had enquired and learned upon what account, and in whose favour such a sign was given; so that this astronomical miracle, besides the political motive which it would suggest of courting such a favourite of heaven, had been sufficient by itself to have led a curious people as far as Jerusalem, that they might see the man for whose sake the sun had forsook his course.

p. 105

How easily have we seen those holy men miscarried by prosperity, against whom no miseries could prevail!

O Hezekiah, what means this impotent ambition? . . . if thy storehouse were as rich as the earth, can thy heart be so vain as to be lifted up with these heavy metals? Didst thou not see, that heaven itself was at thy beck, whilst thou were humbled? and shall a little earthly dross have power over thy soul?

Cf. "The Mourner in Sion," pp. 181–2[5]

. . . I doubt there are too many Christians that with the Epicure place their chief felicity in pleasure; but for sorrow and mourning it is a sowre and harsh thing . . . . But, if, as Christians, we come to weigh both these in the ballance . . . we shall find cause to take up other resolutions; will ye hear what wise *Solomon* says of the point? *Sorrow*, saith he, *is better than laughter; And it is better to go to the house of mourning, than to the house of feasting.* Lo, his very authority alone were enough . . . but withall, he sticks not to give up his reason, why then sorrow is better than laughter? (*For, by the sadness of the countenance the heart is made better*) look to the effects of both, and you shall easily see the difference: sorrow calls our hearts home to God, and our selves, which are apt to run wild in mirth; where did you ever see a man made more holy with worldly pleasure? no, that is apt to debauch him rather; but many a soul hath been bettered with sorrow; for that begins his mortification, recollecting his thoughts to a serious consideration of his spirituall condition, and working his heart to a due remorse for his sin, and a lowly submission to the hand that inflicts it.

p. 40

And here we see how hard it is to stand the shock of prosperity,—and how much truer a proof we give of our strength in that extreme of life, than in the other.

pp. 43–4

"O Hezekiah! . . . How could thy spirit, all-meek and gentle as it was, have ever fallen into this snare? Were thy treasures rich as the earth—What! was thy heart so vain as to be lifted up therewith? Was not all that was valuable in the world—nay, was not heaven itself almost at thy command whilst thou wast humble? and, How was it, that thou couldst barter away all this, for what was lighter than a bubble . . . ?

Sermons, I, 2, pp. 28–30

. . . at certain times it is so necessary a man's mind should be turned towards itself, that rather than want occasions, he had better purchase them at the expence of his present happiness.—He had better, as the text expresses it, *go to the house of mourning*, where he will meet with something to subdue his passions, than to the house of feasting, where the joy and gaity of the place is likely to excite them. . . .

This is the full force of the wise man's declaration.—But to do further justice to his words . . . take a transient view of the two places here referred to . . . . Give me leave . . . to recall both of them for a moment, to your imaginations . . . .

p. 28

. . . mirth and feasting are usually no friends to atchievements of this kind—[virtue]—but that a season of affliction is in some sort a season of piety. . . .

pp. 41–2

When we enter into the house of mourning . . . .Such objects catch our eyes,—they catch likewise our attentions, collect and call home our scattered thoughts, and exercise them with wisdom. A transient scene of distress, . . . how necessarily does it engage it [the mind] to the consideration of the miseries and misfortunes, the dangers and calamities to which the life of man is subject. . . .

5. From *The Remaining Works of That Incomparable Prelate Joseph Hall, D.D.*

From reflections of this serious cast, the thoughts insensibly carry us . . . from considering, what we are— . . . to look forwards at what possibly we shall be. . . .

And why should it be better to go to the house of mourning then to the house of feasting? (*For this is the end of all men, and the living shall lay it to his heart*). The house of mourning hath here principally respect to a funeral; the death which is lamented for, being the end of all flesh, a man is here, and thus, put feelingly in mind of his mortality, which in an house of feasting and jollity is utterly forgotten: By how much then it is better for a man to have his heart kept in order by the meditation of death, then to run wild after worldly vanity; by so much is the house of mourning better then the house of feasting.

pp. 42–3

. . . we shall find it a still more instructive school of wisdom when we take a view of the place in that more affecting light in which the wise man seems to confine it in the text, in which, by the house of mourning, I believe, he means that particular scene of sorrow where there is lamentation and mourning for the dead.

pp. 44–5

The busy and fluttering spirits, which in the house of mirth were wont to transport him from one diverting object to another —see how they are fallen! . . . in this gloomy mansion . . . see, the light and easy heart . . . how pensive it is now . . . . how full of religious impressions . . . we might then safely rest our cause, upon this single evidence, and appeal to the most sensual, whether Solomon has not made a just determination here, in favour of the house of mourning?—not for its own sake, but as it is fruitful in virtue, and becomes the occasion of so much good.

Vol. II, Bk. I, Contemplation 3, pp. 8–9

Man could no sooner see, than he saw himself happy: his eyesight and reason were both perfect at once, and the objects of both were able to make him as happy as he would. . . . He saw the heavens glorious, but afar off: his Maker thought it requisite to fit him with a paradise nearer home. . . . Had man been made only for contemplation, it would have served as well to have been placed in some vast desart, on the top of some barren mountain . . . . Neither was it the purpose of the Creator, that man should but live. Pleasure may stand with innocence. He that rejoiced to see all he had made to be good, rejoiceth to see all that he hath made to be well. God loves to see his creatures happy; our lawful delight is his: They know not God, that think to please him with making themselves miserable.

pp. 24–6

For what purpose do you imagine, has God made us? for the social sweets of the well watered vallies where he has planted us, or for the dry and dismal deserts of a *Sierra Morena?* . . . did the Best of Beings send us into the world for this end— to go weeping through it . . . ? do you think . . . that he who is infinitely happy, can envy us our enjoyments? . . . Consider . . . what provision and accommodation, the Author of our being has prepared for us, that we might not go on our way sorrowing— . . . what powers and faculties he has given us for taking it —what apt objects he has placed in our way to entertain us . . . .[6]

Sermons, IV, 7 (22), p. 29

Whatever is the proportion of misery in this world, it is certain, that it can be no

6. Cf. Wollaston, *op. cit.*, IX, 8, quoted below, pp. 182–3.

duty of religion to increase the complaint . . . .

Sermons, VI, 10 (37), p. 94

. . . God never intended to debar man of
pleasure, under certain limitations.

p. 104

. . . there . . . appears no obligation to
renounce the innocent delights of our beings, or to affect a sullen distaste against
them.—

Sermons, VI, 11 (38), p. 142

. . . —as if religion, which is evidently
calculated to make us happy in this life
as well as the next, was the parent of sul-
lenness and discontent.

WALTER LEIGHTONHOUSE

LEIGHTONHOUSE

"Twelfth Sermon," pp. 429–30[7]

He that soberly sits down, and considers the State and Condition of Man; how that *he is born unto trouble, as the sparks fly upwards,* shall find his Life perpetually surrounded with so many sorrowful Changes and Vicissitudes, that 'twill be matter of the greatest Wonder, how *the Spirit of Man could bear the Infirmities of Nature,* and carry him through the Disappointments of this *Valley of Tears.* And indeed, had not the frame of our Constitution, and the contexture of our Minds been curiously contrived by the Hand of an All-wise Being; did not the Faculties of our upper Region greatly support our tottering building of Clay, 'tis impossible but *the day of our Birth,* would appear to be our greatest Misfortune, and the silent Grave be earnestly sought for, and desired by each thinking son of *Adam.*

p. 440

. . . could we at one view see all the Sufferings of all Ranks and Degrees of Men, from *the Cedar of Libanus, to the humble Shrub upon the Wall,* we should be hard beset to tell, who was the Man amongst that untold Multitude the least *acquainted with Grief* . . . .

Cf. pp. 430–1

. . . although we cannot live exempt from great Tryals and Sufferings, whilst we are cloathed with this Robe of Flesh, yet we are certain, (if we be not wanting to our selves) never to be without a comfortable Support under those Pressures; but even amidst the fluctuating Billows of the *Waters of Marah,* we have the *Anchor of hope to keep us stedfast* . . . And although our sorrowful thoughts should multiply on us . . . yet when we are fully convinc'd, that . . . we shall yet

STERNE

Sermons, vi, 7 (34), pp. 3–5

Whoever seriously reflects upon the state and condition of man, and looks upon that dark side of it, which represents his life as open to so many causes of trouble; . . . that he is born to it as naturally as the sparks fly upwards;—that no rank or degrees of men are exempted from this law of our beings;—but that all, from the high cedar of Libanus to the humble shrub upon the wall, are shook in their turns by numberless calamities and distresses:—when one sits down and looks upon this gloomy side of things, with all the sorrowful changes and chances which surround us,—at first sight,—would not one wonder,—how the spirit of a man could bear the infirmities of his nature, and what it is that supports him, as it does, under the many evil accidents which he meets with in his passage through the valley of tears?—Without some certain aid within us to bear us up,—so tender a frame as ours, would be but ill fitted to encounter what generally befals it in this rugged journey:—and accordingly we find,—that we are so curiously wrought by an all-wise hand, with a view to this,—that in the very composition and texture of our nature, there is a remedy and provision left against most of the evils we suffer . . . .

pp. 10–11

Strengthened with this anchor of hope, which keeps us stedfast . . . however the sorrows of a man are multiplied, he bears up his head, looks towards heaven with confidence, waiting for the salvation of God . . . . He may be troubled, it is true, on every side, but shall not be distressed,—perplexed, yet not in despair . . . .

7. Page references are to the one-volume edition by Walter Leightonhouse, Prebendar, *Twelve Sermons, Preached at the Cathedral Church of Lincoln* (London, 1697). Sterne only made use of the last sermon.

live to see the goodness and deliverance
*of the Lord; we may be troubled on every
side, but we shall not be distressed; perplexed, yet not in despair* . . . .

pp. 431–2

And this we have asserted by . . . that
Kingly Prophet *David,* in the Words of
my Text, *I had fainted, unless I had believed, to see the goodness of the Lord in
the land of the living.*
  Which Psalm was composed by him,
when he was, or had lately been in some
great Distress . . . .

p. 434

. . . upon which he . . . Builds a Rock
of Encouragement, not only for himself,
but for the whole Race of Mankind after
him, to support and comfort them in their
greatest Afflictions.

pp. 434–5

. . . we may suppose it as spoken to a
second Person, and then it will import
thus much; let me admonish thee whoever
thou art, that shalt hereafter fall into any
such Straights or Troubles, to learn, by my
Example, not to be impatient, or despond
presently . . . if the Lord do not send it
[relief] just when thou expectest it; but
wait upon him still with stedfast hope,
and fortifie thy self with a strong Faith in
him.

pp. 459–60

Trust in God who sees all those Conflicts
under which thou labourest, who knows
thy necessities afar off, and *puts all thy
tears into his bottle.* He eyes every careful
Thought and pensive Look, afflictive Sigh,
and Melancholly Groan which thou utter-
est?

Cf. p. 438

'Tis true, indeed, *all things* do not here
come alike to all; but some Mens Sorrows
are enlarg'd . . . whilst others seem to
tread the Stage in a Princely Dress, and
have all their Paths *strewed with Rose-
buds of Delight and Jollity* . . . .

p. 439

And though all appear Serene and Quiet
without, yet *in the midst of laughter, the*

pp. 11–12

The virtue of this had been sufficiently
tried by David, and had, no doubt, been
of use to him in the course of a life full of
afflictions; many of which were so great,
that he declares, that he should verily
have fainted under the sense and apprehension of them, but that he believed to
see the goodness of the Lord in the land
of the living.—

pp. 13–14

. . . all which taught him [David] the
value of the lesson in the text, from which
he had received so much encouragement
himself,—that he transmits it for the benefit of the whole race of mankind after him,
to support them, as it had done him,
under the afflictions which befel him.

pp. 14–15

Trust in God;—as if he had said, Whosoever thou art that shall hereafter fall
into any such straits or troubles as I have
experienced,—learn   by   my   example
where to seek for succour . . . despond
not, and say within thyself . . . why he
vouchsafeth thee not a speedy relief?—
but arm thyself in thy misfortunes with
patience and fortitude;—trust in God,
who sees all those conflicts under which
thou labourest,—who knows thy necessities afar off,—and puts all thy tears into
his bottle;—who sees every careful
thought and pensive look,—and hears
every sigh and melancholy groan thou ut-
terest.—

Sermons, IV, 8 (23), pp. 48–9

But good God! . . . Why doest thou suffer . . . That this man should go clad in
purple, and have all his paths strewed
with rose-buds of delight, whilst so
many mournful passengers go heavily
along . . . ?

Sermons, VII, 17 (44), p. 124

Even in laughter (if you will believe
Solomon) the heart is sorrowful;—*the*

heart may be sorrowful; and the Mind sit drooping, whilst the Countenance is gay: And even he, who is the Object of Envy to those who look upon the Surface of his Estate, appears at the same time worthy of Compassion to those who know his private Recesses.

pp. 442–3

. . . Man in the most deplorable Condition, is mighty ready to believe and hope a Redress. . . . For that Man who labours under the pressing Torture of the Gout, or the Stone, did he believe his Pain equally, without remedy, and without intermission, with what deplorable Lamentations would he languish out his Day? And *how sweet would the clouds*[8] *of the valley be to him?*

pp. 445–6

The Experience which Men have had of God's Former Deliverances, doth strictly oblige us to wait with patience God's own time. The Apostle St. *Paul,* encouraging the *Corinthians* to bear with patience the Tryal incident to human Nature, reminds them of the Deliverance that God did formerly vouchsafe to him and *his fellow labourers, Gaius and Aristarchus,* Acts 19, 29. and thence builds a Fortress of future Trust and Dependance on him; his Life had been in very great Jeopardy at *Ephesus,* where he had like to have been *brought out to the Theatre to have been devoured by wild Beasts;* and indeed had no human means to avert, and consequently to escape it. And therefore he tells them, that he had this advantage by it, that *the more he believed, he should be put to death; the more he was engaged by his deliverance, never to depend on any worldly trust, but only on God, who can rescue from the greatest extremity, even from the grave, or Death it self;* as you may see, 2 Corinth. I. 8, 9, 10 Verses, *For we would not, brethren, have you ignorant of our trouble, which came to us in Asia, that we were pressed out of measure above strength, insomuch that we de-*

mind sits drooping, whilst the countenance is gay:—and even he, who is the object of envy to those who look no further than the surface of his estate,—may appear at the same time worthy of compassion to those who know his private recesses.

Sermons, VI, 7 (34), pp. 6–7

Without . . . an inward resource . . . to trust and hope for redress in the most deplorable conditions,—his [man's] state in this life would be, of all creatures, the most miserable.—When his mind was either wrung with affliction,—or his body lay tortured with the gout or stone,—did he think that in this world there should be no respite to his sorrow;—could he believe the pains he endured would continue equally intense,—without remedy, —without intermission;—with what deplorable lamentation would he languish out his day,—and how sweet, as Job says, would the *clods of the valley be to him?*

pp. 18–21

The conclusion was natural, and the experience which every man has had of God's former loving kindness and protection to him, either in dangers or distress, does unavoidably engage him to think in the same train.—It is observable that the apostle St. Paul, encouraging the Corinthians to bear with patience the trials incident to human nature, reminds them of the deliverances that God did formerly vouchsafe to him, and his fellow labourers, Gaius and Aristarchus;—and on that ground builds a rock of encouragement, for future trust and dependance on him.— His life had been in very great jeopardy at Ephesus,—where he had like to have been brought out to the theatre, to be devoured by wild beasts, and indeed had no human means to avert,—and consequently to escape it;—and therefore, he tells them, that he had this advantage by it, that the more he believed he should be put to death, the more he was engaged by his deliverance, never to depend on any worldly trust, but only on God, who can rescue from the greatest extremity, even from the grave and death itself.—For we would not, brethren, says he, have you ignorant of our trouble, which came to us

---

8. Cf. Job 21.33. The misprinting of "clouds" for "clods" is noted in the table of Errata, facing page 1 in the text.

spaired even of life. But we had the sentence of death in our selves, that we should not trust in our selves, but in God which raiseth the dead: who delivered us from so great a death, and doth deliver: in whom we trust, that he will yet deliver us . . . .

in Asia, that we were pressed out of measure, above our strength, insomuch that we despaired even of life;—but we had the sentence of death in ourselves, that we should not trust in ourselves, but in God, who raiseth the dead, who delivered us from so great a death, and doth deliver, and in whom we trust that he will still deliver us.[9]

pp. 446–8

And indeed a stronger Argument cannot be brought for future Assi[st]ance than past Deliverance; for what ground or reason can I have to distrust the Kindness of that Person who hath always been my Friend and Benefactor? On whom can I better rely for assistance in the day of my Distress, than on him who stood by me in all mine Affliction: And when I was at the very brink of destruction, delivered me out of all my Troubles? Would it not be highly ingrateful, and reflect either upon his Goodness or Sufficiency, to distrust that Providence which hath always had a watchful eye over me; and who, according to his gracious Promises, would never yet leave me nor forsake me? I may, with good ground, depend upon him for relief, who hath been more ready to give, than I to ask; and whose divine Inclinations have been always towards me to do me good; and I may surely trust that God of Mercies, who hath already been so plentiful in his Distribution towards me. *If the former and the latter rain have* hitherto *descended upon the earth in due season, and seed-time, and harvest have never yet fail'd*, why should I not still expect the Fruit of the Earth at it's appointed time? Or, for what reason should I fear either Famine or Scarcity of Bread in the Land?

pp. 21–2

And indeed a stronger argument cannot be brought for future trust, than the remembrance of past protection;—for what ground or reason can I have to distrust the kindness of that person, who has always been my friend and benefactor?

On whom can I better rely for assistance in the day of my distress, than on him who stood by me in all mine affliction?—and, when I was at the brink of destruction, delivered me out of all my troubles? Would it not be highly ungrateful, and reflect either upon his goodness or his sufficiency, to distrust that providence which has always had a watchful eye over me? —and who, according to his gracious promises, will never leave me, nor forsake me; and who, in all my wants, in all my emergencies, has been abundantly more willing to give, than I to ask it.—If the former and the latter rain have hitherto descended upon the earth in due season, and seed time and harvest have never yet failed;—why should I fear famine in the land, or doubt, but that he who feedeth the raven, and providently catereth for the sparrow, should likewise be my comfort?—How unlikely is it that ever he should suffer his truth to fail?

Sermons, II, 12, p. 149

. . . the Psalmist acquaints [us] that his sufferings were . . . grievous;—*That his feet were hurt with fetters*, and the iron entered *even into his soul.*

Cf. p. 452

. . . *Joseph*, whose Feet lay in the Stocks till the Iron entred into his Soul . . . .

pp. 461–4

. . . let us call to mind the loving Kindnesses which we have received of old, and remember the later gracious Vouchsafements of the Almighty. There's not one, I dare say, amongst this numerous Assembly, but can give several Instances of God's Power and his Arm over him; and

Sermons, VI, 7 (34), pp. 25–9

. . . where is the man . . . who looks back . . . upon what has thus happened to him, who could not give you sufficient proofs of God's power, and his arm over him, and recount several cases, wherein the God of Jacob was his help, and the Holy One of Israel his redeemer?

9. Sterne follows Leightonhouse's free rendering of the text rather than the King James version.

could enumerate several Cases wherein *the God of Jacob was his help*, and the *holy one of Israel his Redeemer*. Hast thou ever laid upon the Bed of Languishing, or laboured under any grievous Distemper? Call to mind thy sorrowful pensive Spirit at that time, and add to it, who it was that had *Mercy on thee, that brought thee out of darkness, and the shadow of death, and made all thy bed in thy sickness*. Hath the scantiness of thy Condition hurried thee into great Straights and Difficulties, and brought thee *almost to thy wits end?* Consider who it was that spread thy Table in that Wilderness of Thoughts, and made thy Cup to overflow; who it was that added a Friend of Consolation to thee, and thereby *spake Peace to thy troubled Mind*. Hast thou ever sustained any considerable Damage in thy Stock, or thy Trade? Bethink thy self who it was that repaired those Breaches; or, that gave a serene and contented Mind under those Losses. Hast thou ever been wounded in thy more tender Parts, through the loss of an obliging Husband, or an endearing Friend, or a promising child? Consider whether the *God of Truth* did not approve himself *a Father to thee* when *Fatherless,* or *an Husband* when a *Widow:* and has either *given thee a Name better than of Sons or Daughters,* (or even beyond thy Hopes) made thy remaining tender Branches to grow up tall and glorious, like the *Cedars of Libanus.*

And let the Consideration of these and the like past Deliverances, either to thy Self, Friends, or Acquaintance, keep thee from Fainting, and encourage the[e] to put thy Trust in the Lord for future Mercies. . . . In a Word, let us *hope, even beyond hope* . . . and engage God to be our Redeemer, by an absolute and entire Dependence upon him in our greatest Wants . . . And *although the Figtree should not blossom, neither should Fruit be in the Vine; although the Labour of the Olive should fail, and the Fields should yield no Meat; although the Flock should be cut off from the Fold, and there should be no Herd in the Stalls; yet let us rejoyce in the Lord, let us joy in the God of our Salvation.*

To whom be all Honour, and Glory, now and for ever. AMEN.

Hast thou ever laid upon the bed of languishing, or laboured under a grievous distemper which threatened thy life? Call to mind thy sorrowful and pensive spirit at that time; and add to it, who it was that had mercy on thee, that brought thee out of darkness and the shadow of death, and made all thy bed in thy sickness.—

Hath the scantiness of thy condition hurried thee into great straits and difficulties, and brought thee almost to distraction?—Consider who it was that spread thy table in that wilderness of thought,—who was it made thy cup to overflow,—who added a friend of consolation to thee, and thereby spake peace to thy troubled mind.—Hast thou ever sustained any considerable damage in thy stock or trade?—Bethink thyself who it was that gave thee a serene and contented mind under those losses.—If thou hast recovered,—consider who it was that repaired those breaches,—when thy own skill and endeavours failed . . . . Hast thou ever been wounded in thy more tender parts, through the loss of an obliging husband? —or hast thou been torn away from the embraces of a dear and promising child, by its unexpected death?—

O consider, whether the God of truth did not approve himself a father to thee, when fatherless,—or a husband to thee, when a widow,—and has either given thee a name better than of sons and daughters, or even beyond thy hope, made thy remaining tender branches to grow up tall and beautiful, like the cedars of Libanus.—

Strengthened by these considerations, suggesting the same or like past deliverances, either to thyself,—thy friends or acquaintance,—thou wilt learn this great lesson in the text, in all thy exigencies and difficulties,—to trust God; and whatever befalls thee . . . to speak comfort to thy soul, and to say in the words of Habakkuk the prophet, with which I conclude,—

Although the fig-tree shall not blossom, neither shall fruit be in the vines;— although the labour of the olive shall fail, and the fields shall yield no meat;— although the flock shall be cut off from the fold, and there shall be no herd in the stalls; yet we will rejoice in the Lord, and joy in the God of our salvation.—[1]

To whom be all honour and glory, now and for ever. Amen.

---

1. See Habakkuk, 3.17–18. See also *Life,* pp. 505–06.

JOHN LOCKE (1632–1704)

LOCKE

Essay Concerning Human Understanding,
chap. iii, sec. **25**[2]

I doubt not but if we could discover the figure, size, texture, and motion of the minute constituent parts of any two bodies we should know without trial several of their operations one upon another . . . . Did we know the mechanical affections of the particles of rhubarb, hemlock, opium, and a man . . . we should be able to tell beforehand that rhubarb will purge, hemlock kill, and opium make a man sleep . . . .

chap, x, sec. 1

Though God has given us no innate ideas of himself . . . yet having furnished us with those faculties our minds are endowed with, he hath not left himself without witness: since we have sense, perception, and reason, and cannot want a clear proof of him, as long as we carry *ourselves* about us. Nor can we justly complain of our ignorance in this great point; since he has so plentifully provided us with the means to discover and know him; so far as is necessary to the end of our being, and the great concernment of our happiness.

Cf. *The Reasonableness of Christianity,*
sec. 166[3]

. . . the wisdom and goodness of God has shown itself so visibly to common apprehensions, that it hath furnished us abundantly wherewithal to satisfy the curious and inquisitive.

Cf. sec. 167

Though the works of nature, in every part of them, sufficiently evidence a Deity, yet the world made so little use of their reason, that they saw him not, where even by the impressions of himself he was easy to be found.

STERNE

Sermons, VII, 17 (44), pp. 133–4

Can the deepest enquirers after nature tell us, upon what particular size and motion of parts the various colours and tastes of vegetables depend;—why one shrub is laxative,—another restringent;—why arsenic or hellbore should lay waste this noble frame of ours—or opium lock up all the inroads to our senses,—and plunder us in so merciless a manner of reason and understanding?

Sermons, IV, 11 (26), pp. 145–6

————*The invisible things of him from the creation of the world might be clearly seen and understood, by the things that are made;*————*that is,*————Tho' God by the clearest discovery of himself, had ever laid before mankind such evident proofs of his eternal Being . . . so that what is to be known of his invisible nature, might all along be traced by the marks of his goodness,————and the visible frame and order of the world:————yet . . . tho' they knew God, and saw his image and superscription in every part of his works . . . . So bad a use did they make of the powers given them for this great discovery, that . . . they fell into . . . delusions.

2. Page references are to *An Essay Concerning Human Understanding,* Fraser, A. C., ed. (Oxford, 1894, 2 vols.), Bk. IV.
3. Cf. MacLean, *John Locke and English Literature of the Eighteenth Century,* p. 138.

Essay Concerning Human Understanding, chap. xix, sec. 5

Immediate revelation being a much easier way for men to establish their opinions and regulate their conduct, than the tedious and not always successful labour of strict reasoning, it is no wonder that some have been very apt to pretend to revelation, and to persuade themselves that they are under the peculiar guidance of heaven in their actions and opinions, especially in those of them which they cannot account for by the ordinary methods of knowledge and principles of reason. Hence we see, that, in all ages, men in whom melancholy has mixed with devotion, or whose conceit of themselves has raised them into an opinion of a greater familiarity with God . . . than is afforded to others, have often flattered themselves with a persuasion of an immediate intercourse with the Deity, and frequent communications from the Divine Spirit.

sec. 8

. . . the odd opinions and extravagant actions enthusiasm has run men into were enough to warn them against this wrong principle . . . .

sec. 6

Their minds being thus prepared, whatever groundless opinion comes to settle itself strongly upon their fancies, is an illumination from the Spirit of God, and presently of divine authority: and whatsoever odd action they find in themselves a strong inclination to do, that impulse is concluded to be a call or direction from heaven, and must be obeyed: it is a commission from above, and they cannot err in executing it.

sec. 7

This I take to be properly *enthusiasm,* which, though founded neither on reason nor divine revelation, but rising from the conceits of a warmed or overweening brain, works yet, where it once gets footing, more powerfully on the persuasions and actions of men than either of those two, or both together . . . .

sec. 14

If he [God] would have us assent to the truth of any proposition, he either evi-

Sermons II, 14, pp. 205–06

The last mistake which . . . has misled thousands before these days wherever enthusiasm has got footing . . . is,—the attempting to prove their works, by . . . that extraordinary impulse and intercourse with the Spirit of God which they pretend to . . . . This, I own, is one of the most summary ways of proceeding in this duty of self-examination, and as it proves a man's work in the gross, it saves him a world of sober thought and enquiry after many vexatious particulars.

Sermons, VI, 10 (37), pp. 88–9

Strange force of enthusiasm!—and yet not altogether unaccountable.—For what opinion was there ever so odd, or action so extravagant, which has not, at one time or other, been produced by ignorance,—conceit,—melancholy . . . .

p. 89

When the minds of men happen to be thus unfortunately prepared, whatever groundless doctrine rises up, and settles itself strongly upon their fancies, has generally the ill-luck to be interpreted as an illumination from the spirit of God;—and whatever strange action they find in themselves a strong inclination to do,—that impulse is concluded to be a call from heaven; and consequently,—that they cannot err in executing it.—

Sermons, VI, 11 (38), p. 146

Did these visionary notions of an heated imagination tend only to amuse the fancy, they might be treated with contempt . . . .

dences that truth by the usual methods of natural reason, or else makes it known to be a truth . . . and convinces us that it is from him, by some marks which reason cannot be mistaken in. . . . Every conceit that thoroughly warms our fancies must pass for an inspiration, if there be nothing but the strength of our persuasions, whereby to judge of our persuasions . . . .

Some Thoughts Concerning Education,
sec. 93[4]

The Character of a Sober Man and a Scholar, is . . . what every one expects in a Tutor. This generally is thought enough and is all that Parents commonly look for. But when such an one has emptied out into his Pupil all the Latin, and Logick, he has brought from the University, will that Furniture make him a fine Gentleman?

sec. 212

I confess *Travel* into Foreign Countries has great Advantages, but the time usually chosen to send young Men abroad, is I think, of all other, that which renders them least capable of reaping those Advantages. Those which are propos'd . . . may be reduced to these Two, first Language, secondly an Improvement in Wisdom and Prudence, by seeing Men, and conversing with People of Tempers, Customs, and Ways of living, different from . . . those of his Parish and Neighbourhood.

sec. 213

The time therefore I should think the fittest for a young Gentleman to be *sent abroad,* would be . . . when he is some Years older . . . [and] being thoroughly acquainted with the Laws and Fashions, the natural and moral Advantages and Defects of his own Country, he has something to exchange, with those abroad, from whose Conversation he hoped to reap any Knowledge.

pp. 144–5

Faith, the distinguishing characterstick of a christian, is defined by them not as a rational assent of the understanding, to truths which are established by indisputable authority, but as a violent persuasion of mind . . . .

Sermons, III, 5 (20), p. 155

But you will send an able pilot with your son————a scholar.————

If wisdom can speak in no other language but Greek or Latin,————you do well————or if mathematicks will make a man a gentleman,————or natural philosophy but teach him to make a bow, ————he may be of some service . . . .

pp. 152–4

. . . the passion [for travelling] is no way bad,————but as others are,————in it's mismanagement or excess;————order it rightly the advantages are worth the pursuit; the chief of which are————to learn the languages, the laws and customs, and understand the government and interest of other nations,————to acquire an urbanity and confidence of behaviour . . . to take us out of the company of our aunts and grandmothers, and . . . by shewing us new objects, or old ones in new lights, to reform our judgments . . . .

This is some part of the cargo we might return with; but the impulse of seeing new sights . . . carries our youth too early out, to turn this venture to much account . . . .

pp. 159–60

Conversation is a traffick; and if you enter into it, without some stock of knowledge, to ballance the account perpetually betwixt you,————the trade drops at once: and this is the reason . . . why travellers have so little (especially good) conversation with natives,————owing to their suspicion,—or perhaps conviction, that there is nothing to be extracted from the conversation of young itinerants, worth the trouble of their bad language,—or the interruption of their visits.

---

4. The text here used is that of the fifth edition, enlarged, published in London, 1705.

sec. 215

. . . amongst our young Men, that go abroad under Tutors, what one is there of an hundred, that ever visits any Person of Quality? much less makes an Acquaintance with such, from whose Conversation he may learn, what is good Breeding in that Country, and what is worth observation in it, Though from such Persons it is, one may learn more in one Day, than in a Years rambling from one Inn to another. Nor indeed is it to be wondred. For Men of Worth and Parts will not easily admit the Familiarity of Boys . . . .

pp. 156–9

. . . he [the youth] shall be escorted by one who knows the world . . . he will learn the amount to a halfpenny, of every stage from Calais to Rome;—he will be carried to the best inns,—instructed where there is the best wine . . . .

—And here endeth his pride—his knowledge and his use.

But when your son gets abroad, he will be taken out of his [tutor's] hand, by his society with men of rank and letters, with whom he will pass the greatest part of his time.

Let me observe . . . that company which is really good, is very rare—and very shy . . . .

There is nothing in which we are so much deceived, as in the advantages proposed from our connections with the literati, &c. in foreign parts; especially if the experiment is made before we are matured by years or study.

The Reasonableness of Christianity, sec. 167

In this state of darkness and ignorance [before the coming of Christ] of the true God, vice and superstition held the world; nor could any help be had or hoped for from reason, which could not be heard, and was judged to have nothing to do in the case. . . . And in the crowd of wrong notions, and invented rites, the world had almost lost the sight of the one only true God. The rational and thinking part of mankind, it is true, when they sought after him, found . . . God; but if they acknowledged and worshipped him, it was only in their own minds. . . . Hence we see that reason, speaking never so clearly to the wise and virtuous, had never authority enough to prevail on the multitude. . . .

Sermons, IV, 11 (26), pp. 154–6

Here let us stop a moment and enquire, what was Reason doing all this time, to be so miserably insulted and abused? Where held she her empire whilst her bulwarks were thus born down . . . ?

But tho' reason, you'll say, could not overthrow these popular mistakes,—yet it saw the folly of them, and was at all times able to disprove them.

No doubt it was; and it is certain too, that the more diligent enquirers after truth, did not in fact fall into these absured notions, which by the way, is an observation more to our purpose than theirs, who usually make it, and shews that tho' their reasonings were good, that there always wanted something which they could not supply to give them such weight, as would lay an obligation upon mankind to embrace them, and make that to be a law, which otherwise was but an opinion without force.

sec. 170

. . . it is too hard a task for unassisted reason, to establish morality, in all its parts, upon its true foundations, with a clear and convincing light. . . .

. . . human reason unassisted, failed men in its great and proper business of morality.

pp. 158–9

That the necessities of society, and the impossibilities of its subsisting otherwise, would point out the convenience, or if you will,—the duty of social virtues, is unquestionable:—but I firmly deny, that therefore religion and morality are independent of each other . . . . I cannot conceive how the one . . . can act without the influence of the other . . . .

JOHN NORRIS (1657–1711)

NORRIS	STERNE

"Discourse the Sixth," p. 136[5]

Sermons, v, 2 (29), pp. 38–9

And here not to feign a long Hypothesis of a Sinners being admitted into Heaven, with a particular Description of his Condition and Behaviour there, we need only consider that the Supreme Good is of a *Relative* Nature, as well as any other Good, and consequently the enjoyment of it must necessarily require some Qualification in the Faculty, as well as the enjoyment of any other Good does, something that may render that Good a Good to that particular Faculty. Otherwise tho it may be *possess'd*, yet it can never be *enjoy'd*.

And here, not to feign a long hypothesis, as some have done, of a sinner's being admitted into heaven, with a particular description of his condition and behaviour there,—we need only consider, that the supreme good, like any other good, is of a relative nature, and consequently the enjoyment of it must require some qualification in the faculty, as well as the enjoyment of any other good does;—there must be something antecedent in the disposition and temper, which will render that good a good to that individual,—otherwise though (it is true) it may be possessed,—yet it never can be enjoyed.—

p. 137[6]

pp. 41–3

We see that even in this Life, 'tis very tedious to be in the Company of a Person whose Humour is disagreeable to ours, tho perhaps in other respects of sufficient Worth and Excellency. And how then can we imagine that an ill-disposed Soul should take any Pleasure in God, who is to her infinitely more unlike, and therefore disagreeable, than one Man can be supposed to be to another? For my part, I rather think that should an impure Soul be afforded a Mansion in Heaven, she would be so far from being happy in it, that she would do *Penance* there to all Eternity. For besides that a sensualized Soul would carry such Appetites with her thither for which she could find no suitable Object, which would be a constant Torment; those that she *does* find there would be so disproportionate, that they would rather vex and upbraid, then satisfie her Indigence.

We see, even in the common intercourses of society,—how tedious it is to be in the company of a person whose humour is disagreeable to our own, though perhaps in all other respects of the greatest worth and excellency.—How then can we imagine that an ill-disposed soul . . . should hereafter take pleasure in God . . . ? The consideration of this has led some writers so far, as to say, with some degree of irreverence in the expression,—that it was not in the power of God to make a wicked man happy, if the soul was separated from the body, with all its vicious habits and inclinations unreformed;—which thought, a very able divine in our church has pursued so far, as to declare his belief,—that could the happiest mansion in heaven be supposed to be allotted to a gross and polluted spirit, it would be so far from being happy in it, that it would do penance there to all eternity:—by which he meant, it would carry such appetites along with it, for which there could be found no suitable objects.—A sufficient cause for constant

5. Page references are to the *Practical Discourses upon the Beatitudes* (4th ed. London, 1699).

6. Cf. Tillotson's *Sermons*, Vol. I, No. 8, quoted from, below, pp. 159–60. Also, Clarke, *Sermons*, Vol. VII, No. 5, quoted above, p. 116.

torment;—for those that it found there, would be so disproportioned, that they would rather vex and upbraid it, than satisfy its wants.—

Sermons, v, 1 (28), pp. 21–3

. . . let us not forget that greatest of all happiness, which the text refers to,—. . . peace and content of mind, arising from the consciousness of virtue, . . . and where that is wanting, whatever other enjoyments you bestow upon a wicked man, they will as soon add a cubit to his stature as to his happiness.—In the midst of the highest entertainments,—this, like the handwriting upon the wall, will be enough to spoil and disrelish the feast;—but much more so, when the tumult and hurry of delight is over,—when all is still and silent,—when the sinner has nothing to do but attend its lashes and remorses;—and this, in spite of all the common arts of diversion, will be often the case of every wicked man;—for we can not live always upon the stretch;—our faculties will not bear constant pleasure any more than constant pain;—there will be some vacancies; and when there are, they will be sure to be filled with uncomfortable thoughts and black reflections.—So that, setting aside the great after-reckoning, the pleasures of the wicked are over-bought, even in this world.—

"The Importance of a Religious Life, Considered," pp. 110–11[7]

Indeed a bad Conscience is a Companion troublesome enough even in the midst of the most high-set Enjoyments; 'tis then like the *Hand writing* upon the Wall, enough to spoil and disrelish the *Feast;* but much more when the tumult and hurry of Delight is over, when all is still and silent, when the Sinner has nothing to do, but attend to its lashes and remorses. And this in spite of all the common Arts of Diversion, will be very often the case of every wicked Man; for we cannot live always upon the *Stretch;* our Faculties will not bear constant Pleasure any more than constant Pain; there will be some *Vacancies,* and when there are, they will be sure to be filled up with uncomfortable Thoughts and black Reflections . . . . So that setting aside the great *After-reckoning,* its Pleasures are over-bought even in this World . . . .

p. 111

. . . the practice of . . . Vertue . . . is not destitute even of a *Present* Reward, but carries in hand a sufficient Recompense for all the troubles she occasions. She is pleasant in the *Way* as well as in the *End,* for even her very Ways are Ways of Pleasantness, and all her Paths are Peace. But 'tis her greatest and most distinguishing Glory and Commendation, that she befriends us *Hereafter,* and brings us Peace at the last. And this is a Portion she can never be dis-inherited of, however the Malice of Men or an ill Combination of Accidents may defraud her of the Other.

pp. 25–6

. . . virtue is not even destitute of a present reward,—but carries in her hand a sufficient recompence for all the self-denials she may occasion:—she is pleasant in the way,—as well as in the end;—her ways being ways of pleasantness, and all her paths peace.—But it is her greatest and most distinguished glory,—that she befriends us hereafter, and brings us peace at the last;—and this is a portion she can never be disinherited of,—which may God of his mercy grant us all, for the sake of Jesus Christ.

p. 131

. . . we are generally more impatient of what reflects upon our *Intellectuals,* than of what reflects upon our *Morals.* But cer-

Sermons, iv, 11 (26), pp. 139–40

Strange souls that we are! as if to live well *was* not the greatest argument of Wisdom;—and, as if what reflected upon

7. Page references are to the *Practical Discourses upon Several Divine Subjects,* ii.

tainly to Live well, is the greatest argument of Wisdom, and that which reflects upon our Morals, reflects most of all upon our Understandings.

our morals, did not most of all reflect upon our understandings!

"A Discourse Concerning the Folly of Covetousness," p. 204[8]

Sermons, I, 1, pp. 22-3

. . . and if we do by any extraordinary Fortune meet with any thing in this World that can a little cool and allay the heat of our great Thirst, and refresh the drought of our Spirit, yet we are assured by our Saviour who well understood the World, though he enjoyed but little of it, *John* 4.13. that *Whosoever drinks* . . . And we all find by repeated Experiences, that 'tis so, and our Reason tells us it must be so . . . .

And tho' in our pilgrimage through *this* world—some of us may be so fortunate as to meet with some clear fountains by the way, that may cool for a few moments, the heat of this great thirst of happiness—yet our Saviour, who knew the world, tho' he enjoyed but little of it, tells us, that whosoever drinketh of this water will thirst again:—and we all find by experience it is so, and by reason that it must always be so.

pp. 209-10

Sermons, IV, 8 (23), p. 57

. . . generally are Men most Covetous . . . when they have most Wealth . . . [and are] . . . the more *Empty* for being Full . . . . Strange, that Men should *contract* their *Spirits* upon the *inlargement* of their *Fortunes!* Many indeed are the Temptations and Snares of Wealth; but of all Vices one would think it should not dispose Men to Covetousness, but rather be an Antidote against it . . . .

. . . nay, what is strange, do they [riches] not often tempt men even to covetousness; and tho' amidst all the ill offices which riches do us, one would last suspect this vice, but rather think the one a cure for the other; yet so it is, that many a man contracts his spirits upon the enlargement of his fortune, and is the more empty for being full.

Cf. "A Discourse Concerning Doing God's Will on Earth," p. 272[9]

Sermons, V, 1 (28), p. 12

. . . God is so good and kind as to enjoyn nothing but what is pursuant of the End for which he Created us; that is, our Happiness and Perfection: So kind as to link our Duty and Interest together, and to make those very things the Instances of our Obedience, which are the natural Means, and necessary Causes of our Happiness: So that were we to contrive a way to make our Condition Happy, we could pitch upon no better than what he has already prescribed to us in the Laws which he has given us. So highly consonant and *agreeable* are they to the frame of our Natures, and so absolutely *necessary* are they both to the order of this present World, and to the Happiness of the next.

And in this does the reasonableness of christianity, and the beauty and wisdom of providence appear most eminently towards mankind, in governing us by such laws, as do most apparently tend to make us happy,—and in a word, in making that (in his mercy) to be our duty, which in his wisdom he knows to be our interest . . . .

pp. 11-12

. . . insomuch,—that could we . . . chuse the laws ourselves which we would be bound to observe, it would be impossible for the wit of man to frame any other proposals, which upon all accounts would be more advantageous to our own interests than those very conditions to which we are obliged by the rules of religion and virtue.

---

8. This and the following sermon are also contained in *ibid.*
9. Cf. Tillotson, *Sermons*, Vol. I, No. 6, quoted below, p. 156.

JOHN ROGERS (1679–1729)

ROGERS

Sermon 12, pp. 332–3[1]

Pride was the Passion which made that fatal Breach upon our Innocence, at which Sin and Misery enter'd, and gave our Enemy the Triumph of ruining our Nature. When therefore the Son of God became manifest in the Flesh, to undo this Work of the Devil, he began our Regeneration, by endeavouring to restore the Soul to its original Temper and Humility. Agreeably in his first publick Address to his Followers, we find an Exhortation to this Virtue, as a Disposition necessary to prepare them to be his Disciples: *Blessed are the Poor in Spirit, for theirs is the Kingdom of God.*

p. 336

'Tis our Pride gives a Point to Injuries and Affronts. 'Tis an Opinion of our Merit, and Right to the Observance of the World, that gives every slight Occasion the Power of raising that Ferment in the Soul.

pp. 339–43

. . . it is from Christ we must learn Humility.
But especially are we to learn it from him, because he not only prescrib'd this Virtue, but was himself meek and lowly, the great Pattern and Example of it. . . . Humility is a Virtue which shines with a peculiar Eminence in his Example, and is exhibited to us in every part of his Life and Character. . . . the blessed Jesus came not in a Character to share the Pleasures or Glories of Life with us, to be a Prince or a Ruler on Earth: No, The Meanness of his Birth, the Toils and Indigence of his Life, and the Shame and Ignominy of his Death, are all convincing Arguments that his Kingdom was not of this World. . . . he voluntarily . . .

STERNE

Sermons, IV, 10 (25), p. 119

It is observed by some one, that as pride was the passion through which sin and misery entered the world, and gave our enemy the triumph of ruining our nature, that therefore the Son of God, who came to seek and to save that which was lost, when he entered upon the work of our restoration, he began at the very point where he knew we had failed; and this he did, by endeavouring to bring the soul of man back to it's original temper of Humility; so that his first publick address from the Mount began with a declaration of blessedness to the poor in spirit . . . .

pp. 107–08

With regard to the provocations and offenses, which are unavoidably happening to a man . . . take it as a rule,—as a man's pride is,—so is always his displeasure;—as the opinion of himself rises, —so does the injury,—so does his resentment: 'tis this which gives edge and force to the instrument which has struck him,—and excites that heat in the wound, which renders it incurable.

pp. 120–22

. . . every believer must receive some tincture of the character [of Humility] . . . from the example of so great, and yet so humble a Master, whose whole course of life was a particular lecture to this one virtue; and in every instance of it shewed, that he came not to share the pride and glories of life . . . but . . . appearing himself rather as a servant than a master,—coming, as he continually declared, not to be ministered unto, but to minister; and as the Prophet had foretold in that mournful description of him,—

---

1. The text used here is the one-volume edition of *Twelve Sermons, Preached upon Several Occasions,* by John Rogers, D.D., Late Vicar of St. Giles Cripplegate . . . and Chaplain in Ordinary to his Majesty. A note in the text states that this sermon was "Preach'd before his Majesty at the Royal Chapel at St. James's, April 20th 1729, being the last Sermon the Author preached."

took upon him the Form of a Servant, and, as the Prophet had foretold in that mournful Description of him, he had no Form nor Comliness, nor any Beauty, that we should desire him. . . . [He] submitted to a Condition, below even the common Provisions of Life: *Foxes had Holes, and the Birds of the Air Nests, but the Son of God had not where to lay his Head.* . . . *He came not,* as he says, *to be minister'd unto, but to minister, and to give his Life a Ransom for many.* He gave his Life, and with amazing Resignation humbled himself to the Death of the Cross, the Death of a Slave and a Malefactor.

pp. 348–9

. . . If we expect to find Happiness, we must seek for it at Home, and lay the Foundation of it in our own Humility. . . . The far greater Part of the Miseries we complain of, we create to ourselves. Passion and Impatience hurry us on from one Disquiet to another, the Spur is ever in our Side, and will not suffer us to rest.

p. 350

The Humble provokes no Enemy by Contempt, none by Censure, none by Envy. . . .

p. 358
　A Soul thus resign'd, is carried smoothly down the Stream of Providence; no Temptations of the Passage disquiet him with Desire, and no Dangers alarm his Fears.

to have no form, or comeliness, nor any beauty that they should desire him. The voluntary meanness of his birth,—the poverty of his life,—the low offices in which it was engaged . . . the inconveniences which attended the execution of it, in having no where to lay his head,—all spoke the same language; . . . the tender and pathetick proof he gave of the same disposition at the conclusion and great catastrophe of his suffering,—when a life full of so many instances of humility was crowned with the most endearing one of *humbling himself even to the death of the cross;*—the death of a slave, —a malefactor—drag'd to *Calvary* without opposition,—insulted without complaint.—

p. 106, pp. 110–11

—Rest unto our souls! . . . we have been seeking every where for it, but where there was a prospect of finding it; and that is, within ourselves, in a meek and lowly disposition of heart.
[Men] are so incessantly tortured with the disappointments which their pride and passions have created for them, that tho' they appear to have all the ingredients of happiness in their hands,—they can neither compound or use them:— How should they? the goad is ever in their sides, and so hurries them on from one expectation to another, as to leave them no rest day or night.

p. 108

. . . the humble man . . . provokes no man by contempt; thrusts himself forward as the mark of no man's envy . . . .

p. 118

　A soul thus turned and resigned, is carried smoothly down the stream of providence; no temptations in his passage disquiet him with desire,—no dangers alarm him with fear . . . .

RICHARD STEELE (1672–1729)

STEELE

STERNE

Sermons, II, 15, p. 238

chap. iii, p. 54[2]

The Cordial Drop Heav'n in our Cup has thrown,
To make the nauseous Draught of Life go down.

. . . there is scarce any lot so low, but there is something in it to satisfy the man whom it has befallen; providence having so ordered things, that in every man's *cup,* how bitter soever, there are some cordial drops—some good circumstances, which if wisely extracted are sufficient for the purpose he wants them,—that is, to make him contented, and if not happy, at least resigned.

chap. iv, p. 70

Sermons, II, 12, pp. 156–8

. . . to forgive is the most arduous Pitch human Nature can arrive at; a Coward has often fought, a Coward has often conquer'd, but *a Coward never forgave.* The power of doing that flows from a Strength of Soul conscious of its own Force, whence it draws a certain Safety which its Enemy is not of Consideration enough to interrupt . . . .

. . . when the Mind is in the Contemplation of Revenge, all its Thoughts must surely be tortured with the alternate Pangs of Rancour, Envy, Hatred, and Indignation . . . .

—The brave know only how to forgive;—it is the most refined and generous pitch of virtue, human nature can arrive at.—[3] Cowards have done good and kind actions,—cowards have even fought—nay sometimes even conquered;—but a coward never forgave.—It is not in his nature;—the power of doing it flows only from a strength and greatness of soul, conscious of its own force and security, and above the little temptations of resenting every fruitless attempt to interrupt its happiness. Moreover . . . he [Joseph] was the truest friend likewise to his own happiness and peace of mind; he neither felt that fretful storm of passions, which hurry men on to acts of revenge, or suffered those pangs of horror which pursue it.

. . . the neglected and despised Tenets of Religion are so generous, and in so transcendant and heroic a manner disposed for public Good, that . . . the Christian is as much inclined to your Service when your Enemy, as the moral Man when your Friend.

In this, the excellency of the gospel is said by some one, to appear with a remarkable advantage; "That a christian is as much disposed to love and serve you, when your enemy, as the mere moral man can be, when he is your friend."

2. Page references are to *The Christian Hero* (London, 1766).
3. Sterne inserted a footnote reference here: "Christian hero."

EDWARD STILLINGFLEET (1635–99)

STILLINGFLEET

STERNE

Sermon 15, "Preached before the King, February 24. 1674/5," p. 217[4]

Sermons, v, 6 (33), p. 150

. . . what can we suppose to have greater force and efficacy to restrain men from sin, than what is contained in these fundamentals of Christianity? But we shall find that no *Motives* have ever *been* great enough to restrain those from sin, who have secretly loved it, and only sought pretences for the practice of it.

. . . the wickedness either of the present or past times . . . ought not in reason to reflect dishonour upon christianity, which is so . . . well framed to make us good . . . .

p. 152

. . . the truth of the case being this,— that no motives have been great enough to restrain those from sin who have secretly loved it, and only sought pretences for the practice of it.

Such is the frame and condition of humane nature considered in itself . . . so much stronger are the natural motives to vertue than to vice, that they who look no farther, would expect to find the world much better than it is. For why should we suppose the generality of mankind to betray so much folly, as to act unreasonably and against the common interest of their own kind? as all those do, that yield to the temptations of sin . . . . But on the other side, if men first look into the practice of the World, and there observe the strange prevalency of Vice, and how willing men are to defend as well as to commit it; they would be apt to imagine that either there is no such thing as Reason among men, or that it hath very little influence upon their actions . . . .

pp. 151–2

. . . whoever considers the state and condition of human nature, and upon this view, how much stronger the natural motives are to virtue than to vice, would expect to find the world much better than it is, or ever has been.—For who would suppose the generality of mankind to betray so much folly, as to act against the common interest of their own kind, as every man does who yields to the temptation of what is wrong.—But on the other side,—if men first look into the practice of the world, and there observe the strange prevalency of vice, and how willing men are to defend as well as to commit it,— one would think they believed that all discourses of virtue and honesty were mere matter of speculation for men to entertain some idle hours with;—and say truly, that men seemed universally to be agreed in nothing but in speaking well and doing ill. But this casts no more dishonour upon reason than it does upon revelation . . . .

p. 219

Others think, that all discourses of vertue, and honesty, and true honour, are meer matter of talk for men to entertain some idle hours with, and that men are universally agreed in nothing but in speaking well and doing ill . . . .

Sermons, IV, 11 (26), pp. 159–62

. . . I firmly deny, that . . . religion and morality are independent of each other: they appear so far from it, that I cannot conceive how the one . . . can act without the influence of the other . . . .

Cf. Sermon 15, pp. 218–19

When once the people [of Greece and Rome] had swallowed that pernicious

4. Page references are to *Fifty Sermons Preached upon Several Occasions* (London, 1707). This volume is the first in a folio edition of *The Works of That Eminent and most Learned Prelate, Dr. Edw. Stillingfleet.*

principle, that Morality was no part of their Religion, they had no great regard to the good or evil of their actions . . . . And they were much more encouraged in Wickedness, when the Gods they worshipped were represented on the stage as acting all manner of villainies: and no doubt they thought it a great comfort to them in their debaucheries, that their Gods were as *good fellows* as themselves . . . .

But with different conceptions of the Deity, or such impure ones as they [the ancients] entertained, it is to be doubted whether . . . we should not determine our cases of conscience with much the same kind of casuistry as that of the Libertine in Terence, who . . . argued the matter thus within himself.—If the great Jupiter could not refrain his appetites . . . shall I a mortal . . . pretend to a virtue, which the Father of gods and men could not?

It will scarce admit of a question, Whether vice would not naturally grow bold upon the credit of such an example; or whether such impressions did not influence the lives and morals of many in the heathen world . . . .

Sermon 15, pp. 227–8

. . . From their *present Impunity* in sinning, men are apt to deceive themselves into a continuance in it. This is the account the Wise man hath long since given of mens being hardned in sin; *Because sentence against an evil is not executed speedily; therefore the hearts of the sons of men is fully set in them to do evil*. It seems somewhat hard to understand the consequence, why men should grow more desperately wicked, because God gives them a space to repent? Is it necessary that if God doth punish at all, he must do it presently? that would seem to be rage and fury, or a necessity of nature, and not justice. . . . Why may not God respite the punishment of sinners, when he pleases, to another state, since he hath declared *that he hath appointed a day wherein he will judge the World in righteousness*? . . . . Will . . . **not the** day of his future judgment be a full vindication of his justice? . . . . But all this false way of reasoning ariseth from that gross piece of self-flattery that such do imagine God to be like themselves; *i.e.* as cruel and revengefull as they are: and they presently think, if any persons did offend them at the rate that sinners are said to offend God, and they had so much power in their hands to punish them as he has . . . they would be sure to dispatch them presently; but because they see God doth it not, therefore they conclude that all the talk of God's anger and hatred against sin is without ground: and from hence they take encouragement to sin. So the Psalmist saith in God's name,

Sermons, v, 6 (33), pp. 155–62

To begin with Solomon's account in the text,—that because sentence against an evil work is not executed speedily, therefore the hearts of the sons of men are fully set in them to do evil.—

It seems somewhat hard to understand the consequence, why men should grow more desperately wicked,—because God is merciful and gives them space to repent . . . . Because a vicious man escapes at present, he is apt to draw false conclusions from it . . . as if it was necessary, if God is to punish at all, that he must do it presently; which by the way, would rather seem to bespeak rage and fury of an incensed party, than the determination of a wise and patient judge,— who respites punishment to another state, declaring for the wisest reasons, this is not the time for it to take place in,—but that he has appointed a day for it, wherein he will judge the world in righteousness . . . as to render his future judgment a full vindication of his justice. . . .

Now if you consider, you will find, that all this false way of reasoning doth arise from that gross piece of self-flattery, that such do imagine God to be like themselves, —that is, as cruel and revengeful as they are,—and they presently think, if a fellow creature offended them at the rate that sinners are said to offend God, and they had as much power in their hands to punish and torture them as he has, they would be sure to execute it speedily;— but because they see God does it not, therefore they conclude, that all the talk of God's anger against vice, and his fu-

These things thou didst and I kept silence; and they presently took his *silence* for *consent;* for it follows, and *thou thoughtest that I was altogether such a one as thy self:* but the Psalmist adds, how ill he took this at mens hands, and that he would one day make them know the difference between the forbearance of sinners, and the love of their sins; *but I will reprove thee, and set them in order before thee.* And therefore he bids them be better advised, and *consider this while they forget God, lest he tear them in pieces, and there be none to deliver.*

ture punishment of it,—is mere talk, calculated for the terror of old women and children. . . . Upon which argument, the psalmist, speaking in the name of God,—uses this remonstrance to one under this fatal mistake . . . —these things thou didst, and I kept silence:—And it seems this silence was interpreted into consent; —for it follows,—and thou thoughtest I was altogether such a one as thyself;—but the psalmist adds, how ill he took this at men's hands, and that they should not know the difference between the forbearance of sinners,—and his neglect of their sins;—but I will reprove thee, and set them in order before thee.—Upon the whole of which, he bids them be better advised, and consider, lest, while they forget God, he pluck them away, and there be none to deliver them.—[5]

5. Cf. Tillotson, *Sermons,* Vol. vii, Sermons 148–151, quoted below, pp. 173–4.

JONATHAN SWIFT (1667-1745)

SWIFT   STERNE

Sermons, IV, 12 (27), p. 173

. . . Conscience is nothing else but the knowledge which the mind has within itself . . . and the judgment, either of *approbation* or censure, which it unavoidably makes upon the successive actions of our lives . . . .

pp. 188-9

. . . if you would form a just judgment . . . call in Religion and Morality.—Look —What is written in the law of God?

"On the Testimony of Conscience," p. 24[6]

pp. 176-7

The word *Conscience* properly signifies that Knowledge which a Man hath within himself of his own Thoughts and Actions. And because if a Man judgeth fairly of his own Actions by comparing them with the Law of God, his Mind will either approve or condemn him according as he hath done Good or Evil. . . . Whenever our Conscience accuseth us, we are certainly guilty; but we are not always innocent when it doth not accuse us: For very often, through the Hardness of our Hearts, or the Fondness and Favour we bear to our selves, or through Ignorance, or Neglect, we do not suffer our Conscience to take any Cognisance of several Sins we commit.

I own . . . whenever a man's Conscience does accuse him . . . that he is guilty . . . .
But, the converse of the proposition will not hold true,———namely, That wherever there is guilt, the Conscience must accuse; and, if it does not, that a man is therefore innocent.———

pp. 174-5

. . . did no such thing ever happen, as that the conscience of a man . . . might . . . insensibly become hard . . . . Did this never happen:—or was it certain that self-love could never hang the least bias upon the judgment:— . . . could no such thing as favour and affection enter this sacred court . . .

p. 176

. . . the guilt or innocence of every man's life could be known . . . by no better measure, than the degrees of his own approbation or censure.

pp. 28-9

pp. 193-4

. . . I shall . . . show you the Weakness and Uncertainty of two false Principles which many People set up in the Place of

. . . nothing [is] more common than to see a man, who has no sense at all of religion . . . who would yet take it as the

---

6. Page references are to *Three Sermons by the Reverend Dr. Swift.* Also reprinted in *The Works of Jonathan Swift, D.D.* . . . *with Notes*, Scott, ed., VIII.

Conscience, for a Guide to their Actions.

The first of these false Principles is, what the World usually calls *Moral Honesty*. There are some People, who appear very indifferent as to Religion, and yet have the Repute of being just and fair in their Dealings; and these are generally known by the Character of good Moral Men. But now if you look into the Grounds and Motives of such a Man's Actions, you shall find them to be no other than his own Ease and Interest. For Example: You trust a moral Man with your Money in the Way of Trade, you trust another with the Defence of your Cause at Law, and perhaps they both deal justly with you. Why? Not from any regard they have for Justice, but because their Fortune depends upon their Credit, and a Stain of open publick Dishonesty must be to their Disadvantage. But let it consist with such a Man's Interest and Safety to wrong you, and then it will be impossible you can have any Hold upon him; because there is nothing left to give him a Check, or to put in the Balance against his Profit. For if he hath nothing to govern himself by but the Opinion of the World, as long as he can conceal his Injustice from the World, he thinks he is safe.

Besides, it is found by Experience, that those Men who set up for Morality without regard to Religion, are generally but virtuous in part . . . .

bitterest affront, should you but hint at a suspicion of his moral character,—or imagine he was not conscientiously just, and scrupulous to the uttermost mite. . . . yet were we to look into the grounds of it [i.e. such a man's moral honesty] in the present case, I am persuaded we should find little reason to . . . honour . . . his motive.

Let him declaim as pompously as he can on the subject, it will be found at last to rest upon no better foundation than either his interest, his pride, his ease . . . .[7]

Give me leave to illustrate this by an example.

pp. 195–7

I know the banker I deal with, or the physician I usually call in,[8] to be neither of them men of much religion. . . . Well, ————notwithstanding this I put my fortune into the hands of the one, . . . I trust my life to the honest skill of the other.————Now let me examine what is my reason for this great confidence. ————Why,—in the first place . . . I know their success in the world depends upon the fairness of their characters; ————that they cannot hurt me without hurting themselves more.

But put it otherwise, namely, that . . . a case should happen wherein the one, without stain to his reputation, could secrete my fortune . . . ————or that the other could . . . enjoy an estate by my death, without dishonour to himself or his art.————In this case what hold have I of either of them?—Religion, the strongest of all motives, is out of the question. ————Interest, the next most powerful motive in this world, is strongly against me.————I have nothing left to cast into the scale to ballance this temptation. ————I must lay at the mercy of honour, ————or some such capricious principle.

"The Difficulty of Knowing One's-Self," pp. 10–11[9]

. . . however it cometh to pass, they [men] are wonderfully unacquainted with

Sermons, I, 4, p. 93

Of the many revengeful, covetous, false and ill-natured persons which we com-

---

7. Cf. Tillotson, *Sermons,* Vol. II, No. 27, quoted below, p. 162.
8. The anonymous correspondent to *The Gentleman's Magazine,* Vol. LXXVI, Pt. 1, 407–08, who first noted the resemblances between these two sermons, conjectures that Sterne converts Swift's lawyer into a doctor, for the benefit of Dr. Slop, who hears this sermon read in *Tristram Shandy.*
9. From *The Works of Jonathan Swift, D.D.* . . . *with Notes,* VIII, No. 1.

their own temper and disposition, and know very little of what passeth within them: for, of so many proud, ambitious, revengeful, envying, and ill-natured persons that are in the world, where is there one of them, who, although he hath all the symptoms of the vice appearing upon every occasion, can look with such an impartial eye upon himself, as to believe that the imputation thrown upon him is not altogether groundless and unfair?

plain of in the world, though we all join in the cry against them, what man amongst us singles out himself as a criminal, or ever once takes it into his head that he adds to the number?—or where is there a man so bad, who would not think it the hardest and most unfair imputation to have any of those particular vices laid to his charge?

If he has the symptoms never so strong upon him, which he would pronounce infallible in another, they are indications of no such malady in himself.—

Cf. p. 15

There is nothing more common than to see a wicked man running headlong into sin and folly, against his reason, against his religion, and against his God.

Cf. p. 16

I proceed now . . . to inquire into the grounds and reasons of this ignorance, "and to show whence it comes to pass that man, the only creature in the world that can reflect and look into himself, should know so little of what passeth within him, and be so very much unacquainted even with the standing dispositions and complexions of his own heart."

p. 98

. . . observe how impetuously a man will rush into it [sin], and act against all principles of honour, justice and mercy.—

pp. 80–1

. . . experience and every hour's commerce with the world confirms the truth of this seeming paradox, "That though man is the only creature endowed with reflection, and consequently qualified to know the most of himself—yet so it happens, that he generally knows the least—and with all the power which God has given him of turning his eyes inwards upon himself, and taking notice of the chain of his own thoughts and desires—yet in fact, is generally so inattentive, but always so partial an observer of what passes, that he is as much, nay often, a much greater stranger to his own disposition and true character than all the world besides."

pp. 12–22

To pursue the heart of man through all . . . its several windings and turnings . . . would be a difficult and almost impossible undertaking . . . .
. . . we so very seldom converse with ourselves, and take so little notice of what passeth within us . . . [Let us] retire now and then into the more dark and hidden recesses of the heart . . . .
. . . a man can never find leisure to look into himself, because he doth not set apart some portion of the day for that very purpose . . . .
Thus, let every man look with a severe and impartial eye into all the distinct regions of the heart; and no doubt, several deformities and irregularities, that he

pp. 101–02

. . . let us, I beseech you, assign and set apart some small portion of the day for . . . retiring into ourselves, and searching into the dark corners and recesses of the heart, and taking notice of what is passing there. If a man can bring himself to do this task with a curious and impartial eye, he will quickly find the fruits of it will more than recompense his time and labour. He will see several irregularities and unsuspected passions within him which he never was aware of,—he will discover in his progress many secret turns and windings in his heart to which he was a stranger, which now gradually open and disclose themselves to him upon a nearer view; in these labyrinths he will trace out

never thought of, will open and disclose themselves upon so near a view; and rather make the man ashamed of himself than proud.

such hidden springs and motives for many of his most applauded actions, as will make him rather sorry, and ashamed of himself, than proud.

pp. 95–6

p. 21

. . . let any man look into his own heart, and observe in how different a light, and under what different complexions, any two sins of equal turpitude and malignity do appear to him, if he hath but a strong inclination to the one, and none at all to the other. That which he hath an inclination to, is always drest up in all the false beauty that a fond and busy imagination can give it; the other appeareth naked and deformed, and in all the true circumstances of folly and dishonour.

To conceive this, let any man look into his own heart, and observe in how different a degree of detestation, numbers of actions stand there, though equally bad and vicious in themselves: he will soon find that such of them, as strong inclination or custom has prompted him to commit, are generally dressed out, and painted with all the false beauties which a soft and flattering hand can give them; and that the others, to which he feels no propensity, appear at once naked and deformed, surrounded with all the true circumstances of their folly and dishonour.

JOHN TILLOTSON, ARCHBISHOP OF CANTERBURY (1630–94)

TILLOTSON

STERNE

Vol. i, Sermon 1, p. 353[1]

. . . the jealous and suspicious humour of the generality of men . . . are very apt to suspect that . . . this noise about a God is a mere state engine and a political device, invented at first by some great prince or minister of state, to keep people in awe and order.

Sermons, iii, 6 (21), pp. 167–8

. . . some adventurers . . . might discover that all religions of what denominations or complexions soever, were . . . a contrivance of the Priests and Levites . . . to keep weak minds in fear:—that it's rites and ceremonies . . . were so many different wheels in the same political engine, put in, no doubt, to amuse the ignorant, and keep them in such a state of darkness, as clerical juggling requires.

p. 364[2]

And if there be no superior Being, in whose care of him he [man] may repose his confidence . . . if he have no comfortable expectations of another life to sustain him under the evils and calamities he is liable to in this world, he is certainly of all creatures the most miserable.

Sermons, vi, 7 (34), p. 6

Without such an inward resource, from an inclination, which is natural to man, to trust and hope for redress in the most deplorable conditions,—his state in this life would be, of all creatures, the most miserable.

Vol. i, Sermon 3, pp. 415–16[3]

Religion tends to make men peaceable one towards another. For it endeavours to plant all those qualities and dispositions in men which tend to peace and unity, and to fill men with a spirit of universal love and goodwill. . . . And, in order hereunto, it requires the extirpation of all those passions and vices which render men unsociable and troublesome to one another . . . .
. . . if men would but live as religion requires they should do, the world would be a quiet habitation, a most lovely and desirable place in comparison to what it now is.

Sermons, vii, 14 (40), pp. 33–4

The great end and design of our holy religion . . . was to reconcile us to each other;—by teaching us to subdue all those unfriendly dispositions in our nature, which unfit us for happiness, and the social enjoyment of the many blessings which God has enabled us to partake of in this world . . . . Could Christianity persuade the professors of it into this temper, and engage us, as its doctrine requires . . . after the subduction of the most unfriendly of our passions, to plant, in the room of them, all those (more natural to the soil) humane and benevolent inclinations . . . could this be accomplished,—the world would be worth living in. . . .

Sermon 4, p. 437

. . . to those who are thoroughly convinced of the inconsiderableness of this

Sermons, v, 1 (28), pp. 24–5

. . . always remember to call into our aid, that great and more unanswerable

---

1. Page references are to *The Works of Dr. John Tillotson*, Birch, ed.
2. Cf. Leightonhouse's "Twelfth Sermon," quoted above, p. 135.
3. Cf. Clarke's 14th sermon, Vol. vi, quoted above, p. 114. Since Tillotson's influence upon Sterne was of so profound and far-reaching a nature, it seems advisable to include passages such as this, even though verbal similarities are slight.

short dying life . . . the consideration of a future happiness, and of those everlasting rewards, which shall then be given to holiness and virtue, is certainly the most powerful motive, and the most likely to prevail upon them.

argument . . . [of the] certainty of a future life . . . . However men may differ in their opinions of the usefulness of virtue for our present purposes,—no one was ever so absurd, as to deny it served our best and last interest,—when the little interests of this life were at an end:—upon which consideration we should always lay the great weight which it is fittest to bear, as the strongest appeal, and most unchangeable motive that can govern our actions at all times.

p. 441

God has not been so hard a master to us that we have reason . . . to complain of him. He hath given us no laws but what are for our good; nay, so gracious hath he been to us as to link together our duty and our interest, and to make those very things the instances of our obedience, which are the natural means and causes of our happiness.

Cf. Vol. I, Sermon 6, pp. 469–70[4]

. . . there is nothing in all these laws but what is most reasonable and fit to be done by us, nothing but what if we were to consult our own interest and happiness, and did rightly understand ourselves, we would choose for ourselves . . . . Some virtues plainly tend to the preservation of our health, others to the improvement and security of our estates, all to the peace and quiet of our minds; and . . . to the advancement of our esteem and reputation . . . .

pp. 12–13

. . . in this does the reasonableness of christianity, and the beauty and wisdom of providence appear most eminently towards mankind, in governing us by such laws, as do most apparently tend to make us happy,—and in a word, in making that (in his mercy) to be our duty, which in his wisdom he knows to be our interest,—that is to say, what is most conducive to the ease and comfort of our mind,—the health and strength of our body,—the honour and prosperity of our state and condition . . . .

Sermon 5, p. 457

The Christian religion furnisheth us with the best motives and considerations to patience and contentedness under the evils and afflictions of this life. This was one great design of philosophy, to support men under the evils and calamities which this life is incident to, and to fortify their spirits against sufferings.

Sermons, II, 15, p. 229

. . . there are no principles but those of religion to be depended on in cases of real stress . . . and to bear us up under all the changes and chances to which our life is subject.

p. 223

. . . in most modern languages, the patient enduring affliction has by degrees obtained the name of philosophy, and almost monopolized the word to itself, as if it was the chief end, or compendium of all the wisdom which philosophy had to offer.

p. 457

And to this end the wisest among the heathens racked their wits and cast about

4. Cf. also the passage from Norris' sermon quoted above, p. 144, and Tillotson's 122d sermon, below, p. 171.

every way, they advanced all sorts of principles, and managed very little argument and consideration to the utmost advantage. And yet after all these attempts they have not been able to give any considerable comfort and ease to the mind of man, under any of the great evils and pressures of this life.

p. 457

All the wise sayings and advices which philosophers could muster up to this purpose . . . have helped only to support some few stout and obstinate minds, which, without the assistance of philosophy, would have held up pretty well of themselves.

p. 458

Others have endeavoured to delude their troubles by . . . reasoning, that . . . things are fatal and necessary, and therefore nobody ought to be troubled at them, it being in vain to be troubled at that which we cannot help. And yet perhaps it might as reasonably be said, on the other side, that this very consideration, "that a thing cannot be helped," is one of the justest causes of trouble to a wise man. For it were some kind of comfort if these evils were to be avoided, because then we might be careful to prevent them another time; but if they be necessary, then my trouble is as fatal as the calamity that occasions it; and though I know it in vain to be troubled at that which I cannot help, yet I cannot choose but be afflicted. It was a smart reply that Augustus made to one that ministered this comfort to him of the fatality of things, *Hoc ipsum est* (says he) *quod me malè*

pp. 222–3

And for this reason 'tis observable that there is no subject, upon which the moral writers of antiquity have exhausted so much of their eloquence, or where they have spent such time and pains, as in this of endeavouring to reconcile men to these evils.

pp. 221–2

. . . the wisest of the heathen philosophers had found from observation upon the life of man, that the many troubles and infirmities of his nature, the sicknesses, disappointments, sorrows . . . were in themselves so *great*,—and so *little* solid comfort to be administered from the mere refinements of philosophy in such emergencies, that there was no virtue which required greater efforts, or which was found so difficult to be atchieved upon moral principles . . . .

p. 227

. . . one is led to doubt, whether the greatest part of their heroes, the most renowned for constancy, were not much more indebted to good nerves and spirits, or the natural happy frame of their tempers, for behaving well, than to any extraordinary helps, which they could be supposed to receive from their instructors.

pp. 225–7

The philosophic consolations in sickness, or in affliction . . . were rather in general to be considered as good sayings than good remedies.—. . . that tears and lamentation for the dead were fruitless and absurd;—that to die, was the necessary and unavoidable debt of nature;—and as it could admit of no remedy—'twas impious and foolish to grieve and fret themselves upon it. Upon which sage counsel, as well as many other lessons of the same stamp, the same reflection might be applied, which is said to have been made by one of the roman emperors, to one who administered the same consolation to him on a like occasion—to whom advising him to be comforted, and make himself easy, since the event had been brought about by a fatality and could not be helped,— he replied—"That this was so far from lessening his trouble—that it was the very circumstance which occasioned it."

habet, this was so far from giving any ease to his mind that "this was the very thing that troubled him."

p. 459

Others have tried to divert and entertain the trouble of other men, by pretty and plausible sayings . . . . Now I am apt to imagine that it is but a very small comfort that a plain and ordinary man, lying under a sharp fit of the stone . . . receives from this fine sentence. For what pleasure soever men that are at ease and leisure may take . . . I doubt it is but poor consolation, that a man under great and stinging affliction finds from them.

Cf. Vol. III, p. 249

. . . as if a physician, instead of applying particular remedies to the distemper of his patient, should entertain him with a long discourse of disease in general . . . .

Vol. I, Sermon 5, pp. 459–60

Our religion sets before us not the example of a stupid stoic . . . but an example that lies level to all mankind . . . of "Jesus, the author . . . of our faith . . . ." The assurance of a future blessedness . . . will revive our spirits more in the day of adversity, than all the wise sayings and considerations of philosophy.

Vol. I, Sermon 6, p. 466

One of the great prejudices which men have entertained against the Christian religion is this—that it lays upon men "heavy burdens and grievous to be born," that the laws of it are very strict and severe, and difficult to be kept . . . .

p. 472

Humility, though it may seem to expose a man to some contempt, yet it is truly the readiest way to honour: as, on the contrary, pride is a most improper and absurd means for the accomplishing of the end it aims at . . . . pride and insolence and contempt of others do infallibly defeat their own design. They aim at respect and esteem, but never attain it; for all mankind do naturally hate and slight a proud man.

Sermons, II, 15, p. 225

All which, however fine, and likely to satisfy the fancy of a man at ease, could convey but little consolation to a heart already pierced with sorrow,—nor is it to be conceived how an unfortunate creature should any more receive relief from such a lecture, however just, than a man racked with an acute fit of the gout or stone, could be supposed to be set free from torture, by hearing from his physician a nice dissertation upon his case.

p. 228

. . . and this, not from a stoical stupidity, but a just sense of God's providence, and a persuasion of his justice and goodness in all his dealings.—Such an example, I say, as this, is of more universal use, speaks truer to the heart, than all the heroic precepts, which the pedantry of philosophy have to offer.

Sermons, VI, 10 (37), pp. 85–6

Amongst the many prejudices which at one time or other have been conceived against our holy religion, there is scarce any one which has done more dishonour to christianity, or which has been more opposite to the spirit of the gospel, than this . . . "That the commandments of God *are* grievous."

Sermons, IV, 6 (24), pp. 87–8

Consider a moment,—What is it the proud man aims at?—Why,—such a measure of respect and deference, as is due to his superior merit, &c. &c.

Now, good sense and a knowledge of the world shew us, that how much soever of these are due to a man, allowing he has made a right calculation,—they are still dues of such a nature, that they are not to be insisted upon: Honour and Respect must be a *Free-will offering;* treat them

Vol. 1, Sermon 8, p. 509

. . . the apostle here describes the condition of Christians. It is true, we are born here in this world and live in it, but we belong to another corporation; we are denizens of another country, and free of that city which is above.

    . . . our citizenship is in heaven . . . .

pp. 520–1

. . . it is by the "denying of ungodliness and worldly lusts," and by living "soberly and righteously and godly in this present world," that we are to "wait for the blessed hope." Our Saviour promises this happiness to the pure in heart . . . the Scripture doth exclude all others from any share or portion in this blessedness . . . .

p. 523

All the joys of that place, and delights of that state are purely spiritual, and are only to be relished by those who have purified themselves as God is pure. Heaven is too pure an air for corrupt souls to live and breathe in . . . .

p. 521

To see God is to be happy; but, unless we be like him, we cannot see him. The sight and presence of God himself would be no happiness to that man who is not like to God in the temper and disposition of his mind.

p. 522

And if God should admit us so qualified into the place of happiness, yet we shall bring that along with us which would infallibly hinder us from being happy. Our sensual inclinations and desires would meet with nothing there that would be suitable to them, and we should be perpetually tormented with those appetites which we brought with us out of this world, because we should find nothing there to gratify them withal. . . . So that, if a covetous, or ambitious, or voluptuous man were in heaven, he would be just like

otherwise, and claim them from the world as a tax,—they are sure to be withheld . . . .

Sermons, v, 2 (29), pp. 35–6[5]

It is observable, that St. Peter represents the state of christians under the . . . image, of strangers on earth, whose city and proper home, is heaven:—he makes use of that relation of citizens of heaven, as a strong argument for a pure and holy life,—beseeching them *as* pilgrims and strangers *here*, as men whose interests and connections are of so short a date, and so trifling a nature,—to abstain from fleshly lusts, which war against the soul, that is, unfit it for its heavenly country, and give it a disrelish to the enjoyment of that pure and spiritualized happiness, of which that region must consist, wherein there shall in no wise enter any thing that defileth, neither whatsoever worketh abomination.—

pp. 37–8

The apostle tells us, that without holiness no man shall see God;—by which no doubt he means, that a virtuous life is the only medium of happiness and terms of salvation,—which can only give us admission into heaven.—But some of our divines carry the assertion further, that without holiness,—without some previous similitude wrought in the faculties of the mind, corresponding with the nature of the purest of beings, who is to be the object of our fruition hereafter;—that it is not morally only, but physically impossible for it to be happy,—and that an impure and polluted soul, is not only unworthy of so pure a presence as the spirit of God, but even incapable of enjoying it, could it be admitted.

5. Mr. Cross describes this sermon as "worked over from Tillotson." (*Life*, p. 95.) Tillotson may have suggested the idea to Sterne but closer similarities are to be found in Norris. See above, p. 142.

the rich man in hell, tormented with a continual thirst, and burnt up in the flames of his own ardent desires; and would not be able, amidst all the plenty and treasures of that place, to find so much as one drop of suitable pleasure and delight to quench and allay that heat. So, likewise, our fierce and unruly passions; if we should carry them with us into the other world, how inconsistent would they be with happiness? They would not only make us miserable ourselves, but be a trouble to all those with whom we should converse.

. . . as the apostle says in another sense, "the kingdom of God is not meats and drinks, but righteousness, and peace, and joy in the Holy Ghost." The happiness of heaven consists in such things as a wicked man hath no gust or relish for.

Vol. II, Sermon 12, p. 72

. . . when in doing our duty we directly promote our own happiness, and in serving God do most effectually serve our own interest, what can be imagined to minister more peace and pleasure to the mind of man?

Vol. II, Sermon 14, pp. 112–13

And do we think all this is to be done in an instant . . . ? That we may delay and put off to the last, and yet do all this work well enough? Do we think we can do all this in time of sickness and old age, when we are not fit to do anything; when the spirit of man can hardly bear the infirmities of nature, much less a guilty conscience . . . ? What reasonable or acceptable service can we then perform to God? . . . Consider what a desperate hazard we run by these delays.

Vol. II, Sermon 18, p. 189

. . . God . . . did not think it enough to give us the most perfect laws of holiness and virtue; but hath likewise set before us a living pattern, and a familiar example to excite and encourage us . . . .

pp. 39–40

Preach to a voluptuous epicure, who knows of no other happiness in this world, but what arises from good eating and drinking . . . preach to him of the abstractions of the soul . . . represent to him that saints and angels eat not . . . why, the only effect would be, that the fat glutton would stare a while upon the preacher, and in a few minutes fall fast asleep.

Sermons, VI, 9 (36), pp. 78–9

We have nothing to part with,—but what is not our interest to keep . . . . We have nothing to do for Christ's sake—but what is most for our own . . . that is, to deny ourselves ungodliness . . . and lay such restraints upon our appetites as are for the honour of human nature,—the improvement of our happiness,—our health, —our peace . . . .

Sermons, VI, 10 (37), pp. 111–12

When the edge of appetite is worn down . . . afflictions, or the bed of sickness, will supply the place of conscience;—and if they should fail,—old age will overtake us at last . . . . If there is any thing more to cast a cloud upon so melancholy a prospect as this shews us,—it is surely the difficulty and hazard of having all the work of the day to perform in the last hour;— of making an atonement to God, when we have no sacrifice to offer him, but the dregs and infirmities of those days, when we could have no pleasure in them.

How far God may be pleased to accept such late and imperfect services, are beyond the intention of this discourse.

Sermons, VI, 9 (36), pp. 72–3

. . . it is the great blessing, the peculiar advantage we enjoy under its [Christianity's] institution,—that it affords us not only the most excellent precepts . . . but also it shews us those precepts confirmed by most excellent examples.—

pp. 205–06

To do good, is the most pleasant employment in the world. It is natural, and whatever is so, is delightful. We do like ourselves, whenever we relieve the wants and distresses of others. And therefore this virtue, among all other, hath peculiarly entitled itself to the name of humanity. . . . no man that hath not divested himself of humanity can be cruel and hardhearted to others, without feeling some pain in himself.

Cf. Vol. vi, p. 202

. . . compassion for the sufferings of others, is a virtue so proper to our nature, that it is therefore called humanity, as if it were essential to human nature . . . .

Vol. ii, Sermon 18, pp. 206–07

There is no sensual pleasure in the world comparable to the delight and satisfaction that a good man takes in doing good. . . . Sensual pleasures are not lasting, but . . . leave a sting behind them . . . . But the pleasure of doing good remains after a thing is done . . . and the reflection upon it afterwards does for ever minister joy and delight to us. . . . Solomon, after all his experience of worldly pleasures, pitches at last upon this as the greatest felicity of human life, and the only good use that is to be made of a prosperous and plentiful fortune: . . . "I know that there is no good in them, but for a man to rejoice and do good in his life."

p. 210

He that is charitable to others provides a supply and retreat for himself in the day of distress; for he provokes mankind by his example to like tenderness towards him, and prudently bespeaks the commiseration of others against it comes to be his turn to stand in need of it.

Vol. ii, Sermon 25, p. 401

But how much time every person should allot to this purpose [of prayer], is matter of prudence; and as it need not, so neither indeed can it be precisely determined. . . . some . . . have more leisure and

Sermons, i, 3, pp. 70–1

I think there needs no stronger argument to prove how universally and deeply the seeds of this virtue of compassion are planted in the heart of man, than . . . from the general propensity to pity the unfortunate, we express that sensation by the word *humanity*, as if it were inseparable from our nature. . . . I am perswaded and affirm 'tis still so great and noble a part of our nature, that a man must do great violence to himself, and suffer many a painful conflict, before he has brought himself to a different disposition.

Sermons, i, 5, p. 137

. . . there is no passion so natural . . . as . . . the principle of doing good . . . .

pp. 132–3

Ask the man who has a tear of tenderness always ready to shed over the unfortunate; who, withal, is ready to distribute and willing to communicate: ask him if the best things, which wits have said of pleasure, have expressed what he has felt, when by a seasonable kindness, he has *made the heart of the widow sing for joy.* Mark then the expressions of unutterable pleasure and harmony in his looks; and say, whether Solomon has not fixed the point of true enjoyment in the right place, when he declares, "that he knew no good there was in any of the riches or honours of this world, *but for a man to do good with them in his life.* . . ." Doubtless he had found and seen the insufficiency of all sensual pleasures; how unable to furnish . . . a lasting scheme of happiness: how soon the best of them vanished; the less exceptionable in vanity, but the guilty both *in vanity and vexation of spirit.*

p. 131

. . . many a man has lived to enjoy the benefit of that charity which his own piety projected. . . . When a compassionate man falls, who would not pity him? who, that had the power to do it, would not befriend and raise him up?

Sermons, vii, 16 (43), pp. 88–9

Indeed, as to the frequency of putting this duty [of prayer] formally in practice, as the precept must necessarily have varied according to the different stations in

freedom for it, by reason of their easy condition and circumstances in the world; and therefore are obliged to allow a greater portion of time for the exercises of piety and devotion.

which God has placed us;—so he has been pleased to determine nothing precisely concerning it:—for, perhaps, it would be unreasonable to expect that the day-labourer, or he that supports a numerous family by the sweat of his brow, should spend as much of his time in devotion, as the man of leisure and unbounded wealth.—

Sermons, IV, 12 (27), p. 193

. . . nothing [is] more common than to see a man, who has no sense at all of religion,—who would yet take it as the bitterest affront, should you but hint at a suspicion of his moral character,—or imagine he was not conscientiously just, and scrupulous to the uttermost mite.

pp. 194–7

Let him declaim as pompously as he can on the subject, it will be found at last to rest upon no better foundation than either his interest, his pride, his ease; or some such little and changeable passion . . . .

Give me leave to illustrate this by an example.

I know the banker I deal with, or the physician I usually call in, to be neither of them men of much religion . . . . Well, —notwithstanding this I put my fortune into the hands of one . . . I trust my life to the honest skill of the other.—Now, let me examine what is my reason for this great confidence.—Why,—in the first place, I believe that there is no probability that either of them will employ the power . . . to my disadvantage. . . . I know their success in the world depends upon the fairness of their characters;—that they cannot hurt me without hurting themselves more.

But put it otherwise . . . That a case should happen wherein the one, without stain to his reputation, could secrete my fortune . . . or that the other could send me out of it [the world], and enjoy an estate by my death, without dishonour to himself or his art.—In this case what hold have I of either of them?—Religion, the strongest of all motives, is out of the question.—Interest, the next most powerful motive in this world, is strongly against me.—I have nothing left to cast into the scale to ballance this temptation.[6]

Vol. II, Sermon 27, pp. 456–7

Take away this [religion], and all obligations of conscience cease; and where there is no obligation of conscience, all security of truth, and justice, and mutual confidence among men is at an end. For why should I repose confidence in that man, why should I take his word, or believe his promise, or put any of my interests and concernments into his power, who hath no other restraint upon him but that of human laws, and is at liberty, in his own mind and principles, to do whatever he judgeth to be expedient for his interest, provided he can but do it without danger to himself? . . . every wise man hath reason to be on his guard against those from whom he hath no cause to expect more justice, and truth, and equity in their dealings than he can compel them to by the mere dint and force of laws. For, by declaring themselves free from all other obligations, they give us fair warning what we are to expect at their hands, and how far we may trust them. Religion is the strongest band of human society, and . . . necessary to the welfare and happiness of mankind . . . .

6. Cf. Swift's sermon "On The Testimony of Conscience," quoted above, p. 152.

Vol. II, Sermon 30, pp. 538–9

It requires no subtlety of wit, no skill in antiquity to understand these controversies between us and the church of Rome. . . . and we refer it to the common sense of mankind, which church . . . hath all the right and reason . . . in these debates? . . . they who . . . carry on a worldly design, they who drive a trade of such mighty gain and advantage under pretence of religion, and make such markets of the ignorance and sins of the people; or, we . . . ? for we make no money of the mistakes of the people . . . . We do not . . . pretend a mighty bank and treasure of merits in the church, which they sell to the people for ready money, giving them bills of exchange from the pope to purgatory . . . .

Vol. II, Sermon 31, pp. 559–60

. . . this conceit . . . hath been taken up in good earnest by . . . the church of Rome, whose avowed doctrine it is, That there are some persons so excellently good that they may do more than needs for their own salvation: and therefore, when they have done as much for themselves, as in strict duty they are bound to do . . . they may go to work again for their friends, and begin a new score . . . to be laid up in the public treasury of the church, as so many bills of credit, which the pope by his pardons and indulgences may dispense, and place to whose account he pleases . . . .

p. 561

Let no man therefore think of being good by a deputy, that cannot be contented to be happy, and to be saved the same way, that is to go to hell, and to be tormented there in person, and to go to heaven, and be admitted into that place of bliss only by proxy.

Vol. III, Sermon 33, pp. 47–8

. . . it must be acknowledged to be a very untoward objection against the excellency and efficacy of the Christian religion, that the practice of so many Chris-

Sermons, v, 4 (31), pp. 112–14

. . . how ill the spirit and character of that church [the Roman] resembles that particular part of St. Peter's which has been made the subject of this discourse. . . . instead of the humble declaration in the text . . . you hear a language and behaviour from the Romish court, as opposite to it as insolent words and actions can frame.—

. . . . Think not, as if it were not our own holiness which merits all the homage you can pay us.—It is our own holiness,— the superabundance of it, of which, having more than we know what to do with ourselves,—from works of supererogation, we have transferred the surplus in ecclesiastic ware-houses, and in pure zeal for the good of your souls, have established public banks of merit, ready to be drawn upon at all times.—

Sermons, vi, 10 (37), pp. 98–9

. . . when you examine it [Roman catholicism] minutely, [it] is little else than a mere pecuniary contrivance.—And the truest definition you can give of popery— is,—that it is a system put together and contrived to operate upon men's weaknesses and passions,—and thereby to pick their pockets . . . .

Sermons, II, 14, pp. 204–05

If your works must be proved, you would be advised [by the Romanists] by all means to send them to undergo this operation with some one who knows what he is about . . . to some Convent or religious society, who are in possession of a large stock of good works of all kinds, wrought up by saints and confessors, where you may suit yourself . . . . I shall only add a short remark,—that they who are persuaded to be thus virtuous by proxy, and will prove the goodness of their works only by deputies,—will have no reason to complain against God's justice,—if he suffers them to go to heaven only in the same manner,—that is,—by deputies too.

Sermons, v, 6 (33), p. 150

. . . the wickedness either of the present or past times, whatever scandal and reproach it brings upon christians,—ought not in reason to reflect dishonour upon

tians is so unequal to the perfection of these precepts.

christianity, which is so apparently well framed to make us good,—that there is not a greater paradox in nature,—than that so good a religion should be no better recommended by its professors.

Vol. III, Sermon 36, p. 102

Sermons, II, 8, p. 28

. . . men . . . by some casual hit . . . may attain such a fortune . . . .

. . . as these lucky hits, (as they are called) happen to be for, or against a man . . . .

pp. 103–04

Sermons, VI, 12 (39), pp. 157–8

. . . in human affairs the most likely means do not always attain their end . . . but there is a secret Providence which governs and overrules all things . . . . Now, if a man design victory, what more probable means to overcome in a race than swiftness? what more likely to prevail in war than strength? . . . And yet experience shews that these means, as probable as they seem to be, are not always successful for the accomplishment of their several ends.

With regard to our endeavours,—he [Solomon] shews that the most likely ways and means are not always effectual for the attaining of their end:—that, in general, —the utmost that human councils and prudence can provide for, is to take care, when they contend in a race, that they be swifter than those who run against them; —or when they are to fight a battle, that they be stronger than those whom they are to encounter.—And yet . . . there are secret workings in human affairs, which over-rule all human contrivance . . . .

p. 105

Sermons, II, 8, pp. 33–4

. . . the force of Solomon's reasoning is this—if the swiftest do not always win the race; nor the strongest always overcome in war; if knowledge and learning do not always secure men from want; nor industry always make men rich; nor political skill always raise men to high place; nor any other means that can be instanced in as most probable, do constantly and infallibly succeed: then it must be acknowledged, that there is some other cause which mingles itself with human affairs, and governs all events; and which can, and does when it pleases, defeat the most likely, and bring to pass the most improbable designs: and what else can that be imagined to be, but the secret and overruling providence of Almighty God? When we can find no other, we are very unreasonable if we will not admit this to be the cause of such extraordinary events, but will obstinately impute that to blind necessity or chance, which hath such plain characters upon it of a Divine power and wisdom.

Some, indeed, from a superficial view of this representation of things, have atheistically inferred,—that because there was so much of lottery in this life . . . that the providence of God stood neuter and unconcerned . . . leaving them [our affairs] to the mercy of time and chance, to be furthered or disappointed as such blind agents directed. Whereas in truth the very opposite conclusion follows. For consider, —if a superior intelligent power did not sometimes cross and overrule events in this world,—then our policies and designs in it, would always answer according to the wisdom and stratagem in which they were laid, and every cause, in the course of things, would produce its natural effect without variation. Now, as this is not the case, it necessarily follows from Solomon's reasoning, that, if the race is not to the swift, if knowledge and learning do not always secure men from want, —nor care and industry always make men rich,—nor art and skill infallibly raise men high in the world;—that there is some other cause which mingles itself in human affairs, and governs and turns them as it pleases; which cause can be no other than the first cause of all things,

and the secret and over-ruling providence
of that Almighty God . . . .

p. 111

. . . God doth sometimes thus interpose
to hinder and defeat the most probable
designs of men:—to bring men to an
acknowledgement of his providence, and
of their dependance upon him, and sub-
ordination to him . . . .

p. 35

And no doubt—one reason, why God has
selected to his own disposal, so many
instances . . . where events have run
counter to all probabilities,—was to give
testimony to his providence in governing
the world, and to engage us to a consideration and dependence upon it, for the
event and success of all our undertakings.[7]

Vol. III, Sermon 40, p. 201

That man of himself is not sufficient for
his own happiness, is evident . . . because he is liable to so many evils and
calamities, which he can neither prevent
nor remedy. He is full of wants, which he
cannot supply . . . .

Sermons, II, 10, p. 100

If we consider man as a creature full of
wants and necessities (whether real or
imaginary) which he is not able to supply
of himself, what a train of disappointments, vexations and dependencies are to
be seen, issuing from thence to perplex
and make his being uneasy?—

Vol. III, Sermon 42, pp. 252–5

"To speak evil of no man" . . . is not to
be understood absolutely, to forbid us to
say any thing concerning others that is
bad. This in some cases may be necessary
and our duty, and in several cases very fit
and reasonable. . . .
But then we must take care that this
be done out of kindness, and that nothing
of our own passion be mingled with
it . . . .
. . . when a man is called to give testimony . . . in obedience to the laws . . .
it would be an unpardonable fault in him
to conceal the truth . . . but . . . we
ought to take great care, that the ill character we give of any man be spread no
further than is necessary to the good end
we design in it.

Sermons, III, 2, pp. 56–7

. . . I will forbear to say, because I do
not think it,—that 'tis a breach of Christian charity to think or speak evil of our
neighbor, &c.
—We cannot avoid it: our opinions
must follow the evidence; and we are
perpetually in such engagements and sit-
uations, that 'tis our duty to speak what
our opinions are—but God forbid, that
this ever should be done, but from its
best motive—the sense of what is due to
virtue, governed by discretion and the
utmost fellow feeling . . . .

pp. 256–61

Third place, To consider the evil of
this practice, both in the causes and the
consequences of it.
First . . . ill-nature and cruelty of disposition: and by a general mistake ill-
nature passeth for wit . . . though in
truth they are nothing akin to one another.

Sermons, II, 11, p. 120

This delusive itch for slander, too common in all ranks of people, whether to
gratify a little ungenerous resentment;—
whether oftener out of a principle of lev-
elling from a narrowness and poverty of
soul, ever impatient of merit and superiority in others; whether a mean ambition
or the insatiate lust of being witty, (a

7. Sterne inserted a footnote at the conclusion of this paragraph: "Vid. Tillotson's
sermon on this subject." For a still closer parallel, see, however, Young's sermon, quoted
below, p. 191.

Secondly . . . that many are so bad themselves . . . . They cannot have a good opinion of themselves, and therefore . . . endeavour to bring men to a level . . . .

Thirdly . . . malice and revenge.

Fourthly . . . envy. Men look with an evil eye upon the good that is in others, and think that their reputation obscures them . . . .

Fifthly . . . impertinence and curiosity; an itch of talking and meddling in the affairs of other men . . . . So little do light and vain men consider, that a man's reputation is too great and tender a concernment to be jested withal . . . . For what can be more barbarous, next to sporting with a man's life, than to play with his honour and reputation, which to some men is dearer . . . than their lives? . . . Solomon compares this sort of men to distracted persons: "As a madman, (saith he) who casteth firebrands, and arrows and death . . . and saith, Am I not in sport?" Such and so bad are the causes of this vice.[8]

pp. 257–8

To speak evil of others, is almost become the general entertainment of all companies: and the great and serious business of most meetings and visits . . . . For men generally . . . are secretly pleased with ill reports . . . .

. . . many times when we do not believe it [an ill report] ourselves, we tell it to others, with this charitable caution —that we hope it is not true: but in the mean time we give it our pass, and venture it to take its fortune to be believed or not, according to the charity of those into whose hands it comes.

p. 262

. . . it is an injury that descends to a man's children and posterity; because the good or ill name of the father is derived down to them; and many times the best thing he hath to leave them . . . . Is it no crime by the breath of our mouth at once to blast a man's reputation, and to ruin his children, perhaps to all posterity?

talent in which ill-nature and malice are no ingredients,)—or lastly, whether from a natural cruelty of disposition . . . thus much is certain . . . its growth and progress . . . are as destructive to, as they are unbecoming a civilized people.

pp. 120–1

To pass a hard and ill-natured reflection, upon an undesigning action; to invent, or . . . propagate a vexatious report . . . to plunder an innocent man of his character and good name, a jewel which perhaps he has starved himself to purchase, and probably would hazard his life to secure . . . and all this, as Solomon says of the madman, who casteth firebrands, arrows and death, and saith, Am I not in sport? all this, out of wantonness, and oftener from worse motives . . . .

pp. 125–6

Look into the companies of those whose gentle natures should disarm them,—we shall find no better account. . . . How often does the reputation of a helpless creature bleed by a report—which the party, who is at the pains to propagate it, beholds with so much pity and fellow-feeling,—that she is heartily sorry for it, —hopes in God it is not true;—however, as Arch-bishop Tillotson witily observes upon it, is resolved in the mean time to give the report her pass, that at least it may have fair play to take its fortune in the world,—to be believed or not, according to the charity of those, into whose hands it shall happen to fall.

pp. 120–1

To pass a hard and ill-natured reflection . . . to plunder an innocent man of his character and good name . . . to rob him at the same time of his happiness and peace of mind; perhaps his bread,—the bread may be of a virtuous family . . . .

8. Cf. *Life*, p. 243: " 'Evil Speaking' [II, 11] [is] . . . mainly a restatement of Tillotson's 'Against Evil Speaking' (Vol. III, Sermon 42)."

p. 271

. . . hardly any thing can be so . . . bad, but something may be pleaded in excuse for it . . . .

p. 272

. . . There is yet a more specious plea . . . that men will be encouraged to do ill if they can escape the tongues of men . . . because by this means one great restraint from doing evil would be taken away . . . . For many who will venture upon the displeasure of God, will yet abstain from doing bad things for fear of reproach from men: besides that this seems the most proper punishment of many faults the laws of men can take no notice of.

p. 273

. . . when I have said all I can, there will, I fear, be evil speaking enough in the world to chastise them that do ill: and though we should hold our peace, there will be bad tongues enough to reproach men with their evil doings. . . . I am very much mistaken, if we may not safely trust an ill-natured world that there will be no failure of justice in this kind.

Vol. III, Sermon 48, pp. 411–12

. . . a notion wherein the greatest and the wisest part of mankind did always agree, and therefore may reasonably be presumed to be . . . natural . . . [was] that there is one Supreme Being, the author and cause of all things . . . . yet the idolatry of the heathen plainly shews, that this notion, in process of time, was greatly degenerated, and corrupted into an apprehension of a plurality of gods; though in reason it is evident enough, that there can be no more gods than one; and that one . . . is as sufficient to all purposes whatsoever, as ten thousand deities . . . could possibly be . . . .
Now this multitude of deities, which the fond superstition and vain imagination of men had formed to themselves,

p. 127

But there is nothing so bad which will not admit of something to be said in its defence.

pp. 127–9

And here it may be asked,—Whether the inconvenience and ill effects which the world feels . . . are not sufficiently counterballanced by the real influence it has upon mens lives and conduct?—That if there was no evil-speaking in the world, thousands would be encouraged to do ill . . . were they sure to escape the tongues of men.
That if we take a general view of the world,—we shall find that a great deal of virtue,—at least of the outward appearance of it,—is not so much from any fixed principle, as the terror of what the world will say . . . . No doubt the tongue is a weapon, which does chastise many indecorums, which the laws of men will not reach . . . .

pp. 133–4

To those however, who still believe, that evil-speaking is some terror to evil doers, one may answer, as a great man has done upon the occasion,—that after all our exhortations against it,—'tis not to be feared, but that there will be evil-speaking enough left in the world to chastise the guilty,—and we may safely trust them to an ill-natured world, that there will be no failure of justice upon this score.

Sermons, IV, 11 (26), pp. 150–1

That there was one supreme Being who made this world, and who ought to be worshipped by his creatures . . . Reason, as the Apostle acknowledges, was always able to discover . . . and yet it seems strange, that the same faculty which made the discovery, should be so little able to keep true to its own judgment, and support it long against the prejudices of wrong heads, and the propensity of weak ones, towards idolatry and a multiplicity of gods.
. . . That there was in truth but one God, the Maker and supporter of Heaven and Earth . . . how soon was this simple idea lost, and mankind led to dispose of these attributes inherent in the Godhead, and divide and subdivide them again

were . . . supposed to be . . . parts of the universe . . . parcelled out . . . according to the several parts of the world which several nations made the objects of their worship.

p. 414

But in the midst of all this crowd and confusion of deities . . . the wiser heathen, as Thales, Pythagoras, Socrates, Plato, Aristotle, Tully, Plutarch, and others, preserved a true notion of one supreme God . . . .

Cf. Vol. I, Sermon 1, pp. 356–7

. . . the generality of the philosophers and wise men of all nations and ages did dissent from the multitude in these things. They believed but one supreme Deity. . . . And although they did servilely comply with the people in worshipping God by sensible images and representations; yet it appears by their writings, that they despised this way of worship as superstitious, and unsuitable to the nature of God.

Vol. III, Sermon 53, p. 545

. . . Consider that the surest foundation of public welfare and happiness is laid in the good education of children . . . . And this is a matter of so great concernment both to religion and the civil happiness of a nation, that anciently the best constituted commonwealths did commit this care to the magistrate more than to parents.

When Antipater demanded of the Spartans fifty of their children for hostages, they offered rather to deliver to him twice as many men; so much did they value the loss of their country's education.

Vol. IV, Sermon 68, p. 274

. . . the apostle St. Peter doth . . . earnestly exhort Christians to preserve themselves from fleshly lusts: . . . "Dearly beloved, I beseech you, as strangers and pilgrims, to abstain from fleshly lusts: which war against the soul." . . . Fleshly lusts do not only pollute and defile, but . . . do wholly indispose and unfit us for that pure, and spiritual, and Divine life, which alone can qualify us for our heavenly country and inheritance.

amongst deities, which their own dreams had given substance to;—his eternal power and dominion parcell'd out to gods of the land,—to gods of the sea . . . .

pp. 156–7

. . . it is certain . . . that the more diligent enquirers after truth, did not . . . fall into these absurd notions . . . . 'tis true, the ablest men gave no credit to the multiplicity of gods,—(for they had a religion for themselves, and another for the populace) . . . .

Sermons, I, 5, p. 143

The proper education of poor children . . . [is] the ground-work of almost every other kind of charity . . . .

pp. 145–7

And . . . if we are to trust antiquity . . . this matter has been looked upon of such vast importance to the civil happiness and peace of a people, that some commonwealths, the most eminent for political wisdom, have chose to make a publick concern of it; thinking it much safer to be entrusted to the prudence of the magistrate, than to the mistaken tenderness or natural partiality of the parent.

It was consistent with this . . . in the Lacedaemonians . . . when Antipater demanded of them fifty children, as hostages for the security of a distant engagement, they made this brave and wise answer, "They would not,—they could not consent:—they would rather give him double the number of their best up-grown men" —Intimating, that however they were distressed, they would chuse any inconvenience rather than suffer the loss of their country's education . . . .

Sermons, v, 2 (29), p. 36

. . . St. Peter represents the state of christians under the same image, of strangers on earth . . . beseeching them *as* pilgrims and strangers *here* . . . to abstain from fleshly lusts, which war against the soul, that is, unfit it for its heavenly country, and give it a disrelish to the enjoyment of that pure and spiritualized happiness, of which that region must consist . . . .

Vol. v, Sermon 90, pp. 92–3

. . . Covetousness is likewise evil and unreasonable, because it is an endless and insatiable desire. A covetous mind may propose to itself some certain bounds and limits; and a man may think that when he is arrived to such an estate, and hath raised his fortune to such a pitch, that he will then sit down, contented and satisfied, and will seek after no more. . . . but when he hath attained it he will be still reaching after more . . . the more the covetous man increaseth his estate, the more his desires are enlarged and extended, and he finds continually new occasions and new necessities; and every day as he grows richer, he discovers new wants; and . . . every new accession to his fortune sets his desires one degree farther from rest and satisfaction. . . .

p. 94

. . . contentment doth not arise from the abundance of what a man hath, but it must spring from the inward frame and temper of our minds; and the true way to it is not to enlarge our estate, but to contract our desires . . . otherwise the pursuit is endless . . . .

Vol. v, Sermon 96, p. 185

It is true, indeed, there was a peculiar promise of the Holy Ghost to the apostles and Christians of the first ages, which is not now to be expected . . . yet the effects of . . . God's Holy Spirit is common to all Christians in all ages of the world. . . .

p. 186

The assistance of God's Holy spirit is still necessary to men, to incline and enable them to that which is good; but not in that manner and degree that it was necessary at first . . . .

Vol. v, Sermon 107, p. 392

Miraculous gifts were so ordered by God, that men were merely passive in the receiving of them, and contributed nothing to the obtaining of them. . . . But the case is not the same in the graces of

Sermons, II, 13, pp. 184–5

. . . we scarce see any virtue so hard to be put in practice, and which the generality of mankind seem so unwilling to learn, as this of knowing when they have enough . . . . Aye! but nothing is more easy, you will answer, than to fix this point, and set certain bounds to it.—"For my own part, you will say, I declare, I want and would wish no more, but a sufficient competency of those things, which are requisite to the real uses and occasions of life . . . ." —But recollect how seldom it ever happens, when these points are secured, but that new occasions and new necessities present themselves, and every day as you grow richer, fresh wants are discovered, which rise up before you . . . so that . . . every accession to your fortune, sets your desires one degree further from rest and satisfaction . . . .

p. 186

. . . that devil of a phantom unpossessed and unpossessable, is perpetually haunting you, and stepping in betwixt you and your contentment.—Unhappy creature! to think of enjoying that blessing without moderation! . . . If the ground work is not laid within your own mind, they [wealth and power] will as soon add a cubit to your stature, as to your happiness.

Sermons, VI, 11 (38), pp. 124–5

But besides this plain application of the text to those particular persons and times, when God's spirit was poured down in that signal manner . . . there is something in them to be extended further, which christians of all ages . . . have still a claim and trust in,—and that is, the ordinary assistance and influence of the spirit of God in our hearts, for moral and virtuous improvements;—these, both in their natures as well as intentions, being altogether different from the others . . . conferred upon the disciples of our Lord.—

pp. 125–6

The one were miraculous gifts,—in which the endowed person contributed nothing . . . . In the other case, the helps spoken of were the influences of God's spirit, which upheld us from falling below

God's Spirit, towards the obtaining and improving whereof we ourselves may contribute something . . . the grace of God . . . is indeed the foundation of all the good that is in us: but our different improvements makes different attainments in grace and goodness.

Vol. vi, Sermon 118, p. 37

. . . as God knows, and every man sees it . . . the generality of Christians are very bad, notwithstanding all the influence of that excellent religion which they profess; yet I think it is very evident, men would be much worse without it.

p. 39

If religion be a matter of men's free choice, it is not to be expected that it should necessarily and constantly have its effect upon men; for it works upon us not by a way of force or natural necessity, but of moral persuasion.

p. 40

It cannot be denied, but that Christianity is as well framed to make men good, as any religion can be imagined to be; and therefore, whatever the fault be, it cannot be in the Christian religion that we are not good: so that the bad lives of Christians are no sufficient objection either against the truth or goodness of the Christian doctrine. Besides the confirmation that was given to it by miracles, the excellency of the doctrine, and its proper tendency to make men holy and virtuous, are a plain evidence of its Divine and heavenly original. . . . And all those advantages the Christian religion hath above any religion or institution that ever was in the world. The reasonable and plain rules of a good life are no where so perfectly collected, as in the discourse of our blessed Saviour . . . . No religion ever gave men so full assurance of the mighty rewards and punishments of another world; nor such gracious promises of Divine assistance, and such evidence of it, especially in the piety, and virtue, and patience, and self-denial of the primitive Christians . . . .

the dignity of our nature . . . . Though these gifts are equally called spiritual gifts,—they are not, as in the first case, the entire works of the spirit,—but the calm co-operations of it with our own endeavours . . . .

Sermons v, 6 (33), p. 172

No doubt, there is great room for amendment in the christian world,—and the professors of our holy religion may in general be said to be a very corrupt and bad generation of men,—considering what reasons and obligations they have to be better.—Yet still I affirm, if those restraints were lessened,—the world would be infinitely worse . . . .

pp. 153–4

. . . religion was not to work upon men by way of force and natural necessity,—but by moral persuasion . . . so that, if men have power to do evil, or chuse the good, and will abuse it, this cannot be avoided.—Not only religion, but even reason itself, must necessarily imply a freedom of choice . . . .

p. 150

Let it here . . . be premised,—that the wickedness either of the present or past times, whatever scandal and reproach it brings upon christians,—ought not in reason to reflect dishonour upon christianity, which is so apparently well framed to make us good,—that there is not a greater paradox in nature,—than that so good a religion should be no better recommended by its professors.—

pp. 152–3

. . . if the light of the gospel has not left a sufficient provision against the wickedness of the world,—the true answer is, that there can be none.—'Tis sufficient that the excellency of christianity in doctrine and precepts, and its proper tendency to make us virtuous as well as happy, is a strong evidence of its divine original, —and these advantages it has above any institution that ever was in the world:— it gives the best directions,—the best examples,—the greatest encouragements,— the best helps, and the greatest obligation to gratitude.

And in this does the reasonableness of christianity, and the beauty and wisdom of providence appear most eminently towards mankind, in governing us by such laws, as do most apparently tend to make us happy,—and in a word, in making that (in his mercy) to be our duty, which in his wisdom he knows to be our interest . . . .

pp. 11–12

. . . insomuch,—that could we . . . chuse the laws ourselves which we would be bound to observe, it would be impossible for the wit of man to frame any other proposals, which upon all accounts would be more advantageous to our own interests than those very conditions to which we are obliged by the rules of religion and virtue.

Vol. vi, Sermon 122, pp. 134–5

. . . God, in giving laws to us, hath imposed nothing upon us, but what, in all reason, ought to have been our free choice, if he had not imposed it; nothing but what is for our good, and is in its own nature necessary to make us capable of that happiness which he hath promised to us. And what can be more gracious, than . . . to promise to make us happy for ever, if we will but do that which, upon all accounts, is really best and most for our advantage in this present life?[9]

Vol. vi, Sermon 125, p. 191

. . . the rich man is not here censured for enjoying what he had, for wearing rich apparel, and keeping a great table. This of itself, if it be according to a man's estate and quality, and without intemperance, is so far from being a fault, that it is a commendable virtue.

Sermons, iv, 8 (23), pp. 51–2

———That he had received his good things,—'twas from heaven,———and could be no reproach: with what severity soever the scripture speaks against riches, it does not appear, that the living or faring sumptuously every day, was the crime objected to the rich man . . . the case might be then, as now: his quality and station in the world might be supposed to be such, as not only to have justified his doing this, but, in general, to have required it . . . .[1]

pp. 197–9

It is very observable, how our Saviour chooses to represent to us the discourse between Abraham and the rich man; though there was the greatest difference between them imaginable; the one was in heaven, and the other in hell, yet they treated one another civilly. Abraham is brought in giving the common terms of civility to this wretched wicked man, and calling him son; "Son, remember." . . . "Remember, son, that thou in thy lifetime receivedst thy good things, and Lazarus," &c. . . .

How does this condemn our rudeness and impatience with one another . . . and yet one of the most famous disputes that we find mentioned in Scripture . . . was managed after another fashion; I mean that recorded by St. Jude, between

Sermons, iii, 3 (18), pp. 89–91

We find in the discourse between Abraham and the rich man, tho' the one was in heaven, and the other in hell, yet still the patriarch treated him with mild language:—*Son!*—*Son, remember that thou in thy life time*, &c. &c.—and in the dispute about the body of Moses, between the Arch-angel and the devil, (himself,)

9. Cf. Norris' discourse, quoted above, p. 144.
1. Cf. Clarke's observation on the same subject (Clarke, *Sermons*, Vol. vii, Sermon 12), quoted above, p. 116.

Michael the archangel and the devil: (ver.9.) "Yet Michael the archangel, when, contending with the devil, he disputed about the body of Moses, durst not bring a railing accusation;" **he durst not** allow himself this . . . because it was indecent, and would have been displeasing to God . . . . And yet I may add . . . the devil would have been to hard for him at railing, he was better skilled at that weapon, and more expert at that kind of dispute.

Cf. Vol. iv, Sermon 74, p. 393

In making the same observation, Tillotson here adds, as another reason for the mildness of Michael's language, that "it was so much beneath the dignity and perfection of his nature."

Vol. vi, Sermon 125, p. 208[2]

. . . in Matt. xxv. . . . our Saviour gives us a description of the judgment of the great day: and if that be a true and proper representation of the process of that day, then the grand inquiry will be, what works of charity have been done or neglected by us, and accordingly sentence shall be passed upon us.

Vol. vi, Sermon 131, pp. 341–2[4]

All men naturally desire happiness, and seek after it, and are, as they think, travelling towards it, but generally they mistake their way. Many are eager in the pursuit of the things of this world, and greedily catch at pleasures, and riches, and honour, as if these could make them happy; but when they come to embrace them, they find that they are but clouds and shadows, and that there is no real and substantial felicity in them. "Many say, Who will shew us any good?" meaning the good things of this world . . . but wouldest thou be happy indeed, endeavour to be like the Pattern of happiness, and the Fountain of it; address thyself to him in the prayer of the Psalmist, "Lord, lift thou up upon me the light of thy countenance . . . ."
Many say, "Lo here!" and "Lo there!" that happiness is in a great place, or in a plentiful estate, or in the enjoyment of sensual pleasures and delights; but "be-

St. Jude tells us, he durst not bring a railing accusation against him;—'twas unworthy his high character,—and indeed, might have been impolitick too; for if he had, (as one of our divines notes upon the passage) the devil had been to hard for him at railing,—'twas his own weapon, —and the basest spirits after his example are the most expert at it.

Sermons, i, 3, pp. 72–3

. . . 'Tis observable in many places of scripture, that our blessed Saviour in describing the day of judgment does it in such a manner, as if the great enquiry then, was to relate principally to this one virtue of compassion—and as if our final sentence at that solemnity was to be pronounced exactly according to the degree of it. I was a hungred and ye gave me meat —thirsty and ye gave me drink . . . .[3]

Sermons, i, 1, pp. 1–8

The great pursuit of man is after happiness . . . he searches for it, as for hid treasure—courts it under a thousand different shapes—and though perpetually disappointed,—still persists—runs after and enquires for it afresh—asks every passenger who comes in his way—Who will shew him any good?
He is told by one, to search for it amongst the more gay and youthful pleasures of life . . . .
A second . . . tells the enquirer . . . that happiness lives only in company with the great in the midst of much pomp . . . .
The epicure . . . tells him 'tis in vain to search elsewhere for it, than . . . in the indulgence and gratification of the appetites . . . .
To rescue him from this brutal experiment—ambition takes him by the hand . . . .
In this circle too often does man run,

2. Cf. Clarke, *Sermons*, Vol. vi, No. 17, quoted above, p. 114.   3. *Ibid.*
4. Cf. Clarke, *Sermons*, Vol. ix, No. 15, quoted above, p. 118.

lieve them not;" happiness is something that is nearer and more intimate to us, than any of the things of this world; it is "within thee, in thine heart," and in the very inward frame and disposition of thy mind.

Cf. Vol. I, Sermon 1, p. 363

Man . . . courts happiness in a thousand shapes, and the faster he pursues it, the faster it flies from him. His hopes and expectations are bigger than his enjoyments, and his fears and jealousies more troublesome than the evils themselves which he is so much afraid of.

Vol. VI, Sermon 135, p. 409

Among men folly is looked upon as the greatest defect; it is accounted a greater reproach and disgrace than vice and wickedness; it is of so ill a report in the world, that there are not many but had rather be accounted knaves than fools . . . . wisdom is the greatest perfection next to holiness and goodness; it is usually cried up in the world more than anything else.

Vol. VII, Sermon 147, pp. 67–8

And we continually stand in need of mercy both from God and man. We are liable one to another; and in the change of human affairs, we may be all subject to one another by turns, and stand in need of one another's pity and compassion . . . . To restrain the cruelties, and check the insolences of men, God has so ordered, in his providence, that very often, in this world, men's cruelties "return upon their own heads, and their violent dealings upon their own pates."

Vol. VII, Sermons 148–51, pp. 110–11

Let us consider . . . upon what pretence and colour of reason men encourage themselves in sin, from the long-suffering of God. . . . For when the wise man saith, that "because sentence against an evil work is not executed speedily, therefore the heart of the sons of men is fully set in them to do evil;" he does not intend to

tries all experiments, and generally sits down weary and dissatisfied with them all at last—in utter despair of ever accomplishing what he wants . . . .

In this uncertain and perplexed state . . . Lord! says the psalmist, Lift up the light of thy countenance upon us . . . lighten our eyes . . . and make us know the joy and satisfaction of living in the true faith and fear of thee . . . .

Sermons, VII, 17 (44), p. 127

. . . if the principles of contentment are not within us,—the height of station and worldly grandeur will as soon add a cubit to a man's stature as to his happiness.

Sermons, IV, 11 (26), pp. 137–40

There is no one project to which the whole race of mankind is so universally a bubble, as to that of being thought Wise . . . . there is no injury touches a man so sensibly, as an insult upon his parts and capacity . . . . so that in general you will find it safer to tell a man, he is a knave than a fool . . . .

Strange souls that we are! as if to live well was not the greatest argument of Wisdom . . . .

Sermons, II, 12, pp. 155–6

Without derogating from the merit of his [Joseph's] forbearance, he might be supposed to have cast an eye upon the change and uncertainty of human affairs which he had seen himself, and which had convinced him we are all in another's power by turns, and stand in need of one another's pity and compassion:— and that to restrain the cruelties, and stop the insolences of men's resentments, God has so ordered it in the course of his providence, that very often in this world —our revenges return upon our own heads, and men's violent dealings upon their own pates.

Sermons, V, 6 (33), pp. 155–7

To begin with Solomon's account in the text,—that because sentence against an evil work is not executed speedily, therefore the hearts of the sons of men are fully set in them to do evil.—

insinuate, that God's long-suffering fills the hearts of men with wicked designs and resolutions, and does, by a proper and direct efficacy, harden sinners in their course; but that wicked men, upon some account or other, do take occasion, from the long-suffering of God, to harden themselves in sin; they draw false conclusions from it to impose upon themselves, as if it were really a ground of encouragement; they think they see something in the forbearance of God, and his delay of punishment, which makes them hope for impunity in an evil course, notwithstanding the threatenings of God.

It seems somewhat hard to understand the consequence, why men should grow more desperately wicked,—because God is merciful and gives them space to repent; . . . nor does the wise man intend to insinuate that the goodness and long suffering of God, is the cause of the wickedness of man, by a direct efficacy to harden sinners in their course.—But the scope of his discourse is this, Because a vicious man escapes at present, he is apt to draw false conclusions from it, and from the delay of God's punishment in this life, either to conceive them at so remote a distance, or perhaps so uncertain, that . . . he hopes . . . his fears are greater than his danger;—and from observing some of the worst of men both live and die without any outward testimony of God's wrath,—draws from thence some flattering ground of encouragement for himself . . . .[5]

pp. 129–30

If there be a future judgment, then it is certain, at how great a distance soever it may be.
. . . But it is not certain that it is at such a distance . . . it is, many times, nearer to us than we are aware; and when we think the judgment of God is at a great distance, the Judge may be near, even at the door. . . . Thou dreamest, perhaps, of many years' continuance in this world, and, perhaps, in the height of this vain imagination, "the decree is sealed, and the commandment come forth" to summon thee out of this world . . . .

pp. 167–8

. . . we should . . . consider, that the distance of a thing no way alters the nature of it.—
. . . For though, in our fond imaginations, we dream of living many years upon the earth;—how unexpectedly are we summoned from it?—How oft, in the strength of our age, in the midst of our projects,—when we are promising ourselves the ease of many years?—how oft, at that very time, and in the height of this imagination, is the decree sealed, and the commandment gone forth to call us into another world?—

p. 137

. . . sin never fails to carry its own punishment along with it . . . and makes it a heavy punishment to itself; the conscience of a sinner doth frequently torment him, and his guilt haunts and dogs him wherever he goes; for whenever a man commits a known and wilful sin, he drinks down poison, which, though it may work

pp. 164–5

In all which cases there is a punishment independent of these, and that is, the punishment which a man's own mind takes upon itself, from the remorse of doing what is wrong.—Prima est haec ultio,—this is the first revenge which . . . is sure to follow close upon his heels,[6] and haunts him wheresoever he goes;—

5. Cf. Stillingfleet's sermon No. 15—"Preached before the King, February 24, 1674/5," quoted above, pp. 149–50.
6. An interesting variation of this thought occurs in Richard Duke's *Fifteen Sermons Preach'd on Several Occasions* (3d ed., Oxford, 1730), p. 350: "And the first Vengeance that is executed upon Sin is this very Fear itself of Vengeance. *Prima est haec Ultio*, as even the Heathen Poet witnesses, that the Wicked Wretch receives immediate condemnation from himself. . . ." Since there are no other indications that Sterne may have known or made use of Duke's *Sermons*, the passage is not to be regarded as a possible source.

slowly, yet it will give him many a gripe, and, if no means be used to expel it, will destroy him at last.

for whenever a man commits a wilful bad action,—he drinks down poison, which, though it may work slowly, will work surely, and give him perpetual pains and heart-aches,—and, if no means be used to expel it, will destroy him at last.

Vol. vii, Sermon 169, p. 448

... Zaccheus ... was chief of the publicans ... an office of great odium and infamy among the Jews, they being the collectors of the tribute which the Roman emperor, under whose power the Jews then were, did exact from them.

Sermons, i, 6, p. 164

The publican was one of that order of men employed by the Roman emperors in levying taxes and contributions which were from time to time exacted from Judea as a conquered nation. ... from whatever ... causes it happened—so it was, that the whole set of men were odious, insomuch that the name of a publican was a term of reproach and infamy amongst the Jews.

Vol. vii, Sermon 174, p. 557

... a man's natural actions, I mean, such as surprise us, and do not proceed from deliberation ... do more truly discover the bottom of our hearts ... than those actions which are governed by reason ... and proceed from deliberation.

Sermons, v, 4 (31), pp. 98–9

I would sooner form a judgment of a man's temper from his behaviour on ... little occurrences ... than from the more weighed and important actions, where a man is more upon his guard;— has more preparation to disguise the true disposition of his heart . . . .

Vol. vii, Sermon 175, pp. 575–6

... there is an intimate union and conjunction between the soul and the body, which is the cause of the sympathy which we find to be between them ... it is but reasonable to imagine that ... the body would be affected with the delights and disturbances of the mind . . . .

Sermons, vii, 16 (43), p. 93

... in the present state we are in, we find such a strong sympathy and union between our souls and bodies, that the one cannot be touched or sensibly affected, without producing some corresponding emotion in the other.—

Vol. viii, Sermon 187, p. 213

... whether we [are] ... made up in a more curious and complicated engine, consisting of many secret and hidden springs and wheels, and fitted for greater variety of motions . . . .

Sermons, vi, 7 (34), p. 6

... like a secret spring in a well-contrived machine . . . .

Vol. viii, Sermon 189, p. 254

Seneca writes with wonderful wit and smartness ... about the contempt of the world and wealth; but then ... consider how he flowed in wealth himself, and how intent he was to heap up riches beyond measure.

Sermons, vi, 9 (36), p. 73

A heathen philosopher may talk very elegantly about despising the world, and, like Seneca, may prescribe very ingenious rules to teach us an art he never exercised himself:—for all the while he was writing in praise of poverty, he was enjoying a great estate, and endeavouring to make it greater.

Vol. viii, Sermon 196, pp. 385–6

... these persons [the Apostles] were known to all that dwelt in Jerusalem . . .

their education was known, and the meanness of their condition, that they were simple and illiterate persons, who never had the advantage or opportunity of attaining to this skill in an ordinary way; and, therefore, it must be concluded to have been an extraordinary and supernatural gift.

Sermons, VI, 11 (38), pp. 123–4

. . . our Lord's disciples were illiterate men, consequently unskilled in the arts and acquired ways of persuasion.—Unless this want had been supplied . . . without the gift of tongues they could not have preached the gospel except in Judea . . . . So that without . . . these extraordinary gifts, in the most literal sense of the words, they *could* do nothing.

Vol. VIII, Sermon 199, p. 441

I shall endeavour to open to you the nature of this gift of the Holy Ghost, understanding by it the ordinary influence of the Holy Spirit of God upon the hearts and minds of believers . . . an immediate influence and operation of the Holy Spirit of God upon the minds of men, an inward power, strength, and assistance, communicated to Christians . . . [and] that this power does continually dwell and reside in all true Christians . . . .

pp. 124–6

. . . christians of all ages . . . have still a claim and trust in . . . the ordinary assistance and influences of the spirit of God in our hearts, for moral and virtuous improvements . . . which upheld us from falling below the dignity of our nature:—that divine assistance which graciously kept us from falling, and enabled us to perform the holy professions of our religion. [This gift is] ordinarily what every sincere and well-disposed christian has reason to pray for, and expect . . . .

THOMAS WISE

WISE

Discourse x, "The Great Duty of Charity, or Christian Love," pp. 216–17[7]

Of all which you may take an apt Illustration from St. Paul, in a like comparison he makes with the *natural body:* wherein there are *many Members,* and all have not the same *Office;* but the different Faculties and Operations of each are for the Use and Benefit of the whole. Thus the *Eye* sees not for itself, but for the other Members, and is set up as a Light to direct them. The *Feet* serve to support and carry the other Parts; and the *Hand* acts and labours for them all. . . . And just so is it in the *Body Politic,* or as well in *Civil* as *Spiritual Society* . . . .[8]

STERNE

Sermons, vii, 14 (41), pp. 47–8

This the Apostle hath elegantly set forth to us by the familiar resemblance of the natural body;—wherein there are many members, and all have not the same office; but the different faculties and operations of each, are for the use and benefit of the whole.—The eye sees not for itself, but for the other members;—and is set up as a light to direct them:—the feet serve to support and carry about the other parts; and the hands act and labor for them all. It is the same in states and kingdoms, wherein there are many members . . . .

7. Page references are to *Fourteen Discourses* (London, 1717), by Thomas Wise "and one of the Six Preachers at *Christ-Church* in *Canterbury.*"

8. Cf. Romans 12.4 and I Corinthians 12.12 ff.

WILLIAM WOLLASTON (1660–1724)

WOLLASTON

The Religion of Nature, Sec. 2, Pt. 2, p. 35[9]

Pain considered in itself is a real evil, pleasure a real good. I take this as a *postulatum*, that will without difficulty be granted. . . .

Sec. 2, Pt. 7, p. 37

. . . happiness is something, which . . . must be some kind of pleasure . . . .
One . . . may demand here, whether there may not be happiness without pleasure . . . . But in proper speaking happiness always includes something positive. For *mere* indolence . . . if it be happiness, is a happiness infinitely diminished . . . .

Sec. 5, Pt. 18, p. 110

We are not always certain, who are *good*, who *wicked*. If we trust to fame and reports, these may proceed, on the one hand, from partial friendship, or flattery; on the other, from ill-natured surmises and constructions of things, envy, or malice; and on either, from small matters aggrandized, from mistake, or from the unskilful relation even of *truth* itself . . . .

p. 111

Beside the matters of fact themselves there are many *circumstances* which, before sentence is passed, *ought* to be known and weighed, and yet scarce ever can be known, but to the person *himself* who is concerned. He may have other views, and another sense of things, than his judges have: and what he understands, what he feels, what he intends, may be a *secret* confined to his own brest. A man may through bodily indispositions and faults in his constitution, which it is not in his power to correct, be subject to *starts* and *inadvertencies,* or obnoxious to *snares,* which he cannot be aware of; or

STERNE

Sermons, I, 1, p. 21

. . . I would not be thought . . . as if I was denying the reality of pleasures, disputing the being of them, any more, than one would, the reality of pain—Yet I must observe on this head, that there is a plain distinction to be made betwixt pleasure and happiness. For tho' there can be no happiness without pleasure—yet the converse of the proposition will not hold true.—

Sermons, VII, 17 (44), p. 119

And, first,—what certain and infallible marks have we of the goodness or badness of the bulk of mankind?
If we trust to fame and reports,—if they are good, how do we know but they may proceed from partial friendship or flattery?—when bad, from envy or malice, from ill-natured surmises and constructions of things?—and, on both sides, from small matters aggrandized through mistake,—and sometimes through the unskilful relation of even truth itself?—

pp. 121–3

There are numbers of circumstances which attend every action of a man's life, which can never come to the knowledge of the world,—yet ought to be known, and well weighed, before sentence with any justice can be passed upon him.—A man may have different views and a different sense of things from what his judges have; and what he understands and feels, and what passes within him may be a secret treasured up deeply there for ever.—A man, through bodily infirmity, or some complectional defect, which perhaps is not in his power to correct,—may be subject to inadvertencies,—to starts—and unhappy turns of temper; he may lay open to snares he is not always aware

9. Page references are to *The Religion of Nature, Delineated* (5th ed. London, 1731).

through want of information or proper helps he may labor under *invincible* errors, and act as in the dark: in which cases he may do things, which are in themselves wrong, and yet be innocent, or at least rather to be pitied, than censured with severity . . . .

p. 112

. . . the true characters of men must chiefly depend upon the *unseen* part of their lives; since the truest and best religion is most private, and the greatest wickedness endeavours to be so. Some are modest, and hide their virtues: others hypocritical, and conceal their vices under shews of sanctity, good nature, or something that is *specious*. So that it is many times hard to discern, to which of the two sorts, the *good* or the *bad,* a man ought to be aggregated. . . . It rarely happens, that we are competent judges of the *good* or *bad fortune* of other people. That, which is disagreeable to one, is many times agreeable to another, or disagreeable in a less degree. The misery accruing from any infliction or bad circumstance of life is to be computed . . . according to the resistence and capacity of bearing it, which it meets with. . . . And so the same poverty or disgrace, the same wounds, &c. do not give the *same pain* to all men. . . . a *word* may be more terrible and sensible to tender natures, than a *sword* is to the senseless, or intrepid breed. The same may be said with respect to injoyments: men have different tasts, and the use of the same thing does not beget *equal pleasure* in all. . . .

of; or, through ignorance and want of information and proper helps, he may labour in the dark:—in all which cases, he may do many things which are wrong in themselves, and yet be innocent;—at least an object rather to be pitied than censured with severity and ill-will.

pp. 120–1

. . . the characters of men are not easily penetrated, as they depend often upon the retired, unseen parts of a man's life.— The best and truest piety is most secret, and the worst of actions, for different reasons, will be so too.—Some men are modest, and seem to take pains to hide their virtues; and, from a natural distance and reserve in their tempers, scarce suffer their good qualities to be known:—others, on the contrary, put in practice a thousand little arts to counterfeit virtues which they have not,—the better to conceal those vices which they really have;—and this under fair shews of sanctity, good-nature, generosity, or some virtue or other, —too specious to be seen through. . . . These hints may be sufficient to shew how hard it is to come at the matter of fact:—but one may go a step further,— and say, that even that, in many cases, could we come to the knowledge of it, is not sufficient by itself to pronounce a man either good or bad.

pp. 124–6

Besides this, a man's unhappiness is not to be ascertained so much from what is known to have befallen him,—as from his particular turn and cast of mind, and capacity of bearing it.—Poverty, exile, loss of fame or friends . . . make not equal impressions upon every temper. . . . a hasty word, or an unkind look, to a soft and tender nature, will strike deeper than a sword to the hardened and senseless.—If these reflections hold true with regard to misfortunes,—they are the same with regard to enjoyments:—we are formed differently . . . [and] neither the use or possession of the same enjoyments and advantages, produce the same happiness and contentment . . . .

Cf. p. 112

We do not see the *inward* stings and secret pains, which many of those men carry about them, whose *external* splendor and

pp. 128–30

When a man has got much above us, we take it for granted—that he . . . feels some mighty pleasures from his height;

flourishing estate is so much admired by beholders: nor perhaps sufficiently consider the *silent* pleasures of a lower fortune, arising from temperance, moderate desires, easy reflexions, a consciousness of knowledge and truth; with other pleasures of the *mind,* much greater many times than those of the *body.* . . .

Cf. p. 114

. . . if good and bad men are not respectively treated according to reason in *this life* . . . perhaps it is . . . in order to convince us of the certainty of a future state . . . .

Sec. 5, Pt. 19, p. 124

And further, toward the keeping mankind in order, it is *necessary* there should be some religion profest . . . . And were it not for that sense of virtue, which is *principally* preserved . . . by national *forms* and *habits* of religion, men would soon lose it *all,* run wild, prey upon one another, and do what else the worst of savages do.

Sec. 6, Pt. 17, pp. 139-40

. . . *compassion* appears eminently in them, who upon other accounts are justly reckoned amongst *the best of men:* in some degrees it appears in *almost* all; nay, even sometimes, when they more coolly attend to things, in those hardend and execrable *monsters* of cruelty themselves . . . . The *Pheraean* tyrant, who had never wept over any of those murders he had caused among his own citizens, *wept* when he saw a tragedy but acted in the theatre: the reason was, his attention was caught here, and he more observed the sufferings of *Hecuba* and *Andromache,* than ever he had those of the *Pheraeans;* and more impartially, being no otherwise concerned in them but as a common spectator. Upon this occasion the principle of *compassion,* implanted in human nature, appeared, overcame his habits of cruelty, broke through his petrifaction, and would shew that it could not be totally eradicated. It is therefore according to *nature* to be affected with the sufferings of other

whereas, could we get up to him,—it is great odds whether we should find anything to make us tolerable amends for the pains and trouble of climbing up so high.—. . . To calculate, therefore, the happiness of mankind by their stations . . . is the most deceitful of all rules . . . . Many are the silent pleasures of the honest peasant, who rises chearfully to his labour:—look into his dwelling . . . . the upshot would prove to be . . . that the rich man had the more meat,—but the poor man the better stomach . . . .

p. 132

That things are dealt unequally in this world, is one of the strongest natural arguments for a future state . . . .

Sermons, IV, 11 (26), pp. 162-3

. . . I affirm, if these restraints [i.e., of religion] were taken off, . . . the bulk of mankind . . . would soon come to *live without* God *in the world,* and in a short time differ from Indians themselves in little else but their complexions.

Sermons, I, 5, pp. 137-9

. . . concerning the natural impressions of benevolence . . . a man must do much violence to himself, and suffer many a painful struggle, before he can tear away so great and noble a part of his nature.— Of this antiquity has preserved a beautiful instance in an anecdote of Alexander, the tyrant of Pheres, who thought he had so industriously hardned his heart, as to seem to take delight in cruelty, insomuch as to murder many of his subjects every day, without cause and without pity; yet, at the bare representation of a tragedy which related the misfortunes of Hecuba and Andromache, he was so touched with the fictitious distress which the poet had wrought up in it, that he burst out into a flood of tears. The explication of which inconsistency is easy, and casts as great a lustre upon human nature, as the man himself was a disgrace to it. The case seems to have been this: in *real* life he had been blinded with passions, and thoughtlessly hurried on by interest or resentment:—but here, there was no room for motives of that kind; so that his attention being first caught hold of, and all his vices laid asleep;—then Nature awoke in triumph, and shewed how deeply she had

people: and the contrary is *inhuman* and *unnatural.*

Sec. 9, Pt. 3, p. 174

I must confess however, that our *passions* are so *very apt* to grow upon us, and become exorbitant, if they are not kept under an *exact discipline,* that by way of prevention or caution it is advisable rather to affect a *degree* of apathy, or to recede *more* from the worse extreme. . . .

p. 175

The humoring of *such appetites,* as lie not under the interdict of truth and reason, seems to be the *very means,* by which the Author of nature intended to *sweeten* the journey of life: and a man may upon the road as well muffle himself up against sunshine and blue sky, and expose himself bare to rains and storms and cold, as debar himself of the *innocent delights* of his nature for affected melancholy, want, and pain. . . .

Sec. 9, Pt. 8, p. 201

Consider well the dreadful effects of many *wars,* and all those barbarous desolations, which we read of: what cruel *tyrants* there are, and have been in the world, who . . . *divert themselves* with the pangs and convulsions of their fellow-creatures: what *slavery* is, and *how* men have been brought into that lamentable state . . . . Instances are endless: but, for a *little taste* of the condition of mankind here, reflect upon that story related by *Strabo* (from *Polybius*) and *Plutarch,* where, even by order of the *Roman* senate, P. *Aemylius,* one of the best of them too, at one prefixt hour sacked and destroyd *seventy* cities, unawares, and drove *fifteen myriads* of innocent persons into *captivity;* to be sold, only to raise pay for the merciless soldiers and their own executioners. . . .

p. 202

Look into the history of the *Christian Church,* and her martyrologies: examin

sown the seeds of compassion in every man's breast . . . .

Sermons, VI, 10 (37), p. 96

It is true . . . our passions are apt to grow upon us by indulgence, and become exorbitant, if they are not kept under exact discipline, that by way of caution and prevention, 'twere better at certain times, to affect some degree of needless reserve, than hazard any ill consequences from the other extreme.

pp. 95-6

The humouring of certain appetites, where morality is not concerned, seems to be the means by which the Author of nature intended to sweeten this journey of life,—and bear us up under the many shocks and hard jostlings, which we are sure to meet with in our way.—And a man might, with as much reason, muffle up himself against sun-shine and fair weather, —and at other times expose himself naked to the inclemencies of cold and rain, as debar himself of the innocent delights of his nature, for affected reserve and melancholy.

Sermons, II, 10, pp. 97-9

Consider the dreadful succession of wars in one part or other of the earth . . . consider the horrid effects of them in all those barbarous devastations we read of . . . . For a specimen of this, let us reflect upon the story related by Plutarch, when by order of the Roman senate, seventy populous cities were unawares sacked and destroyed at one prefixed hour, by P. Aemilius, by whom one hundred and fifty thousand unhappy people were driven in one day into captivity, to be sold to the highest bidder to end their days in cruel anguish.[1]—Consider how great a part of our species in all ages down to this, have been trod under the feet of cruel and capricious tyrants . . . . Consider slavery—what it is,—how bitter a draught, and how many millions have been made to drink of it . . . .

pp. 99-100

. . . look into the history of the Romish church and her tyrants, (or rather execu-

---

1. In the later editions of the *Sermons* this illustration was omitted because Sterne had already used it, practically as it stands here, in the preceding sermon. See *Sermons,* II, 9, pp. 70-1.

the prisons of the *inquisition,* the *groans* of which those walls are conscious, and, upon what *slight* occasions men are racked and tortured by the tormentors there: and, to finish this detail . . . as fast as I can, consider the many massacres, persecutions, and miseries consequent upon them, which *false religion* has caused, authorized, sanctified. Indeed the *history* of mankind is little else but the history of uncomfortable, dreadful passages: and a great part of it, however things are palliated and gilded over, is scarcely to be red by a *good natured* man without amazement, horror, tears. . . .

tioners) who seem to have taken pleasure in the pangs and convulsions of their fellow-creatures.——————Examine the prisons of the inquisition, hear the melancholy notes sounded in every cell. . . . Consider how many of these helpless wretches have been haled from thence in all periods . . . to undergo the massacres and flames to which a false and bloody religion has condemned them.[2]

Sermons, IV, 7 (22), p. 4

. . . in some men's lives . . . one evil so rises out of another, and the whole plan and execution of the piece has so very melancholy an air, that a good natured man shall not be able to look upon it, but with tears on his cheeks.

p. 205

. . . like *leaves* one generation drops, and another springs up, to fall again, and be forgotten. . . .[3]

Sermons, II, 10, p. 93

. . . as Homer observes, like leaves, one generation drops, and another springs up to fall again and be forgotten.

Cf. p. 205

Childhood and *youth* are much of them lost in insensibility or trifling . . . .

p. 91

How many of our first years slide by, in the innocent sports of childhood, in which we are not able to make reflections . . . ?—how many more thoughtless years escape us in our youth, when we are unwilling to do it, and are so eager in the pursuit of pleasure as to have no time to spare, to stop and consider them?

Cf. p. 206

. . . perhaps a *family* is increasing, and with it new occasions of *solicitude* are introduced, accompanied with many *fears* and *tender apprehensions.* . . .

p. 92

As families and children increase, so do our affections, and with them are multiplied our cares and toils for their preservation and establishment . . . .

Cf. p. 206

Did he [man] come into the world only to *make his way* through the press, amidst many justlings and hard struggles, with at best only a few deceitful, little, fugacious pleasures interspersed, and so *go out of it* again? Can this be an end worthy a first Cause *perfectly reasonable?* Would even any *man,* of common sense and good nature, send another man upon a *difficult journey,* in which, tho he might perhaps now and then meet with a little smooth

Sermons, I, 2, pp. 24–6

For what purpose do you imagine, has God made us? . . . did the Best of Beings send us into the world . . . to go weeping through it,—to vex and shorten a life short and vexatious enough already? . . . can . . . a being so infinitely kind . . . grudge a mournful traveller, the short rest and refreshments necessary to support his spirits through the stages of a weary pilgrimage? or . . . call him to a severe reckoning, because in his way he

---

2. Cf. *idem,* IV, 12 (27), pp. 201–03; also, Bentley's "Sermon upon Popery," quoted above, p. 105.

3. A footnote gives the Homeric Greek for this passage.

way . . . or be flatterd with some ver-
dures and the smiles of a few daisies on
the banks of the road; yet upon the whole
he must travel through much dirt, take
many wearisom steps . . . and beside
forced all the while to fence against
weather, accidents, and cruel robbers
. . . . I say, would any one send a man
upon *such a journey* as this, *only* that the
man might faint and expire at the end of
it . . . ?

had hastily snatch'd at some little fugacious pleasures, merely to sweeten this uneasy journey of life, and reconcile him to
the ruggedness of the road, and the many
hard justlings he is sure to meet with?
Consider, I beseech you, what provision
and accommodation, the Author of our being has prepared for us, that we might
not go on our way sorrowing . . . what
apt objects he has placed in our way to
entertain us . . . .[4]

p. 207

. . . the case . . . only respects them,
who may be reckond among the *more
fortunate* passengers: and for *one*, that
makes his voyage so well, *thousands* are
tost in tempests and lost. . . .

Sermons, I, 5, pp. 147–8

. . . for one fortunate passenger in life,
who makes his way well in the world
. . . we may reckon thousands who every
day suffer shipwreck, and are lost for
ever.[5]

4. See also Hall's *Contemplations*, Bk. I, No. 1, quoted above, pp. 131–2.
5. Sterne adds a footnote (*Sermons*, II, 10, p. 102): "N.B. Most of these reflections
upon the miseries of life, are taken from Wollaston." The passage to which this acknowledgment of indebtedness refers the reader, however, is not particularly pertinent.

EDWARD YOUNG (1642?–1705)

YOUNG

Vol. I, Sermon 4, pp. 131–2[6]

The Apostle that sometimes compares our Body to a House because of its natural Inhabitant the Soul, does likewise sometimes compare it to a Temple, by reason of its Divine Guest, the Holy Spirit of God: And if ever we will be Temples, indeed 'tis Humility must make the Consecration; 'tis Humility that first distinguishes us from an Unhallowed Pile, that conciliates the Presence of God, and determines his Abode with us. . . .

p. 137

The Cynick *Diogenes* meeting one day with the Excellent *Plato*, habited (as he usually was) in the decent Garb of the Court, snatches his Mantoe from his shoulders, and treads it into the dirt, and cries out, *"Thus I trample upon* Plato's *Pride;"* Plato gently takes up his Garment again, making only this Reply, *" 'Tis true, Diogenes, thou hast trampled upon my Pride, but surely with a greater Pride of thine own"* . . . .

Sermon 11, pp. 366–8

There are Two Opinions which the Devil has been always busy to propagate in the World, as the Two main Pillars of his Kingdom: The First is, That a Sinful Life is a State of true Liberty, and sincere Pleasures, and happy Advantages; The Second is (on the contrary) That a Religious Life is a Servile and Uncomfortable State.

He made the first Breach upon humane Innocence by the former of these Suggestions; when he told *Eve*, That by Eating of the Tree of Knowledge *she should be as God*, that is, she should reap some high and strange felicity from doing that which was forbidden her to do. But we know the Success: *Eve* learnt the difference between Good and Evil by her Transgres-

STERNE

Sermons, III, 2 (17), p. 53

It is a pleasing allusion the scripture makes use of in calling us sometimes a house, and sometimes a temple, according to the more or less exalted qualities of the spiritual guest which is lodged within us . . . . if we are to be temples, 'tis truth and singleness of heart which must make the dedication: 'tis this which must first distinguish them from the unhallowed pile . . . .

Sermons, IV, 9 (24), p. 84

. . . we trample, no doubt too often, upon the pride of Plato's mantle, with as great a pride of our own . . . .

Sermons, V, 1 (28), pp. 3–6[*7]

There are two opinions which the inconsiderate are apt to take upon trust.— The first is—a vicious life, is a life of liberty, pleasure, and happy advantages.— The second is—and which is the converse of the first—that a religious life is a servile and most uncomfortable state.

The first breach which the devil made upon human innocence, was by the help of the first of these suggestions, when he told Eve, that by eating of the tree of knowledge, she should be as God, that is, she should reap some high and strange felicity from doing what was forbidden her.—But I need not repeat the success— Eve learnt the difference between good and evil by her transgression, which she knew not before—but then she fatally

6. Page references are to the *Sermons on Several Occasions.*
7. Passages marked with an asterisk (*) indicate those noted by "O.P.Q." in *The European Magazine;* see above, p. 2.

sion, which she knew not before; but she learnt the Difference to be this, That Good is that that gives the Mind pleasure and assurance; and Evil is that that must necessarily be attended, sooner or later, with shame and sorrow.

As he thus began his Kingdom, so he has carried it on ever since by the same Imposture; that is, by possessing men's minds with vast Expectations of the present Incomes of Sin; and making them dream of golden Mountains, mighty gratifications and advantages they shall meet with in following their Appetites the forbidden way. Whereas on the contrary, there are Seasons wherein all Sinners are ready to confess, that their Counsellor has been a Deceiver, that their Foolish Hearts have been darkned, that their Hopes have been Vain, their Gains no Profit, and all their Enjoyments leading to Bitterness. So little trust is to be given to all the promising Overtures of Sin.

learnt at the same time, that the difference was only this—that good is that which can only give the mind pleasure and comfort—and that evil is that, which must necessarily be attended sooner or later with shame and sorrow.

As the deceiver of mankind thus began his triumph over our race—so has he carried it on ever since by the very same argument of delusion.—That is, by possessing men's minds early with great expectations of the present incomes of sin, —making them dream of wondrous gratifications they are to feel in following their appetites in a forbidden way. . . . This is the opinion which at first too generally prevails—till experience and proper seasons of reflection make us all at one time or other confess—that our counsellor has been (as from the beginning) an imposture—and that instead of fulfilling these hopes of gain and sweetness in what is forbidden—than on the contrary, every unlawful enjoyment leads only to bitterness and loss.

pp. 368–9

To promote the second Opinion, That a Religious Life is a Servile and Uncomfortable State, the Devil suggests to our Thoughts, That true Freedom is to follow our own Humour; That to deny our Appetites is to be Miserable? That not to prosecute our Passions is to be Cowards . . . . That to live by moderate and prescribed Rules is to have no Joy; and therefore that when the Religious Man looks for Joy, he can only see it at the tedious distance of a Future Life: Which were it true, our Nature that is so importunately goaded on with the desire of present Happiness, could not but languish under the discouragement of so Remote an Expectation. But in the mean time the Holy Scriptures give us a quite different prospect of this matter: there we are told, that the *service of* God is true *Liberty;* that the *Yoak of Christ is easy,* in comparison of that which any other Form of Living will bring upon us; that *Religion has Pleasantness in its ways,* as well as Glory in its End; that it will bring us in *Peace and Joy, such as the World cannot give;* and therefore that the Religious Man's Joy does not stand at so tedious a distance, but

pp. 6–8

The second opinion, or, That a religious life is a servile and uncomfortable state, has proved a no less fatal and capital false principle . . . —the foundation of which mistake arising chiefly from this previous wrong judgment—that true happiness and freedom lies in a man's always following his own humour—that to live by moderate and prescrib'd rules, is to live without joy—that not to prosecute our passions is to be cowards—and to forego every thing for the tedious distance of a future life.[8]

Was it true that a virtuous man could have no pleasure but what should arise from that remote prospect—I own we are by nature so goaded on by the desire of present happiness, that was that the case, thousands would faint under the discouragement of so remote an expectation.— But in the mean time the Scriptures give us a very different prospect of this matter. —There we are told that the service of God is true liberty—that the yoke of Christianity is easy in comparison of that yoke which must be brought upon us by any other system of living,—and the text tells of wisdom—by which he means Re-

8. In the Ms. Sterne has crossed out an ending to this paragraph: "will scarce ballance the present Loss—under wch a Man must Languish"

is so present and at hand that it may be felt and tasted every moment. And a Summary Confirmation of all this we meet with in the words of the Text . . . .

The Words . . . lead me to assert the great Advantages of a Religious Life; and to recommend it from the influence it has upon our present well-being . . . .

pp. 381–2

Moral Delight is that which springs from the Conscience of *Well doing:* And though this be a Pleasure that properly belongs to the Good; yet even the Vicious can hardly be insensible of it; because it may be felt to spring from any Single or Casual Act of *Virtue.* As for Example: Let a Man but refresh the Bowels of the needy, or comfort the afflicted, or check an Appetite, or overcome a Temptation, or forgive an Injury, or receive an Affront with Temper and Meekness, and he shall immediately find the tacit Praise of what he has done, darting through his Mind, accompanied with a sincere Delectation. And thus Conscience plays the *Monitor* ev'n to the Loose and Unregenerate in their most Casual Acts of *Well-doing;* and *is like a voice whispering behind them, and saying, This is the way, walk in it.*

Vol. ii, Sermon 3, Pt. 1, p. 86

Peter (we know) was a Man of Precedency, and *Above* the rest of the Disciples: And he was likewise one of such Virtues and Qualifications, as seem to have recommended him to that Precedency, more than did the Advantage of his Years.

pp. 186–7

He was a Man of real and tender Goodness: And this is sufficiently evident from that Passage at his first Admission to our Savior's Acquaintance (St. *Luke* 5.) when being awakened by the miraculous Draught of Fishes, and knowing that the

ligion, that it has pleasantness in its way, as well as glory in its end—that it will bring us peace and joy such as the world cannot give.—So that upon examining the truth of this assertion, we shall be set right in this error, by seeing that a religious man's happiness does not stand at so tedious a distance—but is so present and indeed so inseparable from him, as to be felt and tasted every hour. . . .[9]

pp. 8–9

. . . and of this even the vicious can hardly be insensible, from what he may perceive to spring up in his mind, from any casual act of virtue. And tho' it is a pleasure that properly belongs to the good—yet let any one try the experiment, and he will see what is meant by that moral delight, arising from the conscience of well-doing.—Let him but refresh the bowels of the needy—let him comfort the broken-hearted—or check an appetite, or overcome a temptation—or receive an affront with temper and meekness—and he shall find the tacit praise of what he has done, darting thro' his mind, accompanied with a sincere pleasure—conscience playing the monitor even to the loose and most inconsiderate, in their most casual acts of well-doing, and is, like a voice whispering behind and saying—this is the way of pleasantness—this is the path of peace— walk in it.—[1]

Sermons, v, 4 (31), p. 94*

This great apostle was a man of distinction amongst the disciples,—and was one of such virtues and qualifications, as seem'd to have recommended him more than the advantage of his years, or knowledge.—

pp. 95–6*

On his first admission to our Saviour's acquaintance, he gave a most evident testimony that he was a man of real and tender goodness, when being awakened by the miraculous draught of fishes, as we read in the fifth of St. Luke, and knowing

9. At this point in the Manuscript of Sterne's sermon (*Sermons,* v, 1 [28], p. 8) there occurs the following cancellation: "a Summary Confirmation of wch we meet with in the Text, the plain use of wch shall be at present—to recommend it from the Influence it has upon our present well Being."

1. Cf. Isaiah 30.21.

Author must necessarily be from God, he fell down at his Feet, and broke out into this humble and pious Reflection, *Depart from me, for I am a sinful man, O Lord!* The Censure indeed expresses him a *sinful* Man; but so to censure *himself*, implies more effectually than any thing else could, that he was a Good Man: And though the Words—*Depart from me*—carry in them the Face of Fear, yet he who heard them, and knew the Heart of the Speaker, found that they carried in them a greater measure of Desire; for *Peter* was not willing to be rid of his new Guest, but only longing to be made more worthy of his Conversation.

the author must necessarily be from God, he fell down instantly at his feet,—broke out into this humble and pious reflection; —Depart from me, for I am a sinful man, O Lord!—The censure, you will say, expresses him a sinful man,—but so to censure himself,—with such unaffected modesty, implies more effectually than any thing else could,—that he was not in the common sense of the word,—a sinful, but a good man, who, like the publican in the temple, was no less justified, for a self-accusation extorted merely from the humility of a devout heart jealous of its own imperfections.—And though the words, *depart from me*, carry in them the face of fear,—yet he who heard them, and knew the heart of the speaker, found they carried in them a greater measure of desire. —For Peter was not willing to be discharged from his new guest, but fearing his unfitness to accompany him, longed to be made more worthy of his conversation.—

pp. 87–9

He was a Man of great Love to his Master, and of no less Zeal for his Religion: Of which, from among many, I shall take one Instance out of St. *John* 6. Where, upon the Desertion of several other Disciples, our Saviour puts the Question to the Twelve, *Will ye also go away?* Then (says the Text) *Peter answered him, Lord, whither shall we go? Thou hast the words of eternal life.* An answer so wise and faithful, so evidencing his confirmed Choice of the Better Part, that God seems to have rewarded him for it with the Grace of an immediate Revelation; the Matter whereof follows in the next Words: For thus runs the Text, *Lord, whither shall we go? Thou hast the words of eternal life:* And then it follows—*And we believe, and are sure that thou art Christ, the Son of the living God.* Now if we look into St. *Matth.* 16. 17. we see there what our Saviour pronounces concerning this very Confession, (viz.) *Blessed art thou, Simon Bar-jonah, for Flesh and Blood has not revealed it unto thee, but my Father which is in heaven.* That our Saviour had the words of *eternal life, Peter* was able to deduce from the Principles of Natural Reason; because Reason was able to judge from the Internal Characters of his Doctrine, That it was worthy of God, and accommodated

pp. 109–11

He was a man of great love to his master,—and of no less zeal for his religion, of which, from among many, I shall take one instance out of St. John, with which I shall conclude this account. —Where, upon the desertion of several other disciples,—our Saviour puts the question to the twelve,—Will ye also go away?—Then, says the text, Peter answered and said,—Lord! whither shall we go? Thou hast the words of eternal life,—and we believe, and know that thou art Christ the son of God.—Now, if we look into the gospel, we find what our Saviour pronounced on this very confession.

Blessed art thou, Simon Barjona, for flesh and blood hath not revealed it unto thee,—but my Father which is in heaven. —That our Saviour had the words of eternal life,—Peter was able to deduce from principles of natural reason; because reason was able to judge from the internal marks of his doctrine, that it was worthy God, and accommodated properly to advance human nature and human happiness.—But for all this,—reason could not infallibly determine that the messenger of this doctrine was the Messias, the eternal son of the living God:—to know this required an illumination;—and this illumination, I say, seems to have been vouchsafed at that instant as a reward . . . .

properly to advance Humane Nature to eternal Happiness: but for all this, Reason could not infallibly determine that the Messenger of this Doctrine was therefore the *Messias* . . . the *eternal Son of the living God.* To know this, needed a new Illumination: And this Illumination (I say) it seems God vouchsafed him at that instant, as a Reward of that Faith and Choice which he had then declared.

p. 89

In a word—*Peter* was a Man of Sincerity, Firmness, and Constancy: And for this we need no farther Testimony than that of our Saviour, in conferring upon him the Symbolical Name of *Cephas,* i.e. *a Rock.*

pp. 89–90

Thus much of his Character being premised, I may be *bold* to affirm of this his Resolution in the Text, that it was as Honest a one, that is, both as Just in the Matter, and as Sincere in the Intention, as ever was made by any of Mankind . . . and yet this Resolution miscarried, and ended only in the Shame of the Resolver. . . .

His character will not suffer us to imagine he made it in a braving Dissimulation: No, himself proved himself sufficiently in earnest, by his subsequent behaviour in the Garden; where he drew his Sword against a whole Band of Men, and thereby made it appear that he had less concern for his own Life, than he had for his Master's Safety.

Would we know then how this Resolution came to be abortive? The Reason was purely this—*Peter* grounded it upon too much Confidence in Himself; he never doubted of himself, but that he had power to perform that which he did so honestly resolve; and this was the . . . original of all his failure.

pp. 90–1

He resolved honestly, I say; but none may presume to say he resolved wisely: For his Lord had just admonish'd him of his peril of Lapsing, (v. 31.) *All ye shall be offended because of me this night:* To which *Peter* answers confidently, *Though all should be offended, yet will not I be offended:* To check this Trust in himself,

pp. 108–09

He denied his master.—But in all instances of his life, but that, was a man of the greatest truth and sincerity;—to which part of his character our Saviour has given an undeniable testimony, in conferring on him the cymbolical name of Cephas, a rock . . . .

pp. 102–03

. . . The resolve was noble and dutiful to the last degree,—and I make no doubt as honest a one—that is, both as just in the matter, and as sincere in the intention, as ever was made by any of mankind;—his character not suffering us to imagine he made it in a braving dissimulation:—no; —for he proved himself sufficiently in earnest by his subsequent behaviour in the garden, when he drew his sword against a whole band of men, and thereby made it appear, that he had less concern for his own life, than he had for his master's safety.—How then came his resolution to miscarry?—The reason seems purely this:—Peter grounded the execution of it upon too much confidence in himself,—doubted not but his will was in his power, whether God's grace assisted him or not;—surely thinking, that what he had courage to resolve so honestly, he had likewise ability to perform.—This was his mistake . . . .

pp. 101–02

Our Lord, before he was betrayed, had taken occasion to admonish his disciples of the peril of lapsing,—telling them, 31st verse,—All ye shall be offended because of me this night.—To which Peter answering, with a zeal mix'd with too much confidence,—That though all should be offended, yet will I *never be offended;*—

Our Saviour rejoyns—That *He* in particular should lapse in a manner more scandalous than all the rest; *Verily I say unto thee, before the Cock crow thou shalt deny me thrice:* But *Peter* looking upon this Monition no farther than as it imply'd a Reproach to his Faith, and his Love, and his Courage, he summons them up all to form this final Resolve, *Tho' I should die with thee, yet will I not deny thee.*

to check this trust in himself,—our Saviour replies, that he in particular should deny him *thrice.*—But Peter looking upon this monition no farther than as it implied a reproach to his faith, and his love, and his courage;—stung to the heart to have them called in question by his Lord,—he hastily summons them all up to form his final resolution,—Though I should die with thee, yet will I not deny thee.—

pp. 91–2

It should have been remembred that he who had precaution'd him was *the Searcher of Hearts, and needed not that any should testifie of Man, because he knew what was in Man.* And therefore in Wisdom *Peter* ought rather to have distrusted his own Heart . . . . It ought to have been remembered that his Lord had said before—*Without me ye can do nothing* . . . .

p. 104

The great apostle had not considered, that he who precautioned him was the searcher of hearts,—and needed not that any should testify of man, for he knew what was in man:—he did not remember, that his Lord had said before,—Without me ye can do nothing . . . .

p. 92

. . . and our Lord, to rebuke him, did no other than leave him to *his own strength to perform it;* and this was in effect the same as to leave him under the necessity of *not* performing it.

p. 104

. . . and his Lord to rebuke and punish him for it, did no other than leave him to his own strength to perform it;—which, in effect, was almost the same as leaving him to the necessity of not performing it at all.

p. 105

He would not doubt but that his Will was in his own Power, and that his Executing Faculties were under the power of his Will; so that what he had Courage to Resolve, he had likewise Ability to Perform. . . .

p. 105

. . . that the execution of all our faculties were under the power of his will . . . .

p. 103

. . . surely thinking, that what he had courage to resolve so honestly, he had likewise ability to perform.

p. 107

'Tis true, that though we are born Ignorant, we can make our selves Skilful; we can acquire Arts and Sciences by our own Diligence and Study: But the Case is not the same in respect of Goodness. We can acquire Arts and Sciences, because we lie under no Connate Indisposition to that Acquirement; for Nature, though it be corrupt, yet still is curious and busie after Knowledge, but to Goodness we have naturally an Indisposition that is Invincible: Lusts within and Temptations without set up such a firm Confederacy

Sermons, VI, 11 (38), pp. 133–4

It is true,—though we are born ignorant, —we can make ourselves skillful;—we can acquire arts and sciences by our own application and study.—But the case is not the same in respect of goodness.—We can acquire arts and sciences, because we lay under no natural indisposition or backwardness to that acquirement.—For nature, though it be corrupt, yet still is curious and busy after knowledge.—But it does not appear, that to goodness and sanctity of manners we have the same natural propensity.—Lusts within, and temp-

against it, as we are never able to surmount in our own Strength.

p. 109

. . . no Man *stands* in Goodness; he is
only upheld and supported *there,* and
graciously kept upright . . . .

pp. 109–10

. . . the Apostle . . . *Rom.* 11.20 . . .
expresses the Manner how even the best
of Men do stand (*viz.*) *Thou standest by
Faith.* Now he that stands by Faith stands
not by Himself; because Faith is properly
a Recumbency or Rest upon *another.* But
to make the matter clearer, the Apostle illustrates it by a Resemblance (*ver.* 17.)
wherein he instructs us, that a Good Man
stands, as the *Branch of a wild Olive does,*
when it is *grafted into the Good* Olive
Tree; and that is, not in its *own* Virtue,
but in Virtue of the *Root;* and *such* a Root
as is naturally *not its own.* It is Remarkable that the Apostle, in that Passage, calls
a Bad Man a *Wild Olive Tree:* a Wild
Olive *Tree;* not barely a *Branch,* but a
Tree; which having a Root of its own,
supports it *self,* and stands in its own
Strength, and brings forth its own Fruit;
and so does Man in respect of the wild
and sour fruit of an ill Conversation: He
is a *Tree;* has a Root of his own, and Sap
and Vegetation, and Seminal Fruitfulness,
and Power to bring it forth: But in respect
of Good, he is only a Branch; and all his
Fruitfulness, and all his Support, depend
upon the Influence and Communications
of God. You may see both the Doctrine
and the Illustration of it, yet more fully
exprest by our Saviour in the beginning
of the 15*th Chapter* of St. *John.*

pp. 116–17

. . . this very Doctrine was familiarly
espoused by the Wise Men among the
Heathen. Who, as they found by Conscious Experience, That it was as little in
a Man's Power to make himself Virtuous
. . . so they espoused this Belief of God's
Assisting Men to Probity of Manners, as a
Truth deducible from the first Principles
of Reason. Accordingly *Plato* delivers it
as a Rule received from *Socrates,* and laid
down as a Fundamental in his Morality.
That *Virtue was* . . . *a Divine Distribution;* and that Education, Precepts, Example, and Practical Diligence, were only

tations without, set up so strong a confederacy against it, as we are never able to
surmount by our own strength.—However
firmly we may think we stand,—the best
of us are upheld, and graciously kept upright . . . .

pp. 118–20

In the 11th chapter to the Romans, where
the manner is explained in which a christian stands by faith,—there is . . . [an]
illustration made use of . . . where St.
Paul instructs us,—that a good man stands
as the branch of a wild olive does, when
it is grafted into a good olive tree;—and
that is,—it flourishes not through its own
virtue, but in virtue of the root,—and such
a root as is naturally not its own.

It is very remarkable in that passage,—
that the apostle calls a bad man a wild
olive *tree;*—not barely a branch, (as in
the other case) but a tree, which having
a root of its own, supports itself, and
stands in its own strength, and brings
forth its own fruit.—And so does every
bad man in respect of the wild and sour
fruit of a vicious and corrupt heart.—According to the resemblance,—if the
apostle intended it,—he is a tree,—has a
root of his own,—and fruitfulness, such as
it is, with a power to bring it forth without help. But in respect of religion, and
the moral improvements of virtue and
goodness,—the apostle calls us, and reason tells us, we are no more than a branch;
and all our fruitfulness, and all our support,—depend so much upon the influence and communications of God,—that
without him we can do nothing,—as our
Saviour declares in the text.

pp. 135–6

Whether it was from a conscious experience of this truth in themselves . . .
or that it was, in some measure, deducible
from the principles of reason,—in the
writings of some of the wisest of the
heathen philosophers, we find the strongest traces of the persuasion of God's
assisting men to virtue and probity of
manners.—One of the greatest masters of
reasoning amongst the ancients acknowledges, that nothing great and exalted can
be achieved, sine divino afflatu;—and
Seneca, to the same purpose,—nulla mens
bona sine deo;—that no soul can be

partial Advances towards it; but that the State was got and finished by the Concurrence of God. And what can be more express, and withal more venerable, than that of *Seneca,* when he says, *Nulla sine Deo mens bona, No Soul can be Good without the Divine Assistance.*

good without divine assistance. . . . And though, in vindication of human liberty, it is as certain on the other hand,—that education, precepts, examples, pious inclinations, and practical diligence, are great and meritorious advances towards a religious state;—yet the state itself is got and finished by God's grace; and the concurrence of his spirit upon tempers thus happily pre-disposed . . . .

Vol. II, Sermon 3, Pt. 2, p. 147

Wish therefore we may, that Virtue were more *cheap,* or more *easie* to us; but we ought to remember, That at the same time we wish *away* that which gives Virtue her best Title both to present Commendation and future Reward.

p. 131

We come not into the world equipt with virtues, as we do with talents;—if we did, we should come into the world with that which robbed virtue of its best title both to present commendation and future reward.—

pp. 131-2

Again, we depend upon God for all the Event and Success of our Undertakings: And this is another Instance which God has selected to his own Disposal, and exempted from the ordinary Laws of Nature, on purpose to give Testimony to his Providence in governing the World. For undoubtedly, it is but suitable to Nature's Law, that the *Race should be to the Swift, and the Battle to the Strong;* That the best Contrivances and Means should have the best Success. And yet it often falls out otherwise in the Case of Man; where the wisest Projects are defeated, and the most hopeful Means are controul'd; and *Time and Chance happens unto all: Time and Chance, i.e.* At sundry Times sundry Events fall out, which they who look no farther than the Events themselves, call *Chance,* because they fall out quite contrary both to their Intentions and their Hopes; though at the same time, in respect of God's Providence over-ruling in these Events, it were profane to call them Chance, for they are pure Designation.

Sermons, II, 8, pp. 35-6

And no doubt—one reason, why God has selected to his own disposal, so many instances as this, where events have run counter to all probabilities,—was to give testimony to his providence in governing the world, and to engage us to a consideration and dependence upon it, for the event and success of all our undertakings.[2] For undoubtedly—as I said,—it should seem but suitable to nature's law, that the race should ever be to the swift,—and the battle to the strong;—it is reasonable that the best contrivances and means should have best success,—and since it often falls out otherwise in the case of man, where the wisest projects are overthrown,—and the most hopeful means are blasted, and time and chance happens to all;—You must call in the deity to untye this knot, —for though at sundry times—sundry events fall out,—which we who look no further than the events themselves, call chance, because they fall out quite contrary both to our intentions and our hopes, —though at the same time, in respect of God's providence overruling in these events; it were profane to call them chance, for they are pure designation, and though invisible, are still the regular dispensations of the superintending power of . . . [the] Almighty being . . . .

---

2. Sterne here inserted a footnote: "Vid. Tillotson's sermon on this subject." But there is no passage in Tillotson's "Success not Always Answerable to the Probability of Second Causes" (Tillotson, *Sermons,* Vol. III, No. 36) which so closely parallels Sterne as this one from Young. See above, p. 165.

Index

Abbey, C. J., 80n, 84n, 85n
Addison, Joseph, 15n, 76
Allestree, Richard, 73
Atterbury, Francis, 9, 100n
Atterbury, Lewis, 10

Bagehot, Walter, 5, 6, 90
Baxter, Richard, 10, 73
Behrmann, Friedrich, 1
Bentley, Richard, 6, 7, 8, 50
—— contemporary reputation, 86–7
—— early recognition of his influence upon Sterne, 2, 4, 87
—— indebtedness of Sterne to, extent of, 4n, 7, 38–9, 52n, 71, 87, 105–7
Berkeley, George, 10
Black, Clementia, 77n
Blackall, Ofspring, 10, 100n
Blair, James, 100n
—— contemporary reputation, 85
—— indebtedness of Sterne to, extent of, 16, 22–3, 24–5, 65–6, 71, 85, 108–9
Bolingbroke, Henry St. John, 10
Bossuet, Jacques Benigne, 11
Boswell, James, 9–10, 76, 80
Bragge, Francis, 73
Browne, Sir Thomas, 9
Bull, George, 75
Burder, William, 9
Burnet, Gilbert, 4, 5n
Burton, Robert, 2, 9
Butler, Joseph, 8, 50
—— contemporary reputation, 86
—— indebtedness of Sterne to, extent of, 38, 52n, 71, 86, 110–11

Chandler, Samuel, 10
Chillingworth, William, 10
Clarke, Samuel, 6, 7, 8, 32, 50, 57, 67n, 70, 83, 93, 100n
—— contemporary reputation, 10, 70, 80–1
—— indebtedness of Sterne to, extent of, 23–4, 34, 37, 39, 52, 65–6, 69, 71, 72, 80, 112–22
—— Sterne's acknowledgment of indebtedness to, 3, 69, 80
Clarke, T. E. S., 4n
Clement, Père, 99
Cooper, Thomas, 76n

Cross, Wilbur L., 1, 6, 9n, 50n, 56
—— critical comments about the *Sermons*, 6, 7, 19n, 35, 51n, 52–3, 57, 59, 79, 80n, 99, 159n, 166n
Cudworth, Ralph, 10
Curtis, Lewis Perry, 1, 9n, 58

De Froe, Arie, 1n
De Isla, José Francisco, 2, 3n, 8
Dodd, William, 10
Doddridge, Philip, 88–9
Donne, John, the younger, 74
Duke, Richard, 174n

Earle, John, 11, 75
Erasmus, Desiderius, 9

Feltham, Owen, 16n
Ferriar, John, 5, 7
—— attitude toward Sterne's plagiarisms in the *Sermons*, 77, 81
—— Sterne's plagiarisms, investigations of, 1–2, 68, 83, 126n, 127n
Fitzgerald, Percy, 3n, 4–5, 6, 7, 8, 84n
Foster, James, 14–15, 57, 90n
—— contemporary reputation, 86–7
—— indebtedness of Sterne to, extent of, 16, 71, 87, 123–4
Foxcroft, H. C., 4n
Franklin, Benjamin, 78

Garat, D. J., 82n
Garvie, A. E., 74n
Goldsmith, Oliver, 76

Hales, John, 10
Hall, Joseph, 5n, 6, 7, 8, 11, 13, 50
—— contemporary reputation, 81–2
—— early recognition of his influence upon Sterne, 2, 4
—— indebtedness of Sterne to, extent of, 37–8, 43n, 51, 58, 67–8, 72, 125–32
Hammond, Henry, 10, 90n
Hartley, Lodwick, 1n
Hill, George B., 79n
Hoadly, Benjamin, 10
Hutton, W. H., 87n

Jackson, Robert W., 96
Jackson, William, 84n
Jackson, William Spencer, 56n

Jebb, R. C., 87n
Johnson, Dr. Samuel, 9–10, 76, 78–9, 88
Jortin, John, 10
Josepheus, Flavius, 59

La Bruyère, Jean de, 11
La Rochefoucauld, François de, 11, 15n
Leighton, Robert, 4, 5n
Leightonhouse, Walter, 6, 8, 9, 11, 32, 45, 60, 67n, 73
—— confused with Robert Leighton, 4n, 5n
—— contemporary reputation, 84
—— indebtedness of Sterne to, extent of, 28–30, 34, 52, 69, 71, 83, 84, 85, 133–7
Linley, Ozias, 77
Locke, John, 7, 8, 50, 70, 85
—— indebtedness of Sterne to, extent of, 34, 37n, 38, 52n, 57, 72, 83, 138–41
—— Sterne's acknowledgment of indebtedness to, 82
Lucas, Richard, 73

Maack, Rudolf, 1
MacCarthy, Desmond, 96–7
MacLean, Kenneth, 83, 138n
Manton, Thomas, 73
Marchant, E. C., 85n
Melville, Lewis, 6
Montaigne, Michael Seigneur de, 9
Motley, D. E., 85n
Mudge, Zachariah, 10, 93n

Nelson, Robert, 10, 73
Newman, John Henry, 35
Norris, John, 6, 7, 8, 9, 27, 31–2, 50, 67n, 93n
—— contemporary reputation, 85–6
—— early recognition of his influence upon Sterne, 3, 4, 85–6
—— indebtedness of Sterne to, extent of, 21n, 25–7, 32, 52n, 65–6, 70, 86, 142–4

Ogden, Samuel, 10, 73, 100, 100n
Ollard, S. L., 54–6
Overbury, Sir Thomas, 11
Overton, J. H., 80n, 84n, 85n

Patrick, Simon, 9, 10, 12–13
Paull, H. M., 74, 74n, 77
Pepys, Samuel, 87
Pope, Alexander, 75, 86

Quennell, Peter, 1n, 90

Rogers, John, 9, 73
—— contemporary reputation, 85
—— indebtedness of Sterne to, extent of, 13–14, 16, 71, 85, 145–6
Root, Robert Kilburn, 91

Saintsbury, George, 6, 7
Saunders, Frederick, 77n, 84n
Scott, Sir Walter, 5, 66n
Secker, Thomas, 35, 53, 90n
Seed, Jeremiah, 10, 35, 93n
Seward, John, 44n
Shaftesbury, Anthony Ashley Cooper, 10
Sharp, John, 100n
Sherlock, Thomas, 10
Sherlock, William, 10
Sichel, Walter, 6, 7
Sinclair, John, 77n
Smaldridge, George, 10
Sotheran (and Todd), 8, 66, 71, 80n
South, Robert, 9
Sprat, Thomas, 100n
Stapfer, Paul, 5, 97
Steele, Richard, 8
—— indebtedness of Sterne to, extent of, 66–7, 72, 84, 147
—— Sterne's acknowledgment of indebtedness to, 3, 84, 147n
Stephen, Leslie, 5, 82n, 85n, 86n, 87n
Sterne, Laurence
—— Bible, his use of, 39–44
—— biographical notes on those from whom he plagiarized, with an evaluation of his indebtedness to each, 78–89
—— borrowed material, importance of, in the posthumously published *Sermons*, 34–6
in the *Sermons* edited by Sterne, 36–9
—— borrowed material, Sterne's practice of rewriting, 27–31, 45–9
—— commonplace book, his possible use of, 65–70
—— criteria used to determine his indebtednesses, 11–15
—— critical treatment of the *Sermons*, inadequacy of former, 4–8
—— early charges of plagiarisms in the *Sermons*, 1–3
—— as parish priest, 55–6
—— plagiarism in sermon writing, earlier attitudes toward, 74–8
—— preaching, what he admired in, 98–100
subjects he preferred to deal with, 94–8
—— *Sermon* manuscripts, non-existence of, 50n

—— *Sermons of Mr. Yorick*,
  those whose dates of composition are known, 50
  methods used to determine when the others may have been written, 50–7
  autobiographical accounts of how they were composed, $9n$, 17–18, 68–9, 99–100
  length of, 100–01
—— theology,
  extent of his readings in, 70–3
  not a deist, 91–2
—— York Minster Library, his use of, 9
Stillingfleet, Edward, 10, $67n$, $100n$
—— contemporary reputation, 87–8
—— indebtedness of Sterne to, extent of, 16, 30, 34, $37n$, 71, 88, 148–50
Swift, Jonathan, 8, 50, 56, $100n$
—— early recognition of his influence upon Sterne, 2, 3, 4
—— indebtedness of Sterne to, extent of, $37n$, 38, $52n$, 71, 83, 151–4

Taylor, Jeremy, $100n$
Teerink, Herman, $56n$
Thackeray, William M., 5, 90
Theophrastus, 11
Tillotson, John, 6, 8, 9, 10, 27, 28, $31n$, 50, 57, 60, $67n$, 92, 93, $100n$
—— contemporary reputation, 70, 78–80, 87–8
—— indebtedness of Sterne to, extent of, 7, 21–2, 34, 37, 52, 58, 62, 65–6, 69, 71–2, 87–8, 155–76
  Sterne's acknowledgment of indebtedness to, 3, 79

Todd (and Sotheran), 8, 66, 71, $80n$
Toland, John, 10
Traill, Henry D., 5–6, 7, $42n$
Trapp, Joseph, 10
Trusler, John, 76

Veneer, John, 11

Walker, P. C., $54n$
Waterland, Daniel, 9, $100n$
Watkins, W. C. B., $1n$
Wells, Edward, 10
Wesley, John, 85
Whichcote, Benjamin, 10
Wise, Thomas, 14–15
—— contemporary reputation, 84
—— indebtedness of Sterne to, extent of, 16, 71, 84, 177
Wishart, William, 95–6
Wollaston, William, 6, 8, 50, $67n$
—— contemporary reputation, 82
—— indebtedness of Sterne to, extent of, 34, 35–6, 51–2, 59, 72, 178–83
—— Sterne's acknowledgment of indebtedness to, 3, 82
Work, James Aiken, $1n$, $9n$

Yoseloff, Thomas, $1n$
Young, Edward, $4n$, $5n$, 6, 8, 11, 30, 68, $100n$
—— contemporary reputation, 85
—— early recognition of his influence upon Sterne, 2, $85n$
—— indebtedness of Sterne to, extent of, 19–21, 34, 52, 58, 65–6, 69, 71, 85, 91–2, 184–91